Mediterranean Instant Pot Cookbook

550 Quick and Healthy Instant Pot Recipes That Will Make Your Life Easier

Alexia Burns

Table of contents

11

Introduction

The Mediterranean diet has gained a lot of popularity during the last years because of its multiple benefits and advantages. This diet is the best way to lose weight, improve your health and look amazing.
This diet is based on the foods people in countries like Greece or Italy consume. Therefore, this diet is based on the consumption of all types of veggies, seeds, fruits, grains, legumes, fish, seafood, eggs, poultry, pork, cheese, yogurt and some beef. Also, don't forget to consume as many fruits as possible and a glass of wine from time to time.

On the other hand, if you opt for such a diet, you can forget about eating refined oils, processed foods, processed meat, sodas, candies, white bread and pasta and any product labeled low fat or diet.

As you can see for yourself, the Mediterranean diet is easy to follow and it allows you to consume a lot of amazing foods. As long as you eat what you are allowed, you will soon enjoy this diet's benefits.
If you made the decision to start a Mediterranean diet, then this next collection is exactly wheat you need. We thought you could use a cooking journal that contains some exception Mediterranean meals made using one simple kitchen tool: the instant pot.

The instant pot is probably one of the best tools available on the market these days. It allows you to cook in a simple, fast and accessible manner. You will obtain perfectly cooked meals in a matter of minutes.
So, don't wait any longer. Start a Mediterranean diet right away and enjoy cooking some of the best meals in your instant pot.

Have fun and enjoy cooking the Mediterranean way!

Mediterranean Diet Instant Pot Breakfast Recipes

Zucchini and Eggs Mix
Preparation time: 10 minutes|**Cooking time:** 20 minutes|**Servings:** 2

Ingredients:
- 2 zucchinis, grated
- 1 tablespoon olive oil
- 2 shallots, chopped
- 4 eggs, whisked
- A pinch of salt and black pepper
- 1 teaspoon oregano, dried
- ½ teaspoon basil, dried
- ½ teaspoon sweet paprika

Directions:
Set the instant pot on Sauté mode, add the oil, heat it up, add the shallots and sauté for 2 minutes. Add the zucchinis and the other ingredients except the eggs, whisk and cook for 3 minutes more. Add the eggs, whisk, put the lid on and cook on High for 15 minutes. Release the pressure naturally for 10 minutes, divide the mix between plates and serve.

Nutrition: calories 331, fat 17.7, fiber 8.7, carbs 43.1, protein 7

Quinoa Bowls
Preparation time: 10 minutes|**Cooking time:** 20 minutes|**Servings:** 4

Ingredients:
- 1 tablespoon avocado oil
- 1 cup quinoa
- 2 cups water
- ½ cup baby kale
- ½ teaspoon oregano, dried
- ½ cup cherry tomatoes, halved
- A pinch of salt and black pepper

Directions:
Set the instant pot on Sauté mode, add the oil, heat it up, add the quinoa and toast for 5 minutes. Add the water, kale and the other ingredients, toss, put the lid on and cook on High for 15 minutes. Release the pressure naturally for 10 minutes, divide the mix into bowls and serve.

Nutrition: calories 217, fat 10, fiber 5, carbs 15, protein 14

Veggie Bowls

Preparation time: 10 minutes|**Cooking time:** 20 minutes|**Servings:** 2

Ingredients:

- 2 spring onions, chopped
- 1 zucchini, cubed
- 1 cup cherry tomatoes, halved
- 1 eggplant, cubed
- 1 tablespoon olive oil
- ½ cup tomato passata
- ½ teaspoon basil, dried
- 1 tablespoon oregano, chopped
- A pinch of salt and black pepper
- 1 tablespoon chives, chopped

Directions:

Set the instant pot on Sauté mode, add the oil, heat it up, add the spring onions, basil, zucchini, eggplant and tomatoes, stir and cook for 5 minutes. Add the rest of the ingredients, toss, put the lid on, cook on High for 15 minutes, release the pressure naturally for 10 minutes, divide into bowls and serve.

Nutrition: calories 223, fat 12, fiber 5, carbs 15, protein 5

Banana and Avocado Oatmeal

Preparation time: 10 minutes|**Cooking time:** 12 minutes|**Servings:** 4

Ingredients:

- 2 cups old fashioned oats
- 1 banana, peeled and mashed
- 1 big avocado, peeled, pitted and cubed
- ½ teaspoon nutmeg, ground
- 3 cups almond milk
- 2 teaspoons cinnamon powder

Directions:

In your instant pot, combine the oats with the milk, banana and the other ingredients, toss, put the lid on and cook on High for 12 minutes. Release the pressure naturally for 10 minutes, divide the oatmeal into bowls and serve for breakfast.

Nutrition: calories 371, fat 12, fiber 2, carbs 5, protein 5

Cheddar Eggs Ramekins

Preparation time: 10 minutes|**Cooking time:** 25 minutes|**Servings:** 4

Ingredients:

- 8 eggs, whisked
- 1 cup heavy cream
- ½ cup cheddar cheese, shredded
- 2 spring onions, chopped
- ½ teaspoon sweet paprika
- A pinch of salt and black pepper
- ½ teaspoon garlic powder
- 2 tablespoons chives, chopped
- ½ cup red bell pepper, chopped
- ½ cup water

Directions:

In a bowl, combine the eggs with the cream and the other ingredients except the cheese and the water, whisk well and divide into 4 ramekins. Put the water in the instant pot, add the trivet inside, add put the ramekins inside, sprinkle the cheese on top, put the lid on and cook on High for 25 minutes. Release the pressure naturally for 10 minutes, and serve for breakfast.

Nutrition: calories 367, fat 13, fiber 3, carbs 15, protein 12

Spinach Frittata

Preparation time: 5 minutes|**Cooking time:** 20 minutes|**Servings:** 4

Ingredients:

- 8 eggs, whisked
- 1 cup baby spinach
- 1 red onion, chopped
- ½ teaspoon oregano, dried
- ½ teaspoon cumin, ground
- ½ teaspoon sweet paprika
- A pinch of salt and black pepper
- 1 tablespoon olive oil

Directions:

Set the instant pot on Sauté mode, add the oil, heat it up, add the onion and sauté for 5 minutes. Add the spinach and the other ingredients except the eggs and stir. Add the eggs, toss a bit, spread into the pot, put the lid on and cook on High for 15 minutes. Release the pressure fast for 5 minutes, divide the frittata between plates and serve.

Nutrition: calories 253, fat 4.9, fiber 2, carbs 26.4, protein 23.6

Mushroom Oatmeal

Preparation time: 10 minutes|**Cooking time:** 20 minutes|**Servings:** 4

Ingredients:
- ½ pound mushrooms, sliced
- 1 red onion, chopped
- 1 cup steel cut oats
- 2 cups veggie stock
- 2 tablespoons olive oil
- 1 red chili, minced
- A pinch of salt and black pepper
- 1 carrot, peeled and grated
- ½ teaspoon sweet paprika

Directions:
Set the instant pot on Sauté mode, add the oil, heat it up, add the onion and chili and cook for 5 minutes. Add the rest of the ingredients, toss, put the lid on and cook on High for 15 minutes. Release the pressure naturally for 10 minutes, divide the mix into bowls and serve.

Nutrition: calories 342, fat 12, fiber 5, carbs 16, protein 15

Berry and Barley Bowls

Preparation time: 10 minutes|**Cooking time:** 25 minutes|**Servings:** 4

Ingredients:
- 1 cup pearl barley
- 2 cups almond milk
- ¼ teaspoon raw honey
- 1 cup blueberries
- ½ cup strawberries
- 2 teaspoons vanilla extract

Directions:
In the instant pot, combine the barley with the milk, berries and the other ingredients, toss, put the lid on and cook on High for 25 minutes. Release the pressure naturally for 10 minutes, divide the mix into bowls and serve.

Nutrition: calories 197, fat 2, fiber 3, carbs 36, protein 6

Sweet Potato Bowls
Preparation time: 10 minutes|**Cooking time:** 20 minutes|**Servings:** 4

Ingredients:
- ½ pound sweet potatoes, peeled, and cubed
- 2 spring onions, chopped
- 1 tablespoon olive oil
- 1 cup baby spinach
- ½ teaspoon sweet paprika
- A pinch of salt and black pepper
- 1 cup cherry tomatoes, halved
- 3 tablespoons Greek yogurt
- 1 teaspoon oregano, dried

Directions:
Set the instant pot on Sauté mode, add the oil, heat it up, add the spring onions, paprika and the oregano, stir and sauté for 5 minutes. Add the sweet potatoes and cook for 5 minutes more. Add the rest of the ingredients, toss, put the lid on and cook on High for 10 minutes. Release the pressure naturally for 10 minutes, divide the mix into bowls and serve.

Nutrition: calories 438, fat 13, fiber 9, carbs 64, protein 26

Walnut and Quinoa Bowls
Preparation time: 10 minutes|**Cooking time:** 20 minutes|**Servings:** 4

Ingredients:
- 1 cup quinoa
- 2 cups almond milk
- ½ cup walnuts, chopped
- 1 tablespoon raisins
- ½ teaspoon vanilla extract
- 1 teaspoon cinnamon powder

Directions:
In your instant pot, combine the quinoa with the milk, walnuts and the other ingredients, toss, put the lid on and cook on High for 20 minutes. Release the pressure naturally for 10 minutes, divide the mix into bowls and serve.

Nutrition: calories 224, fat 12, fiber 5, carbs 15, protein 5

Tomato Eggs Mix

Preparation time: 10 minutes|**Cooking time:** 15 minutes|**Servings:** 4

Ingredients:
- 1 tablespoon olive oil
- 8 eggs, whisked
- 1 cup cherry tomatoes, halved
- A pinch of salt and black pepper
- 1 red onion, chopped
- 1 teaspoon chili powder
- ½ teaspoon sweet paprika
- A pinch of salt and black pepper
- 1 tablespoon chives, chopped

Directions:
Set the instant pot on Sauté mode, add the oil, heat it up, add the onion, chili powder and paprika and sauté for 2 minutes. Add the eggs and the other ingredients, toss, put the lid on and cook on High for 13 minutes. Release the pressure naturally for 10 minutes, divide the eggs mix between plates and serve.

Nutrition: calories 300, fat 12, fiber 6, carbs 16, protein 6

Basil Tomato Salad

Preparation time: 10 minutes|**Cooking time:** 15 minutes|**Servings:** 4

Ingredients:
- ½ pound cherry tomatoes, halved
- 1 tablespoon avocado oil
- 2 spring onions, chopped
- 1 tablespoon basil, chopped
- 1 avocado, peeled, pitted and cubed
- A pinch of salt and black pepper
- 1 tablespoon chives, chopped

Directions:
Set the instant pot on Sauté mode, add the oil, heat it up, add the spring onions and cook for 2 minutes. Add the tomatoes and the other ingredients, toss the mix, put the lid on and cook on High for 13 minutes. Release the pressure naturally fro 10 minutes, divide the mix into bowls and serve.

Nutrition: calories 424, fat 23, fiber 12, carbs 42, protein 15

Banana Salad

Preparation time: 5 minutes|**Cooking time:** 8 minutes|**Servings:** 2

Ingredients:

- 2 bananas, peeled and sliced
- ¼ cup almond milk
- 1 cup blackberries
- 1 teaspoon cinnamon powder
- 2 teaspoons raw honey
- 1 teaspoon vanilla extract
- ½ teaspoon nutmeg, ground

Directions:

In your instant pot, combine the bananas with the berries and the other ingredients, toss gently, put the lid on and cook on High for 8 minutes. Release the pressure fast for 5 minutes, divide the salad into bowls and serve for breakfast.

Nutrition: calories 305, fat 19, fiber 5, carbs 29, protein 8

Zucchini Casserole

Preparation time: 10 minutes|**Cooking time:** 25 minutes|**Servings:** 4

Ingredients:

- 1 tablespoon olive oil
- 1 red onion, chopped
- ½ pound zucchinis, cubed
- ½ pound pork sausage, chopped
- 2 garlic cloves, minced
- 8 eggs, whisked
- ½ teaspoon oregano, dried
- ½ teaspoon basil, dried
- ½ teaspoon chili powder
- A pinch of salt and black pepper
- 1 tablespoon chives, chopped

Directions:

Set the instant pot on Sauté mode, add the oil, heat it up, add the onion, sausage, garlic and chili powder and sauté for 5 minutes. Add the zucchinis and the other ingredients, toss, spread into the pot, put the lid on and cook on High for 20 minutes more. Release the pressure naturally for 10 minutes, divide the casserole between plates and serve.

Nutrition: calories 356, fat 29, fiber 2, carbs 3, protein 18

Peppers Spread

Preparation time: 10 minutes|**Cooking time:** 20 minutes|**Servings:** 4

Ingredients:
- 1 pound red bell peppers, roughly cubed
- 1 cup heavy cream
- 1 red onion, chopped
- 1 tablespoon olive oil
- 1 tablespoon sesame seeds paste
- 1 teaspoon onion powder
- ¼ teaspoon sweet paprika
- A pinch of salt and black pepper
- 1 tablespoon chives, chopped

Directions:

Set the instant pot on Sauté mode, add the oil, heat it up, add the onion, onion powder and paprika and cook for 3 minutes. Add the bell peppers and the other ingredients, toss, put the lid on and cook on High for 17 minutes. Release the pressure naturally for 10 minutes, transfer the mix to a blender, pulse well, divide into bowls and serve.

Nutrition: calories 203, fat 12, fiber 4, carbs 15, protein 4

Apple Oatmeal

Preparation time: 10 minutes|**Cooking time:** 20 minute|**Servings:** 4

Ingredients:
- 1 cup apples, cored and cubed
- 1 cup steel oats
- 2 cups almond milk
- 2 teaspoons raw honey
- 1 teaspoon vanilla extract
- 1 teaspoon cinnamon powder

Directions:

In your instant pot, combine the apples with the oats and the other ingredients, toss, put the lid on and cook on High for 20 minutes. Release the pressure naturally for 10 minutes, divide into bowls, and serve.

Nutrition: calories 200, fat 8, fiber 5, carbs 6, protein 10

Eggplant Spread

Preparation time: 10 minutes|**Cooking time:** 20 minutes|**Servings:** 4

Ingredients:
- 1 pound eggplant
- 1 cup water
- 1 tablespoon olive oil
- 2 spring onions, chopped
- ½ teaspoon oregano, dried
- ½ teaspoon sweet paprika
- A pinch of salt and black pepper
- 1 tablespoon chives, chopped

Directions:
Put the water in the instant pot, add the trivet , put the eggplants inside, put the lid on and cook on High for 20 minutes. Release the pressure fast for 5 minutes, cool the eggplant down, peel and transfer to a blender. Add the other ingredients, pulse well, divide into bowls and serve.

Nutrition: calories 200, fat 12, fiber 6, carbs 7, protein 9

Spinach and Chickpeas Salad

Preparation time: 5 minutes|**Cooking time:** 15 minutes|**Servings:** 4

Ingredients:
- 1 cup canned chickpeas, drained and rinsed
- ½ pound baby spinach
- 1 yellow onion, chopped
- 1 tablespoon olive oil
- ½ teaspoon cumin, ground
- ½ teaspoon oregano, dried
- 1 tablespoon chives, chopped
- A pinch of salt and black pepper

Directions:
Set the instant pot on Sauté mode, add the oil, heat it up, add the onion and sauté for 3 minutes. Add the chickpeas and the other ingredients, toss, put the lid on and cook on High for 12 minutes. Release the pressure fast for 5 minutes, divide the salad into bowls and serve for breakfast.

Nutrition: calories 170, fat 10, fiber 4, carbs 7, protein 9

Chili Eggs Mix

Preparation time: 10 minutes|**Cooking time:** 15 minutes|**Servings:** 4

Ingredients:
- 1 tablespoon olive oil
- 1 red onion, chopped
- 8 eggs, whisked
- ½ cup cherry tomatoes, cubed
- ½ cup black olives, pitted and cubed
- 2 tablespoons chives, chopped
- 1 teaspoon chili powder
- A pinch of salt and black pepper

Directions:

Set the instant pot on Sauté mode, add the oil, heat it up, add the onion and chili powder and sauté for 5 minutes. Add the eggs and the other ingredients, toss, put the lid on and cook on High for 10 minutes. Release the pressure naturally for 10 minutes, divide everything between plates and serve.

Nutrition: calories 181, fat 11, fiber 2, carbs 6, protein 9

Zucchini Muffins

Preparation time: 10 minutes|**Cooking time:** 20 minutes|**Servings:** 4

Ingredients:
- 3 eggs, whisked
- 1 cup almond milk
- 1 tablespoon avocado oil
- ½ teaspoon nutmeg, ground
- 1 cup almond flour
- ½ teaspoon baking powder
- 1 cup zucchinis, grated
- 1 cup water
- Cooking spray

Directions:

In a bowl, combine the eggs with the milk, oil and the other ingredients except the water and the cooking spray, whisk well and divide into a muffin tin. Add the water to the instant pot, put the trivet into the pot, put the muffin tins inside, put the lid on and cook on High for 20 minutes. Release the pressure naturally for 10 minutes, divide the muffins between plates and serve for breakfast.

Nutrition: calories 188, fat 11, fiber 6, carbs 9, protein 7

Salsa Eggs

Preparation time: 10 minutes|**Cooking time:** 20 minutes|**Servings:** 4

Ingredients:
- 1 tablespoon olive oil
- 1 red onion, chopped
- 8 eggs, whisked
- A pinch of salt and black pepper
- ½ cup mild salsa
- ¼ cup green onions, chopped
- 1 tablespoon basil, chopped

Directions:
Set the instant pot on Sauté mode, add the oil, heat it up, add the onion and sauté for 5 minutes. Add the eggs and the rest of the ingredients, toss, put the lid on and cook on High for 15 minutes. Release the pressure naturally for 10 minutes, divide the mix into bowls and serve for breakfast.

Nutrition: calories 200, fat 8, fiber 5, carbs 7, protein 11

Zucchini Salad

Preparation time: 10 minutes|**Cooking time:** 15 minutes|**Servings:** 2

Ingredients:
- 1 tablespoon avocado oil
- 2 zucchinis, sliced
- ½ cup tomatoes, cubed
- 2 spring onions, chopped
- 1 tablespoon oregano, chopped
- ½ teaspoon chili powder
- 1 red onion, chopped
- 1 teaspoon sweet paprika
- A pinch of salt and black pepper

Directions:
Set the instant pot on Sauté mode, add the oil, heat it up, add the spring onions and red onion and sauté for 5 minutes. Add the zucchinis and the other ingredients, toss, put the lid on, and cook on High for 10 minutes. Release the pressure for 10 minutes, divide the salad into bowls and serve for breakfast.

Nutrition: calories 200, fat 12, fiber 5, carbs 6, protein 8

Beans Spread

Preparation time: 10 minutes|**Cooking time:** 20 minutes|**Servings:** 4

Ingredients:
- 1 cup canned white beans, drained and rinsed
- 3 tablespoons olive oil
- 1 yellow onion, chopped
- 1 cup veggie stock
- 1 tablespoon lemon juice
- ½ teaspoon chili powder
- A pinch of salt and black pepper
- 1 tablespoon tahini paste
- 1 teaspoon cumin, ground

Directions:

Set the instant pot on Sauté mode, add 1 tablespoon oil, heat it up, add the onion, chili powder and cumin and sauté for 2 minutes. Add the beans and the stock, toss, put the lid on and cook on High for 18 minutes. Release the pressure naturally for 10 minutes, drain the beans, transfer to a blender, add the rest of the ingredients, pulse well, divide into bowls and serve as a morning spread

Nutrition: calories 180, fat 8, fiber 5, carbs 8, protein 6

Vanilla Berry Oatmeal

Preparation time: 5 minutes|**Cooking time:** 20 minutes|**Servings:** 4

Ingredients:
- 1 teaspoon vanilla extract
- 1 cup steel cut oats
- 2 cups almond milk
- ½ cup blackberries
- 2 tablespoons brown sugar

Directions:

In your instant pot, combine the oats with the milk and the other ingredients, toss, put the lid on and cook on High for 20 minutes. Release the pressure fast for 5 minutes, divide the mix into bowls and serve for breakfast.

Nutrition: calories 173, fat 5, fiber 2, carbs 5, protein 5

Avocado Salad

Preparation time: 5 minutes|**Cooking time:** 8 minutes|**Servings:** 4

Ingredients:
- 2 avocados, peeled, pitted and cubed
- 1 cup cherry tomatoes, halved
- 1 tablespoon olive oil
- 2 spring onions, chopped
- A pinch of salt and black pepper
- 1 tablespoon oregano, chopped
- 1 tablespoon lime juice

Directions:
In your instant pot, combine the avocados with the tomatoes, oil and the other ingredients, toss gently, put the lid on and cook on High for 8 minutes. Release the pressure fast for 5 minutes, divide into bowls and serve for breakfast.

Nutrition: calories 167, fat 8, fiber 4, carbs 6, protein 10

Chia Pudding

Preparation time: 10 minutes|**Cooking time:** 15 minutes|**Servings:** 4

Ingredients:
- 3 tablespoons chia seeds
- 2 cups almond milk
- 1 tablespoon brown sugar
- ½ teaspoon vanilla extract
- 1 mango, peeled and cubed

Directions:
In your instant pot, combine the almond milk with the chia seeds and the other ingredients, toss, put the lid on and cook on High for 15 minutes. Release the pressure naturally for 10 minutes, divide the pudding into bowls and serve for breakfast.

Nutrition: calories 180, fat 11, fiber 2, carbs 4, protein 7

Rice Pudding

Preparation time: 10 minutes|**Cooking time:** 25 minutes|**Servings:** 4

Ingredients:
- 1 cup white rice
- 2 cups almond milk
- 2 tablespoons brown sugar
- 1 teaspoon vanilla extract
- 1 teaspoon nutmeg, ground
- 1 teaspoon cinnamon powder

Directions:
In your instant pot, combine the rice with the milk and the other ingredients except the cinnamon, stir, put the lid on and cook on High for 25 minutes. Release the pressure naturally for 10 minutes, divide the rice into bowls, sprinkle the cinnamon on top and serve.

Nutrition: calories 201, fat 11, fiber 2, carbs 5, protein 10

Mango Smoothie Bowls

Preparation time: 10 minutes|**Cooking time:** 15 minutes|**Servings:** 4

Ingredients:
- 1 cup mango, peeled, cubed
- 1 cup almond milk
- ½ cup heavy cream
- 2 tablespoons brown sugar
- 2 teaspoons vanilla extract

Directions:
In your instant pot, combine the mango with the milk and the other ingredients, toss, put the lid on and cook on High for 15 minutes. Release the pressure naturally for 10 minutes, blend the mix, divide into bowls and serve for breakfast.

Nutrition: calories 200, fat 8, fiber 2, carbs 7, protein 10

Orange Spread

Preparation time: 5 minutes|**Cooking time:** 12 minutes|**Servings:** 4

Ingredients:
- 1 cup heavy cream
- 1 cup oranges, peeled and cut into segments
- 2 tablespoons brown sugar
- ¼ teaspoon vanilla extract
- ½ teaspoon ginger, grated

Directions:

In your instant pot, combine the oranges with the cream and the other ingredients, toss, put the lid on and cook on High for 12 minutes. Release the pressure fast for 5 minutes, blend using an immersion blender, divide the mix into bowls and serve for breakfast.

Nutrition: calories 190, fat 4, fiber 2, carbs 8, protein 10

Tomato Omelet

Preparation time: 10 minutes|**Cooking time:** 20 minutes|**Servings:** 4

Ingredients:
- 8 eggs, whisked
- 1 cup cherry tomatoes, halved
- 1 tablespoon olive oil
- 1 red onion, chopped
- ½ teaspoon cumin, ground
- ½ teaspoon basil, dried
- A pinch of salt and black pepper
- ½ teaspoon chili powder
- 1 tablespoon cilantro, chopped

Directions:

Set the instant pot on Sauté mode, add the oil, heat it up, add the onion, cumin, basil and chili powder, stir and sauté for 5 minutes. Add the eggs and the other ingredients, toss and spread, put the lid on and cook on High for 15 minutes. Release the pressure naturally for 10 minutes, divide the omelet between plates and serve for breakfast.

Nutrition: calories 211, fat 12, fiber 5, carbs 6, protein 10

Avocado and Tomato Bowls

Preparation time: 5 minutes|**Cooking time:** 12 minutes|**Servings:** 4

Ingredients:
- 1 cup avocado, peeled, pitted and cubed
- 1 cup cherry tomatoes, halved
- 1 tablespoon olive oil
- 2 spring onions, chopped
- ¼ cup tomato passata
- A pinch of salt and black pepper
- ½ tablespoon chives, chopped

Directions:
Set the instant pot on Sauté mode, add the oil, heat it up, add the spring onions and sauté for 2 minutes.Add the cherry tomatoes and the other ingredients, toss, put the lid on and cook on Low for 10 minutes. Release the pressure fast for 5 minutes, divide the mix into bowls and serve.

Nutrition: calories 152, fat 4, fiber 3, carbs 6, protein 9

Creamy Figs Mix

Preparation time: 5 minutes|**Cooking time:** 10 minutes|**Servings:** 4

Ingredients:
- 1 cup figs, halved
- 2 teaspoons brown sugar
- 2 cups heavy cream
- ½ teaspoon vanilla extract
- ½ teaspoon cinnamon powder

Directions:
In your instant pot, combine the figs with the cream and the other ingredients, toss gently, put the lid on and cook on Low for 10 minutes. Release the pressure fast for 5 minutes, divide into bowls and serve for breakfast.

Nutrition: calories 161, fat 7, fiber 3, carbs 5, protein 5

Ginger Eggs Mix

Preparation time: 10 minutes|**Cooking time:** 15 minutes|**Servings:** 4

Ingredients:
- 8 eggs, whisked
- 1 yellow onion, chopped
- 2 spring onions, chopped
- 1 tablespoon olive oil
- ½ cup heavy cream
- 1 tablespoon ginger, grated
- A pinch of salt and black pepper
- 1 tablespoon chives, chopped

Directions:
Set the instant pot on Sauté mode, add the oil, heat it up, add the onion and spring onions and sauté for 2 minutes. Add the ginger and cook for 3 minutes more. Add the eggs mixed with the other ingredients, whisk everything, put the lid on and cook on High for 10 minutes. Release the pressure naturally for 10 minutes, divide the mix between plates and serve.

Nutrition: calories 170, fat 6, fiber 4, carbs 8, protein 10

Mango Quinoa Mix

Preparation time: 10 minutes|**Cooking time:** 20 minutes|**Servings:** 4

Ingredients:
- 1 cup quinoa
- 3 cups coconut milk
- ½ cup mango, peeled, pitted and cubed
- 1 tablespoon brown sugar
- 1 teaspoon vanilla extract

Directions:
In your instant pot, combine the quinoa with the milk and the other ingredients, toss, put the lid on and cook on High for 20 minutes. Release the pressure naturally for 10 minutes, divide the mix into bowls and serve.

Nutrition: calories 180, fat 5, fiber 5, carbs 7, protein 6

Lime Rice Pudding Mix

Preparation time: 5 minutes|**Cooking time:** 20 minutes|**Servings:** 4

Ingredients:
- 1 cup white rice
- 2 cups almond milk
- 2 tablespoons brown sugar
- 1 tablespoon lime juice
- 1 tablespoon cinnamon powder

Directions:
In your instant pot, combine the rice with the milk and the other ingredients, toss, put the lid on and cook on High for 20 minutes. Release the pressure fast for 5 minutes, divide into bowls and serve for breakfast.

Nutrition: calories 172, fat 5, fiber 4, carbs 7, protein 6

Garlic Green Beans and Eggs

Preparation time: 10 minutes|**Cooking time:** 20 minutes|**Servings:** 4

Ingredients:
- ½ pound green beans, trimmed and halved
- 8 eggs, whisked
- 2 garlic cloves, minced
- 1 red onion, chopped
- ½ teaspoon oregano, dried
- 2 tablespoons avocado oil
- 1 teaspoon turmeric powder
- 1 tablespoon chives, chopped

Directions:
Set the instant pot on Sauté mode, add the oil, heat it up, add the garlic, onion, oregano and turmeric and sauté for 3 minutes. Add the beans and cook for another 2 minutes. Add the eggs and the rest of the ingredients, toss, put the lid on and cook on High for 15 minutes. Release the pressure naturally for 10 minutes, divide between plates and serve.

Nutrition: calories 190, fat 7, fiber 2, carbs 5, protein 7

Tomato and Quinoa Bowls

Preparation time: 10 minutes|**Cooking time:** 20 minutes|**Servings:** 4

Ingredients:

- 1 cup quinoa
- 2 cups veggie stock
- 1 cup cherry tomatoes, halved
- 1 tablespoon oregano, chopped
- 1 yellow onion, chopped
- 1 tablespoon olive oil
- 1 tablespoon basil, chopped
- A pinch of salt and black pepper

Directions:

Set the instant pot on Sauté mode, add the oil, heat the it up, add the onion and oregano and cook for 5 minutes. Add the quinoa, tomatoes and the other ingredients, toss, put the lid on and cook on High for 15 minutes. Release the pressure naturally for 10 minutes, divide the mix into bowls and serve for breakfast.

Nutrition: calories 193, fat 6, fiber 3, carbs 6, protein 6

Broccoli Spread

Preparation time: 10 minutes|**Cooking time:** 20 minutes|**Servings:** 4

Ingredients:

- 1 pound broccoli florets
- ½ cup Greek yogurt
- ¼ cup veggie stock
- 1 yellow onion, chopped
- 2 garlic cloves, minced
- 1 tablespoon olive oil
- 1 tablespoon lemon juice
- 1 tablespoon pine nuts, toasted
- ½ teaspoon chili powder
- 1 tablespoon chives, chopped
- A pinch of salt and black pepper

Directions:

Set the instant pot on Sauté mode, add the oil, heat it up, add the onion, garlic and chili powder and sauté for 5 minutes. Add the broccoli and the other ingredients except the hives and the yogurt, toss, put the lid on and cook on High for 15 minutes. Release the pressure naturally for 10 minutes, add the yogurt, blend the mix using an immersion blender, divide the salad into bowls and serve as a spread with the chives sprinkled on top.

Nutrition: calories 200, fat 12, fiber 2, carbs 5, protein 9

Eggs and Veggie Salad
Preparation time: 5 minutes|**Cooking time:** 10 minutes|**Servings:** 4

Ingredients:
- 1 cup tomato, cubed
- ¼ cup veggie stock
- ½ cup black olives, pitted and cubed
- 1 tablespoon olive oil
- 1 cup baby spinach
- 1 tablespoon lemon juice
- 2 spring onions, chopped
- 4 eggs, hard boiled, peeled and cut into wedges
- 2 tablespoons balsamic vinegar
- A pinch of salt and black pepper

Directions:

In the instant pot, combine the tomatoes with the olives and the other ingredients except the eggs, toss gently, put the lid on and cook on High for 10 minutes. Release the pressure fast for 5 minutes, divide into bowls, add the eggs in each serving and serve for breakfast.

Nutrition: calories 221, fat 6, fiber 4, carbs 7, protein 10

Strawberry Yogurt Mix
Preparation time: 5 minutes|**Cooking time:** 8 minutes|**Servings:** 4

Ingredients:
- 1 cup strawberries, halved
- 2 cups Greek yogurt
- 1 teaspoon vanilla extract
- 3 teaspoons raw honey
- 1 avocado, peeled, pitted and cubed
- 1 teaspoon cinnamon powder

Directions:

In your instant pot, combine the berries with the yogurt and the other ingredients, toss, put the lid on and cook on High for 8 minutes. Release the pressure fast for 5 minutes, divide the mix into bowls and serve for breakfast.

Nutrition: calories 190, fat 7, fiber 4, carbs 7, protein 5

Millet and Berries Mix
Preparation time: 10 minutes|**Cooking time:** 20 minutes|**Servings:** 4

Ingredients:
- 1 cup millet
- 2 cups coconut milk
- ½ cup blackberries
- 1 tablespoon brown sugar
- 1 tablespoon lime zest, grated
- 2 teaspoons vanilla extract

Directions:
In your instant pot, combine the millet with the milk and the other ingredients, toss, put the lid on and cook on High for 20 minutes. Release the pressure naturally for 10 minutes, divide into bowls and serve for breakfast,

Nutrition: calories 192, fat 6, fiber 3, carbs 6, protein 9

Creamy Avocado Mix
Preparation time: 4 minutes|**Cooking time:** 5 minutes|**Servings:** 2

Ingredients:
- 1 cup avocado, peeled, pitted and cubed
- 1 cup heavy cream
- ½ teaspoon vanilla extract
- 1 tablespoon walnuts, chopped
- 2 tablespoons brown sugar

Directions:
In your instant pot, combine the avocado with the cream and the other ingredients, toss, put the lid on and cook on High for 5 minutes. Release the pressure fast for 4 minutes, toss, divide the mix into bowls and serve for breakfast.

Nutrition: calories 198, fat 7, fiber 5, carbs 7, protein 8

Hot Eggplant Frittata

Preparation time: 10 minutes|**Cooking time:** 20 minutes|**Servings:** 4

Ingredients:

- 1 eggplant, cubed
- 1 tablespoon olive oil
- 1 red chili pepper, chopped
- 1 red onion, chopped
- ½ teaspoon coriander, ground
- 1 teaspoon turmeric powder
- 1 teaspoon chili powder
- 8 eggs, whisked
- A pinch of salt and black pepper
- 1 tablespoon chives, chopped

Directions:

Set your instant pot on sauté mode, add the oil, heat it up, add the onion, chili pepper and chili powder and sauté for 5 minutes. Add the eggplant and the rest of the ingredients, toss, spread well into the pot, put the lid on and cook on High for 15 minutes. Release the pressure naturally for 10 minutes, divide the mix between plates and serve.

Nutrition: calories 201, fat 9, fiber 4, carbs 7, protein 10

Tomato and Fennel Bowls

Preparation time: 10 minutes|**Cooking time:** 20 minutes|**Servings:** 4

Ingredients:

- 2 tablespoons olive oil
- 1 yellow onion, chopped
- ½ pound cherry tomatoes, halved
- ¼ cup tomato passata
- 1 fennel bulb, sliced
- ½ cup kalamata olives, pitted and cubed
- Juice of ½ lime
- A pinch of salt and black pepper
- 1 teaspoon cumin, ground
- 1 teaspoon fennel seeds, crushed

Directions:

Set your instant pot on sauté mode, add the oil, heat it up, add the onion, fennel, cumin and fennel seeds and sauté for 5 minutes. Add the rest of the ingredients, toss, put the lid on and cook on High for 15 minutes. Release the pressure naturally for 10 minutes, divide everything into bowls and serve.

Nutrition: calories 222, fat 13, fiber 4, carbs 7, protein 10

Cauliflower and Rice Pudding

Preparation time: 10 minutes|**Cooking time:** 25 minutes|**Servings:** 4

Ingredients:

- 1 cup white rice
- 2 cups veggie stock
- 1 yellow onion, chopped
- 1 cup cauliflower florets
- 1 tablespoon olive oil
- A pinch of salt and black pepper
- ½ teaspoon sweet paprika
- ½ teaspoon chili powder
- Zest of 1 lime, grated
- 1 tablespoon cilantro, chopped

Directions:

Set the instant pot on Sauté mode, add the oil, heat it up, add the onion and sauté for 5 minutes. Add the rice, stock and the other ingredients, toss, put the lid on and cook on High fro 20 minutes. Release the pressure naturally for 10 minutes, divide the mix into bowls and serve for breakfast.

Nutrition: calories 200, fat 7, fiber 5, carbs 7, protein 10

Carrot Scramble

Preparation time: 10 minutes|**Cooking time:** 20 minutes|**Servings:** 4

Ingredients:

- 1 cup carrots, peeled and grated
- 8 eggs, whisked
- 1 red onion, chopped
- 1 tablespoon olive oil
- ½ teaspoon sweet paprika
- ½ teaspoon oregano, dried
- A pinch of salt and black pepper
- 1 tablespoon chives, chopped

Directions:

Set the instant pot on Sauté mode, add the oil, heat it up, add the onion and sauté for 5 minutes. Add the carrots and the other ingredients, toss well, put the lid on and cook on High for 15 minutes. Release the pressure naturally for 10 minutes, divide everything between plates and serve.

Nutrition: calories 200, fat 7, fiber 3, carbs 7, protein 10

Eggplant and Mushroom Salad

Preparation time: 10 minutes|**Cooking time:** 15 minutes|**Servings:** 4

Ingredients:
- 2 spring onions, chopped
- 1 eggplant, roughly cubed
- 2 tablespoons olive oil
- 2 garlic cloves, minced
- 1 tablespoon oregano, chopped
- ½ pound mushrooms, halved
- 2 tablespoons lime juice
- Salt and black pepper to the taste

Directions:

Set your instant pot on sauté mode, add the oil, heat it up, add the spring onions and garlic and cook for 2 minutes. Add the eggplant and the rest of the ingredients, toss, put the lid on and cook on High for 13 minutes. Release the pressure naturally for 10 minutes, divide the mix into bowls and serve.

Nutrition: calories 221, fat 11, fiber 5, carbs 7, protein 8

Creamy Mango Pomegranate Mix

Preparation time: 10 minutes|**Cooking time:** 10 minutes|**Servings:** 4

Ingredients:
- 1 cup mango, peeled, pitted and cubed
- ½ cup heavy cream
- ½ cup pomegranate seeds
- 1 teaspoon vanilla extract
- 1 teaspoon cinnamon powder

Directions:

In your instant pot, combine the mango with the cream and the other ingredients, toss, put the lid on and cook on High for 10 minutes. Release the pressure naturally for 10 minutes, divide the mix into bowls and serve.

Nutrition: calories 180, fat 4, fiber 3, carbs 7, protein 10

Greek Grapes Mix

Preparation time: 5 minutes|**Cooking time:** 5 minutes|**Servings:** 2

Ingredients:
- 1 cup grapes, halved
- 1 tablespoon lime juice
- 1 tablespoon lime zest, grated
- 2 cups Greek yogurt
- 1 teaspoon vanilla extract

Directions:
In your instant pot, combine the grapes with the lime juice and the other ingredients, toss gently, put the pressure lid on and cook on High for 5 minutes. Release the pressure fast for 5 minutes, divide the mix into bowls and serve for breakfast.

Nutrition: calories 181, fat 11, fiber 4, carbs 7, protein 9

Nuts and Rice

Preparation time: 5 minutes|**Cooking time:** 20 minutes|**Servings:** 4

Ingredients:
- ½ cup brown rice
- 1 and ½ cups almond milk
- ¼ cup walnuts, chopped
- 1 teaspoon vanilla extract
- 1 teaspoon cinnamon powder

Directions:
In your instant pot, combine the rice with the milk and the other ingredients, toss, put the lid on and cook on High for 20 minutes. Release the pressure fast for 5 minutes, divide into bowls and serve for breakfast.

Nutrition: calories 200, fat 8, fiber 5, carbs 7, protein 9

Quinoa and Olives Mix

Preparation time: 10 minutes|**Cooking time:** 20 minutes|**Servings:** 4

Ingredients:

- 1 cup quinoa
- 2 cups veggie stock
- ½ cup black olives, pitted and halved
- ½ cup kalamata olives, pitted and halved
- ½ teaspoon sweet paprika
- ½ teaspoon chili powder
- 2 spring onions, chopped
- 1 red onion, chopped
- 1 tablespoon olive oil
- A pinch of salt and black pepper
- 2 tablespoons parsley, chopped

Directions:

Set the instant pot on Sauté mode, add the oil, heat it up, add the spring and red onion and sauté for 5 minutes. Add the quinoa, stock and the other ingredients, toss, put the lid on and cook on High for 15 minutes. Release the pressure naturally for 10 minutes, divide the mix into bowls and serve for breakfast.

Nutrition: calories 181, fat 7, fiber 6, carbs 8, protein 11

Chickpeas and Olives Bowls

Preparation time: 10 minutes|**Cooking time:** 20 minutes|**Servings:** 4

Ingredients:

- 1 cup canned chickpeas, drained and rinsed
- 1 cup kalamata olives, pitted and halved
- ½ cup cherry tomatoes, halved
- ¼ cup veggie stock
- A pinch of salt and black pepper
- 1 teaspoon turmeric powder
- 1 red onion, chopped
- 1 tablespoon olive oil
- 1 tablespoon chives, chopped

Directions:

Set the instant pot on Sauté mode, add the oil, heat it up, add the onion and turmeric and cook for 5 minutes. Add the chickpeas and the other ingredients, toss, put the lid on and cook on High for 15 minutes. Release the pressure naturally for 10 minutes, divide into bowls and serve.

Nutrition: calories 171, fat 8, fiber 4, carbs 6, protein 8

42

Lentils and Rice Bowls

Preparation time: 10 minutes|**Cooking time:** 20 minutes|**Servings:** 4

Ingredients:

- 1 cup brown rice
- ½ cup canned lentils, drained and rinsed
- 1 yellow onion, chopped
- ½ cup heavy cream
- ½ teaspoon sweet paprika
- 2 tablespoons olive oil
- 1 cup veggie stock
- 2 tablespoons lime juice
- ¼ teaspoon cumin, ground
- A pinch of salt and black pepper
- ¼ cup chives, chopped

Directions:

Set the instant pot on Sauté mode, add the oil, heat it up, add the onion, paprika and cumin, stir and sauté for 5 minutes. Add the rice, lentils and the rest of the ingredients, toss, put the lid on and cook on High for 15 minutes. Release the pressure naturally for 10 minutes, divide the mix into bowls and serve for breakfast.

Nutrition: calories 200, fat 12, fiber 3, carbs 5, protein 9

Ground Lamb Bowls\

Preparation time: 10 minutes|**Cooking time:** 20 minutes|**Servings:** 4

Ingredients:

- 1 pound lamb stew meat, ground
- 1 red onion, chopped
- ½ teaspoon sweet paprika
- ½ teaspoon mint, ground
- ½ cup tomato passata
- 2 tablespoons olive oil
- 1 teaspoon rosemary, dried
- 1 teaspoon cumin, ground
- 1 teaspoon chili powder
- A pinch of salt and black pepper
- 1 tablespoon oregano, chopped

Directions:

Set the instant pot on Sauté mode, add the onion, meat, mint and paprika, stir and brown for 5 minutes. Add the passata and the other ingredients, toss, put the lid on and cook on High for 15 minutes. Release the pressure naturally for 10 minutes, divide the mix into bowls and serve for breakfast.

Nutrition: calories 273, fat 13, fiber 3, carbs 6, protein 14

Brussels Sprouts and Sweet Potato Bowls

Preparation time: 10 minutes|**Cooking time:** 20 minutes|**Servings:** 4

Ingredients:

- 1 cup Brussels sprouts, trimmed and halved
- 1 cup sweet potatoes, peeled and cubed
- 1 tablespoon olive oil
- 1 red onion, chopped
- ½ cup tomato passata
- 1 teaspoon sweet paprika
- ½ teaspoon cumin, ground
- ½ teaspoon coriander, ground
- 1 tablespoon cilantro, chopped

Directions:

Set the instant pot on Sauté mode, add the oil, heat it up, add the onion, paprika, cumin and coriander, stir and cook for 5 minutes. Add the sprouts and the other ingredients, toss, put the lid on and cook on High for 15 minutes. Release the pressure naturally for 10 minutes, divide everything into bowls and serve for breakfast.

Nutrition: calories 200, fat 12, fiber 4, carbs 7, protein 8

Zucchini and Seeds Bowls

Preparation time: 10 minutes**Cooking time:** 15 minutes**Servings:** 4

Ingredients:

- 2 zucchinis, roughly cubed
- 1 tablespoon olive oil
- 1 red onion, chopped
- 1 tablespoon pumpkin seeds
- ¼ cup heavy cream
- 1 tablespoon cilantro, chopped
- ½ cup black olives, pitted and halved
- A pinch of salt and black pepper

Directions:

Set the instant pot on Sauté mode, add the oil, heat it up, add the onion and sauté for 2 minutes. Add the zucchinis, seeds and the other ingredients, toss, put the lid on and cook on High for 13 minutes. Release the pressure naturally for 10 minutes, divide the mix into bowls and serve.

Nutrition: calories 171, fat 11, fiber 5, carbs 9, protein 5

Cauliflower Salad

Preparation time: 10 minutes**Cooking time:** 20 minutes**Servings:** 4

Ingredients:

- 2 cups cauliflower florets
- 1 cup shallots, minced
- 2 garlic cloves
- 1 tablespoon olive oil
- ½ cup heavy cream
- ½ teaspoon turmeric powder
- 2 tablespoons mayonnaise
- 1 tablespoon chives, chopped
- Salt and black pepper to the taste

Directions:

Set the instant pot on Sauté mode, add the oil, heat it up, add the garlic and the shallots, stir and cook for 5 minutes. Add the cauliflower and the rest of the ingredients except the chives, toss, put the lid on and cook on High for 15 minutes. Release the pressure naturally for 10 minutes, divide everything into bowls and serve for breakfast with the chives sprinkled on top.

Nutrition: calories 200, fat 11, fiber 4, carbs 7, protein 9

Sweet Potato and Eggs Hash

Preparation time: 10 minutes**Cooking time:** 20 minutes**Servings:** 4

Ingredients:

- 2 sweet potatoes, peeled and cubed
- 8 eggs, whisked
- 1 tablespoon avocado oil
- 2 tablespoons Greek yogurt
- 1 red onion, chopped
- 2 teaspoons Italian seasoning
- 1 teaspoon sage, chopped
- 1 tablespoon parsley, chopped
- A pinch of salt and black pepper

Directions:

Set the instant pot on Sauté mode, add the oil, heat it up, add the onion, seasoning and sage and cook for 5 minutes. Add the potatoes, eggs and the other ingredients, toss well, put the lid on and cook on High for 15 minutes. Release the pressure naturally for 10 minutes, divide between plates, and serve for breakfast.

Nutrition: calories 161, fat 7, fiber 4, carbs 8, protein 11

Mango and Spinach Salad

Preparation time: 5 minutes**Cooking time:** 6 minutes**Servings:** 4

Ingredients:

- 1 pound baby spinach
- 2 mangoes, peeled, pitted and cubed
- ¼ cup Greek yogurt
- 2 spring onions, chopped
- 1 tablespoon olive oil
- 1 cup cherry tomatoes, halved
- A pinch of salt and black pepper
- 1 tablespoon balsamic vinegar
- 1 tablespoon lime zest, grated

Directions:

Set the instant pot on Sauté mode, add the oil, heat it up, add the onion and sauté for 2 minutes. Add the mango, spinach and the other ingredients, toss, put the lid on and cook on High for 4 minutes. Release the pressure fast for 5 minutes, divide the salad into bowls and serve for breakfast.

Nutrition: calories 200, fat 9, fiber 5, carbs 7, protein 10

Pesto Scramble

Preparation time: 10 minutes**Cooking time:** 15 minutes**Servings:** 4

Ingredients:

- 1 yellow onion, chopped
- 8 eggs, whisked
- 2 tablespoons basil pesto
- 1 tablespoon avocado oil
- ¼ cup heavy cream
- 1 teaspoon turmeric powder
- Salt and black pepper to the taste
- 1 tablespoon chives, chopped

Directions:

Set your instant pot on Sauté mode, add oil, heat it up, add the onion and turmeric and cook for 2 minutes. Add the eggs mixed with the other ingredients, toss well, put the lid on and cook on High for 13 minutes. Release the pressure naturally for 10 minutes, divide the mix between plates and serve.

Nutrition: calories 188, fat 11, fiber 6, carbs 7, protein 9

Mediterranean Diet Instant Pot Lunch Recipes
Tomato Stew

Preparation time: 5 minutes**Cooking time:** 20 minutes**Servings:** 4
Ingredients:

- 1 pound tomatoes, cut into wedges
- 1 red onion, chopped
- 1 tablespoon olive oil
- 2 garlic cloves, minced
- 1 cup veggie stock
- 1 teaspoon chili powder
- ½ teaspoon turmeric powder
- ½ cup tomato passata
- 2 tablespoons parsley, chopped
- 1 tablespoon basil, chopped
- A pinch of salt and black pepper

Directions:
Set the instant pot on Sauté mode, add the oil, heat it up, add the onion and the garlic and cook for 5 minutes. Add the tomatoes and the other ingredients, toss gently, put the lid on and cook on High for 15 minutes. Release the pressure fast for 5 minutes, divide the stew into bowls and serve.
Nutrition: calories 181, fat 7.3, fiber 1.4, carbs 4.6, protein 1.1

Chickpeas Stew

Preparation time: 10 minutes**Cooking time:** 25 minutes**Servings:** 4
Ingredients:

- 1 cup canned chickpeas, drained and rinsed
- 1 red onion, chopped
- 2 garlic cloves, minced
- 2 tablespoons olive oil
- A pinch of salt and black pepper
- 14 ounces canned tomatoes, chopped
- 1 bunch cilantro, chopped
- 2 cups veggie stock
- ½ teaspoon chili powder
- ½ teaspoon sweet paprika

Directions:
Set the instant pot on Sauté mode, add the oil, heat it up, add the onion and the garlic and cook fro 5 minutes. Add the chickpeas, tomatoes and the other ingredients, toss, put the lid on and cook on High for 20 minutes. Release the pressure naturally for 10 minutes, divide the stew into bowls and serve.
Nutrition: calories 671, fat 15.6, fiber 27.5, carbs 87.5, protein 27.1

Chicken and Rice

Preparation time: 10 minutes**Cooking time:** 30 minutes**Servings:** 4

Ingredients:

- 1 pound chicken breast, skinless, boneless and cubed
- 1 tablespoon olive oil
- 1 red onion, chopped
- 2 garlic cloves, minced
- 1 cup white rice
- 2 cups chicken stock
- ½ teaspoon turmeric powder
- ½ teaspoon sweet paprika
- ½ teaspoon oregano, dried
- Zest of 1 lemon, grated
- Juice of ½ lemon
- 2 tablespoons parsley, chopped
- A pinch of salt and black pepper

Directions:

Set the instant pot on Sauté mode, add the oil, heat it up, add the onion and the garlic and cook for 5 minutes. Add the meat and brown for 5 minutes more. Add the rice, stock and the other ingredients, toss well, put the lid on and cook on High for 20 minutes. Release the pressure naturally for 10 minutes, divide everything between plates and serve.

Nutrition: calories 342, fat 17.4, fiber 16.5, carbs 27.7, protein 26.4

Pork and Zucchini Hash

Preparation time: 10 minutes**Cooking time:** 30 minutes**Servings:** 4

Ingredients:

- 1 pound pork stew meat, cubed
- 2 zucchinis, cubed
- 1 tablespoon olive oil
- 1 yellow onion, chopped
- Juice of 1 lime
- 1 teaspoon oregano, dried
- A pinch of salt and black pepper
- 1 teaspoon garlic powder
- 2 garlic cloves, minced
- ½ cup tomato passata
- ½ teaspoon Italian seasoning
- 1 tablespoon oregano, chopped
- 1/3 cup parsley, chopped

Directions:

Set the instant pot on Sauté mode, add the oil, heat it up, add the onion, garlic, garlic powder and Italian seasoning, stir and cook fro 5 minutes. Add the meat and brown for 5 minutes more. Add the rest of the ingredients, toss, put the lid on and cook on High fro 20 minutes. Release the pressure naturally for 10 minutes, divide into bowls and serve for lunch.

Nutrition: calories 435, fat 18.5, fiber 13.6, carbs 27.8, protein 25.6

Shrimp and Quinoa Bowls

Preparation time: 5 minutes**Cooking time:** 25 minutes**Servings:** 4

Ingredients:

- 1 cup quinoa
- 2 cups chicken stock
- ½ pound shrimp, peeled and deveined
- 1 red onion, chopped
- 1 tablespoon olive oil
- ½ teaspoon coriander, ground
- ½ teaspoon sweet paprika
- ½ teaspoon chili powder
- A pinch of salt and black pepper
- 1/3 cup parsley, chopped
- Juice of ½ lemon

Directions:

Set the instant pot on Sauté mode, add the oil, heat it up, add the onion and sauté for 2 minutes. Add the quinoa, stock and the other ingredients except the shrimp, toss, put the lid on and cook on High fro 18 minutes. Release the pressure fast for 5 minutes, set the pot on Sauté mode again, add the shrimp, toss, cook for 5 more minutes, divide everything into bowls and serve.

Nutrition: calories 253, fat 11.5, fiber 3.4, carbs 16.5, protein 23.2

Chicken and Peppers

Preparation time: 10 minutes**Cooking time:** 25 minutes**Servings:** 4

Ingredients:

- 1 pound chicken breast, skinless, boneless and cubed
- 1 yellow onion, chopped
- ¼ cup chicken stock
- 1 tablespoon olive oil
- ½ teaspoon chili powder
- ½ teaspoon hot paprika
- 2 tablespoons mustard
- 1 red bell pepper, cut into strips
- 1 orange bell pepper, cut into strips
- 2 tablespoons balsamic vinegar
- ¼ cup parsley, chopped

Directions:

Set the instant pot on Sauté mode, add the oil, heat it up, add the onion and the meat and brown for 5 minutes. Add the rest of the ingredients, toss, put the lid on and cook on High fro 20 minutes. Release the pressure naturally for 10 minutes, divide everything between plates and serve for lunch.

Nutrition: calories 266, fat 12.2, fiber 4.5, carbs 15.7, protein 3.7

Turkey and Veggie Medley

Preparation time: 10 minutes**Cooking time:** 30 minutes**Servings:** 4

Ingredients:

- 2 garlic cloves, minced
- 1 yellow onion, chopped
- 1 pound turkey breast, skinless, boneless and cubed
- 1 tablespoon olive oil
- ¼ teaspoon red pepper flakes, crushed
- ½ teaspoon sweet paprika
- ½ teaspoon oregano, dried
- 1 cup cherry tomatoes, halved
- 1 zucchini, cubed
- 1 eggplant, cubed
- ¼ teaspoon garlic powder
- 2 tablespoons lemon juice
- ¼ cup parsley, chopped

Directions:

Set the instant pot on Sauté mode, add the oil, heat it up, add the garlic and the onion and cook for 5 minutes. Add the meat and brown fro 5 minutes more. Add the rest of the ingredients, toss, put the lid on and cook on High for 20 minutes. Release the pressure naturally for 10 minutes, divide between plates and serve for lunch.

Nutrition: calories 364, fat 16.8, fiber 5.5, carbs 26.8, protein 23.4

Eggplant Stew

Preparation time: 10 minutes**Cooking time:** 25 minutes**Servings:** 4

Ingredients:

- 2 eggplants, roughly cubed
- 2 tablespoons olive oil
- 1 red onion, chopped
- 2 garlic cloves, minced
- 1 cup cherry tomatoes, halved
- 1 tablespoon rosemary, chopped
- ½ teaspoon cumin, ground
- 1 tablespoon thyme, chopped
- Zest and juice of 1 lemon
- A pinch of salt and black pepper
- 1 cup tomato passata
- ½ cup veggie stock
- 1 tablespoon parsley, chopped

Directions:

Set the instant pot on Sauté mode, add the oil, heat it up, add the onion and the garlic and cook for 5 minutes. Add the eggplant and the other ingredients, toss gently, put the lid on and cook on High for 20 minutes. Release the pressure naturally for 10 minutes, divide the stew into bowls and serve.

Nutrition: calories 512, fat 16.4, fiber 17.5, carbs 78, protein 17.2

Shrimp Mix

Preparation time: 5 minutes**Cooking time:** 10 minutes**Servings:** 4

Ingredients:

- 1 pound shrimp, peeled and deveined
- 1 cup cherry tomatoes, halved
- 1 tablespoon avocado oil
- 2 scallions, chopped
- ½ teaspoon turmeric powder
- ½ teaspoon chili powder
- ½ cup chicken stock
- 1 tablespoon lime juice
- 1 tablespoon tomato paste
- A pinch of salt and black pepper
- ¼ cup parsley, chopped

Directions:

Set the instant pot on Sauté mode, add the oil, heat it up, add the scallions, turmeric and chili powder, stir and cook for 3 minutes. Add the shrimp and the other ingredients, toss, put the lid on and cook on High for 7 minutes. Release the pressure fast for 5 minutes, divide everything into bowls and serve.

Nutrition: calories 281, fat 12.7, fiber 1.7, carbs 5.8, protein 36.5

Lamb and Tomato Mix

Preparation time: 10 minutes**Cooking time:** 25 minutes**Servings:** 4

Ingredients:

- 1 pound lamb stew meat, ground
- 1 cup cherry tomatoes
- ¼ cup tomato passata
- 1 red onion, chopped
- 1 tablespoon olive oil
- 1 tablespoon lime juice
- ½ teaspoon oregano, dried
- A pinch of salt and black pepper
- ¼ cup chives, chopped

Directions:

Set the instant pot on Sauté mode, add the oil, heat it up, add the onion and the meat and cook for 5 minutes. Add the rest of the ingredients, toss, put the lid on and cook on High for 20 minutes. Release the pressure naturally for 10 minutes, divide everything into bowls and serve.

Nutrition: calories 354, fat 19.2, fiber 4.5, carbs 24.7, protein 11.2

Chicken and Quinoa Stew

Preparation time: 10 minutes**Cooking time:** 30 minutes**Servings:** 4
Ingredients:

- 2 cups chicken stock
- 1 cup quinoa
- 1 pound chicken breast, skinless, boneless and cubed
- 1 yellow onion, chopped
- ½ cup tomato passata
- 1 tablespoon olive oil
- ½ teaspoon sweet paprika
- ½ teaspoon red pepper flakes, crushed
- 1 cup carrots, chopped
- ½ cup dill, chopped
- Salt and black pepper to the taste

Directions:

Set the instant pot on Sauté mode, add the oil, heat it up, add the onion and the meat and cook for 5 minutes. Add the quinoa and the rest of the ingredients, toss, put the lid on and cook on High for 25 minutes. Release the pressure naturally for 10 minutes, divide into bowls and serve for lunch.

Nutrition: calories 263, fat 18.5, fiber 4.5, carbs 19.8, protein 14.5

Lentils Soup

Preparation time: 10 minutes**Cooking time:** 30 minutes**Servings:** 4
Ingredients:

- 2 cups canned lentils, drained and rinsed
- 6 cups chicken stock
- 1 yellow onion, chopped
- 1 tablespoon olive oil
- 1 carrot, peeled and sliced
- Juice of 1 lime
- ¼ cup dill, chopped
- Salt and black pepper to the taste
- ½ teaspoon sweet paprika

Directions:

Set the instant pot on Sauté mode, add the oil, heat it up, add the onion and the carrot and sauté for 5 minutes. Add the lentils and the other ingredients, toss, put the lid on and cook on High for 25 minutes. Release the pressure naturally for 10 minutes, divide into bowls and serve.

Nutrition: calories 264, fat 17.5, fiber 4.8, carbs 28.7, protein 16.3

Peppers and Tomato Soup

Preparation time: 10 minutes**Cooking time:** 25 minutes**Servings:** 4

Ingredients:

- ½ pound tomatoes, chopped
- 1 cup roasted peppers, chopped
- 1 red onion, chopped
- 1 tablespoon olive oil
- 2 garlic cloves, minced
- 6 cups veggie stock
- A pinch of salt and black pepper
- 2 tablespoons tomato paste
- ¼ cup parsley, chopped

Directions:

Set the instant pot on Sauté mode, add the oil, heat it up, add the onion and the garlic and cook for 5 minutes. Add the tomatoes and the other ingredients, toss, put the lid on and cook on High for 20 minutes. Release the pressure naturally for 10 minutes, blend the mix using an immersion blender, divide into bowls and serve.

Nutrition: calories 273, fat 11.2, fiber 3.4, carbs 15.7, protein 5.6

Chickpeas Soup

Preparation time: 10 minutes**Cooking time:** 25 minutes**Servings:** 4

Ingredients:

- 1 red onion, chopped
- 2 tablespoons olive oil
- 1 cup canned chickpeas, drained and rinsed
- 5 cups veggie stock
- 1 carrot, sliced
- ½ cup cilantro, chopped
- 2 tablespoons ginger, grated
- 1 teaspoon turmeric powder
- 28 ounces canned tomatoes and juice, crushed
- A pinch of salt and black pepper

Directions:

Set the instant pot on Sauté mode, add the oil, heat it up, add the ginger and the onion and cook for 5 minutes. Add the chickpeas and the other ingredients, toss, put the lid on and cook on High for 20 minutes. Release the pressure naturally for 10 minutes, divide the soup into bowls and serve.

Nutrition: calories 238, fat 7.3, fiber 6.3, carbs 32, protein 14

Green Beans Soup

Preparation time: 10 minutes**Cooking time:** 25 minutes**Servings:** 4

Ingredients:

- 1 red onion, chopped
- 1 tablespoon olive oil
- 1 cup carrots, chopped
- 1 pound green beans, trimmed and halved
- 6 cups veggie stock
- ½ teaspoon turmeric powder
- ½ teaspoon chili powder
- 1 teaspoon thyme, dried
- A pinch of salt and black pepper

Directions:

Set the instant pot on Sauté mode, add the oil, heat it up, add the onion and turmeric and cook for 5 minutes. Add the green beans and the other ingredients, toss, put the lid on and cook on High for 20 minutes. Release the pressure naturally for 10 minutes, divide the soup into bowls and serve.

Nutrition: calories 264, fat 17.5, fiber 4.5, carbs 23.7, protein 11.5

Beans Soup

Preparation time: 10 minutes**Cooking time:** 25 minutes**Servings:** 4

Ingredients:

- 1 yellow onion, chopped
- 1 cup canned red kidney beans, drained and rinsed
- ½ cup pinto beans, drained and rinsed
- 6 cups veggie stock
- 2 tablespoons parsley, chopped
- 1 tablespoon olive oil
- ¼ cup celery, chopped
- ¼ teaspoon thyme, dried
- ½ teaspoon basil, dried
- ½ teaspoon rosemary, dried
- A pinch of salt and black pepper

Directions:

Set the instant pot on Sauté mode, add the oil, heat it up, add the onion and sauté for 5 minutes. Add the beans and the other ingredients, toss, put the lid on and cook on High for 20 minutes. Release the pressure naturally for 10 minutes, divide into bowls and serve.

Nutrition: calories 300, fat 11.3, fiber 3.4, carbs 17.5, protein 10

Shrimp Stew

Preparation time: 10 minutes**Cooking time:** 10 minutes**Servings:** 4

Ingredients:

- 1 tablespoon olive oil
- 1 pound shrimp, peeled and deveined
- 1 red onion, chopped
- 2 spring onions, chopped
- 1 cup tomato passata
- 1 red bell pepper, chopped
- 1 green bell pepper, chopped
- 1 red chili, chopped
- 2 garlic cloves, minced
- ¼ cup parsley, chopped
- A pinch of salt and black pepper

Directions:

Set the instant pot on Sauté mode, add the oil, heat it up, add the onion and spring onion and sauté for 5 minutes. Add the shrimp and the other ingredients, toss, put the lid on and cook on High for 5 minutes more. Release the pressure naturally for 10 minutes, divide the stew into bowls and serve.

Nutrition: calories 363, fat 2, fiber 5, carbs 18, protein 40

Quinoa and Veggies Soup

Preparation time: 10 minutes**Cooking time:** 20 minutes**Servings:** 4

Ingredients:

- 1 cup quinoa
- 5 cups veggie stock
- 2 scallions, chopped
- 1 carrot, peeled and cubed
- 1 zucchini, cubed
- 1 eggplant, cubed
- ½ cup cherry tomatoes halved
- 1 green bell pepper, cubed
- ½ teaspoon chili powder
- A pinch of salt and black pepper
- 1 tablespoon lime juice
- 1 tablespoon parsley, chopped

Directions:

In your instant pot, combine the quinoa with the stock, scallions and the other ingredients, toss, put the lid on and cook on High for 20 minutes. Release the pressure naturally for 10 minutes, divide the soup into bowls and serve.

Nutrition: calories 300, fat 12.2, fiber 5.4, carbs 16.5, protein 12.2

Lime Turkey Soup

Preparation time: 10 minutes**Cooking time:** 30 minutes**Servings:** 6

Ingredients:

- 1 pound turkey breast, skinless, boneless and cubed
- 1 yellow onion, chopped
- 1 tablespoon olive oil
- Juice of 1 lime
- A pinch of salt and black pepper
- ½ teaspoon cumin, ground
- ½ teaspoon oregano, dried
- ½ cup tomato passata
- 4 cups chicken stock
- 2 celery stalks, chopped
- ¼ cup cilantro, chopped

Directions:

Set the instant pot on Sauté mode, add the oil, heat it up, add the onion and the meat and cook for 5 minutes. Add the rest of the ingredients, toss, put the lid on and cook on High for 25 minutes more. Release the pressure naturally fro 10 minutes, divide the soup into bowls and serve.

Nutrition: calories 276, fat 1, fiber 21, carbs 48, protein 17

Zucchini Cream

Preparation time: 10 minutes**Cooking time:** 20 minutes**Servings:** 4

Ingredients:

- 1 pound zucchinis, roughly chopped
- ½ cup heavy cream
- 3 scallions, chopped
- 1 tablespoon garlic, minced
- ½ teaspoon ginger, grated
- ½ teaspoon turmeric powder
- ½ teaspoon coriander, ground
- 2 tablespoons olive oil
- 4 cups chicken stock
- 1 tablespoon dill, chopped
- Salt and black pepper to the taste

Directions:

Set the instant pot on Sauté mode, add the oil, heat it up, add the garlic, scallions and ginger and sauté for 5 minutes. Add the zucchinis and the other ingredients except the cream, whisk, put the lid on and cook on High for 15 minutes. Release the pressure naturally for 10 minutes, add the cream, blend the soup using an immersion blender, divide into bowls and serve.

Nutrition: calories 182, fat 7.6, fiber 1.5, carbs 12.6, protein 2.3

Spinach Cream Soup

Preparation time: 10 minutes**Cooking time:** 15 minutes**Servings:** 4

Ingredients:

- 1 yellow onion, chopped
- 1 pound baby spinach
- 2 tablespoons olive oil
- ½ cup carrots, chopped
- 1 zucchini, chopped
- 6 cups veggie stock
- 1 cup heavy cream
- 1 tablespoon basil, chopped
- Salt and black pepper to the taste

Directions:

In your instant pot, combine the spinach with the onion, oil and the other ingredients, toss, put the lid on and cook on High for 15 minutes. Release the pressure naturally for 10 minutes, blend the soup using an immersion blender, divide into bowls and serve.

Nutrition: calories 471, fat 8.2, fiber 19.4, carbs 76.5, protein 27.6

Broccoli Cream

Preparation time: 10 minutes**Cooking time:** 25 minutes**Servings:** 4

Ingredients:

- 1 pound broccoli florets
- 1 red onion, chopped
- 1 tablespoon olive oil
- 1 teaspoon garlic powder
- ½ teaspoon cumin, ground
- 1 cup heavy cream
- 4 cups chicken stock
- Salt and black pepper to the taste
- 1 tablespoon cilantro, chopped

Directions:

Set the instant pot on Sauté mode, add the oil, heat it up, add the onion and garlic powder and cook for 5 minutes. Add the broccoli and the other ingredients, toss, put the lid on and cook on High for 20 minutes. Release the pressure naturally for 10 minutes, blend the soup using an immersion blender, divide into bowls and serve.

Nutrition: calories 243, fat 17, fiber 2.3, carbs 41.1, protein 13.7

White Beans Soup

Preparation time: 10 minutes**Cooking time:** 30 minutes**Servings:** 4

Ingredients:

- 1 yellow onion, chopped
- 2 carrots, peeled and cubed
- 2 cups canned white beans, drained and rinsed
- 6 cups veggie stock
- A pinch of salt and black pepper
- ½ teaspoon turmeric powder
- ½ teaspoon sweet paprika
- 1 tablespoon olive oil
- 1 bay leaf
- 2 tablespoons tomato paste
- 1 tablespoon cilantro, chopped

Directions:

Set the instant pot on Sauté mode, add the oil, heat it up, add the onion and carrots and sauté for 5 minutes. Add the beans and the other ingredients, toss, put the lid on and cook on High for 25 minutes more. Release the pressure naturally for 10 minutes, ladle the soup into bowls and serve.

Nutrition: calories 273, fat 16.3, fiber 8.4, carbs 15.6, protein 7.4

Mixed Veggie Soup

Preparation time: 10 minutes**Cooking time:** 20 minutes**Servings:** 4

Ingredients:

- 2 tablespoons olive oil
- 2 red onions, chopped
- 1 zucchini, cubed
- 1 eggplant, cubed
- ½ cup cherry tomatoes, halved
- 1 carrot, peeled and cubed
- 6 cups chicken stock
- Zest of 1 lemon, grated
- Juice of ½ lemon
- ½ cup basil, chopped
- Salt and black pepper to the taste

Directions:

Set the instant pot on Sauté mode, add the oil, heat it up, add the onions and sauté for 5 minutes. Add the zucchini and the other ingredients, toss, put the lid on and cook on High for 15 minutes. Release the pressure naturally fro 10 minutes, divide the soup into bowls and serve.

Nutrition: calories 274, fat 11.1, fiber 4.5, carbs 16.5, protein 4.5

Leeks Soup

Preparation time: 10 minutes**Cooking time:** 20 minutes**Servings:** 4

Ingredients:

- 3 leeks, sliced
- 1 yellow onion, chopped
- 1 tablespoon olive oil
- 4 cups veggie stock
- ½ teaspoon sweet paprika
- A pinch of nutmeg, ground
- ½ teaspoon chili powder
- Salt and black pepper to the taste

Directions:

Set the instant pot on Sauté mode, add the oil, heat up, add the leeks and the onion and sauté for 5 minutes. Add the stock and the other ingredients, toss, put the lid on and cook on High for 15 minutes. Release the pressure naturally for 10 minutes, ladle the soup into bowls and serve.

Nutrition: calories 310, fat 15.3, fiber 8.7, carbs 24.6, protein 18.4

Lamb and Leeks Soup

Preparation time: 10 minutes**Cooking time:** 25 minutes**Servings:** 4

Ingredients:

- 1 pound lamb meat, cubed
- 2 leeks, sliced
- 1 red onion, chopped
- 2 tablespoons olive oil
- 5 cups water
- 2 tablespoons dill, chopped
- A pinch of salt and black pepper
- ½ teaspoon turmeric powder
- 1 cup baby spinach

Directions:

Set the instant pot on Sauté mode, add the oil, heat it up, add the onion and the leeks and sauté for 2 minutes. Add the meat and brown for 3 minutes more. Add the rest of the ingredients, toss, put the lid on and cook on High for 20 minutes. Release the pressure naturally for 10 minutes, ladle the soup into bowls and serve.

Nutrition: calories 275, fat 28.5, fiber 1, carbs 2.8, protein 5

Kale Soup

Preparation time: 10 minutes**Cooking time:** 20 minutes**Servings:** 4
Ingredients:

- 1 tablespoon olive oil
- 1 carrot, chopped
- 1 yellow onion, chopped
- ½ pound baby kale
- 4 cups chicken stock
- 1 teaspoon oregano, dried
- ½ cup tomato passata
- Salt and black pepper to the taste
- ½ tablespoon chives, chopped

Directions:

Set the instant pot on Sauté mode, add the oil, heat it up, add the onion and the carrot and sauté for 5 minutes. Add the kale and the other ingredients, toss, put the lid on and cook on High for 15 minutes. Release the pressure naturally for 10 minutes, divide the soup into bowls and serve.

Nutrition: calories 564, fat 26.5, fiber 15.4, carbs 37.4, protein 26.6

Salmon Soup

Preparation time: 10 minutes**Cooking time:** 20 minutes**Servings:** 4
Ingredients:

- 2 tablespoons olive oil
- 1 yellow onion, chopped
- 5 cups chicken stock
- 1 pound salmon fillets, boneless, skinless and cubed
- ½ teaspoon turmeric powder
- ½ teaspoon basil, dried
- ½ teaspoon sweet paprika
- ¼ tablespoon chives, chopped
- ½ cup heavy cream
- A pinch of salt and black pepper

Directions:

Set the instant pot on Sauté mode, add the oil, heat it up, add the onion , turmeric and paprika and sauté for 5 minutes. Add the fish, stock and the other ingredients, toss gently, put the lid on and cook on High for 15 minutes. Release the pressure naturally for 10 minutes, ladle the soup into bowls and serve.

Nutrition: calories 198, fat 8.1, fiber 1, carbs 4.2, protein 26.4

Shrimp and Tomato Soup

Preparation time: 10 minutes**Cooking time:** 12 minutes **Servings:** 6

Ingredients:

- ½ pound tomatoes, cubed
- 1 pound shrimp, peeled and deveined
- 4 cups chicken stock
- 1 yellow onion, chopped
- 2 tablespoons olive oil
- ½ cup parsley, chopped
- 2 garlic cloves, minced
- 1 teaspoon cumin, ground
- Juice of ½ lemon
- ½ teaspoon ginger, grated
- A pinch of salt and black pepper

Directions:

Set the instant pot on Sauté mode, add the oil, heat it up, add the onion and the garlic and cook for 2 minutes. Add the tomatoes, shrimp and the other ingredients, toss, put the lid on and cook on High for 10 minutes. Release the pressure naturally for 10 minutes, ladle the soup into bowls and serve.

Nutrition: calories 300, fat 15.4, fiber 4.5, carbs 29.5, protein 15.4

Garlic Tomato Cream

Preparation time: 10 minutes**Cooking time:** 25 minutes**Servings:** 4

Ingredients:

- 2 pounds tomatoes, peeled and chopped
- 2 tablespoons olive oil
- 1 red onion, chopped
- 1 cup heavy cream
- 3 cups veggie stock
- 6 garlic cloves, minced
- A pinch of salt and black pepper
- ½ teaspoon red pepper flakes
- ½ cup basil, chopped

Directions:

Set the instant pot on Sauté mode, add the oil, heat it up, add the onion and garlic and cook for 5 minutes. Add the tomatoes and the other ingredients except the cream, stir, put the lid on and cook on High fro 20 minutes. Release the pressure naturally for 10 minutes, transfer the soup to a blender, add the cream, pulse well, divide into bowls and serve.

Nutrition: calories 237, fat 10, fiber 3.4, carbs 15.3, protein 7.

Shrimp and Zucchini

Preparation time: 5 minutes**Cooking time:** 12 minutes**Servings:** 4

Ingredients:

- 2 garlic cloves, minced
- 1 pound shrimp, peeled and deveined
- 1 red onion, chopped
- 1 tablespoon olive oil
- 1 zucchini, cubed
- 1 tablespoon balsamic vinegar
- Salt and black pepper to the taste
- 1 teaspoon red pepper flakes, crushed
- ¼ cup chicken stock
- 1 tablespoon chives, chopped

Directions:

Set the instant pot on Sauté mode, add the oil, heat it up, add the onion and the garlic and cook for 2 minutes Add the shrimp and the other ingredients, toss, put the lid on and cook on High for 10 minutes Release the pressure fast for 5 minutes, divide the mix between plates and serve.

Nutrition: calories 264, fat 9.3, fiber 1.2, carbs 2.3, protein 1.2

Potatoes Stew

Preparation time: 10 minutes**Cooking time:** 25 minutes**Servings:** 4

Ingredients:

- 1 carrot, peeled and sliced
- 1 tablespoon olive oil
- 1 pound gold potatoes, peeled and roughly cubed
- 1 yellow onion, chopped
- 2 garlic cloves, minced
- ½ teaspoon smoked paprika
- ½ teaspoon oregano, dried
- Salt and black pepper to the taste
- 14 ounces canned tomatoes, chopped
- ½ cup chives, chopped

Directions:

Set the instant pot on Sauté mode, add the oil, heat it up, add the onion and the garlic and cook for 5 minutes. Add the carrot, potatoes and the other ingredients, toss, put the lid on and cook on High for 20 minutes. Release the pressure naturally for 10 minutes, divide the stew into bowls and serve.

Nutrition: calories 325, fat 17.3, fiber 6.8, carbs 26.4, protein 16.4

Lamb and Tomato Mix

Preparation time: 10 minutes**Cooking time:** 30 minutes**Servings:** 4

Ingredients:
- 2 pounds lamb shoulder, cubed
- ½ pound tomatoes, cubed
- 1 tablespoon olive oil
- 1 red onion, chopped
- Salt and black pepper to the taste
- ½ cup chicken stock
- ¾ cup green olives, pitted and sliced
- 1 tablespoon cilantro, chopped

Directions:

Set the instant pot on Sauté mode, add the oil, heat it up, add the onion and the meat and brown for 5 minutes Add the tomatoes and the other ingredients, toss, put the lid on and cook on High for 25 minutes Release the pressure naturally fro 10 minutes, divide the stew into bowls and serve.

Nutrition: calories 411, fat 17.4, fiber 8.4, carbs 25.5, protein 34.3

Parsley Potato Soup

Preparation time: 10 minutes**Cooking time:** 30 minutes**Servings:** 4

Ingredients:
- 1 pound gold potatoes, peeled and roughly cubed
- 1 tablespoon olive oil
- 1 yellow onion, chopped
- 5 cups chicken stock
- Salt and black pepper to the taste
- 2 garlic cloves, minced
- 2 teaspoons thyme, dried
- ½ teaspoon turmeric powder
- 1 tablespoons parsley, chopped

Directions:

Set the instant pot on Sauté mode, add the oil, heat it up, add the onion and the garlic and sauté for 5 minutes. Add the potatoes and the other ingredients, toss, put the lid on and cook on High for 25 minutes more. Release the pressure naturally for 10 minutes, divide the soup into bowls and serve.

Nutrition: calories 372, fat 17.3, fiber 5.5, carbs 28.4, protein 17.4

Shrimp and Peas

Preparation time: 10 minutes**Cooking time:** 20 minutes**Servings:** 4

Ingredients:

- 2 spring onions, chopped
- 1 pound shrimp, peeled and deveined
- 1 cup green peas
- 1 tablespoon olive oil
- ¼ cup tomato passata
- 2 tablespoons lemon juice
- 2 tablespoons parsley, chopped
- Salt and black pepper to the taste

Directions:

Set the instant pot on Sauté mode, add the oil, heat it up, add the onions and cook for 2 minutes. Add the peas and the other ingredients except the shrimp, toss and cook for 10 minutes more. Add the shrimp, put the lid on and cook on High for 8 minutes. Release the pressure naturally for 10 minutes, divide the mix between plates and serve.

Nutrition: calories 293, fat 11.2 fiber 3.4, carbs 27, protein 4.45

Ginger Lamb Stew

Preparation time: 10 minutes**Cooking time:** 35 minutes**Servings:** 4

Ingredients:

- 2 pounds lamb stew meat, cubed
- ½ cup beef stock
- 1 tablespoon olive oil
- 3 scallions, chopped
- ½ cup mint, chopped
- A pinch of salt and black pepper
- ½ teaspoon turmeric powder
- 1 carrot, peeled and sliced
- 2 sweet potatoes, peeled and cubed
- 1 celery rib, chopped
- 1 tablespoon ginger, grated
- 1 cup apricots, dried and halved
- 2 tablespoons Greek yogurt

Directions:

Set the instant pot on Sauté mode, add the oil, heat up, add the scallions and the meat and brown for 5 minutes. Add the rest of the ingredients, toss, put the lid on and cook on High for 30 minutes. Release the pressure naturally for 10 minutes, divide the stew into bowls and serve.

Nutrition: calories 355, fat 14.3, fiber 6.7, carbs 22.6, protein 15.4

Chicken and Barley Soup

Preparation time: 10 minutes**Cooking time:** 30 minutes**Servings:** 4

Ingredients:

- ½ cup barley
- 1 pound chicken breast, skinless, boneless and cubed
- 1 yellow onion, chopped
- 1 tablespoon olive oil
- 6 cups chicken soup
- A pinch of salt and black pepper
- 2 teaspoons oregano, dried
- 2 tablespoons lime juice
- ½ tablespoon parsley, chopped

Directions:

Set the instant pot on Sauté mode, add the oil, heat it up, add the meat and the onion and brown for 5 minutes Add the rest of the ingredients, toss, put the lid on and cook on High for 25 minutes. Release the pressure naturally for 10 minutes, ladle the soup into bowls and serve.

Nutrition: calories 360, fat 10.2, fiber 4.7, carbs 43.3, protein 22.3

Turmeric Turkey Soup

Preparation time: 10 minutes**Cooking time:** 30 minutes**Servings:** 4

Ingredients:

- 2 tablespoons olive oil
- 1 pound turkey breast, skinless, boneless and cubed
- 1 yellow onion, chopped
- 1 tablespoon olive oil
- 5 cups chicken stock
- 2 teaspoons mustard seeds, ground
- 2 teaspoons garlic, minced
- ¼ teaspoon turmeric powder
- A pinch of salt and black pepper
- 2 tablespoons cilantro, chopped

Directions:

Set the instant pot on Sauté mode, add the oil, heat it up, add the onion and the meat and sauté for 5 minutes. Add the rest of the ingredients, toss, put the lid on and cook on High for 25 minutes. Release the pressure naturally for 10 minutes, divide the soup into bowls and serve.

Nutrition: calories 189, fat 8.3, fiber 3.4, carbs 11.7, protein 4.5

Lamb and Plums Mix

Preparation time: 10 minutes**Cooking time:** 30 minutes**Servings:** 4
Ingredients:

- 3 garlic cloves, minced
- 1 yellow onion, chopped
- 2 pounds lamb stew meat, cubed
- 2 tablespoons olive oil
- 1 cup plums, pitted and halved
- 2 cups water
- ½ teaspoon sweet paprika
- ½ teaspoon chili flakes, crushed
- ½ teaspoon turmeric powder
- 3 tablespoons cilantro, chopped
- Salt and black pepper to the taste
- 1 teaspoon ginger, grated

Directions:

Set the instant pot on Sauté mode, add the oil, heat it up, add the onion and the garlic and cook for 5 minutes. Add the meat and cook for 5 minutes more. Add the rest of the ingredients, toss, put the lid on and cook on High for 20 minutes. Release the pressure naturally for 10 minutes, divide the stew into bowls and serve.

Nutrition: calories 309, fat 25.4, fiber 4, carbs 15.3, protein 6.7

Sea Bass and Eggplant Mix

Preparation time: 10 minutes**Cooking time:** 20 minutes**Servings:** 4
Ingredients:

- 1 pound sea bass fillets, boneless, skinless and cubed
- 2 eggplants, cubed
- 1 tablespoon avocado oil
- 1 red onion, sliced
- ½ teaspoon chili powder
- ½ teaspoon coriander, ground
- 2 tablespoons cilantro, chopped
- 2 garlic cloves, minced
- ½ teaspoon sweet paprika
- ½ cup chicken stock
- A pinch of salt and black pepper

Directions:

Set the instant pot on Sauté mode, add the oil, heat it up, add the onion and chili powder and sauté for 5 minutes. Add the fish and the other ingredients, toss gently, put the lid on and cook on High for 15 minutes. Release the pressure naturally for 10 minutes, divide the mix between plates and serve.

Nutrition: calories 272, fat 15, fiber 3.6, carbs 14, protein 2.3

Asparagus Soup

Preparation time: 10 minutes**Cooking time:** 12 minutes**Servings:** 4

Ingredients:
- 1 pound asparagus, trimmed and halved
- 4 cups chicken stock
- 1 yellow onion, chopped
- 1 cup cherry tomatoes, halved
- ½ teaspoon chili powder
- ½ teaspoon turmeric powder
- 1 tablespoon cilantro, chopped
- 1 tablespoon chives, chopped
- Salt and black pepper to the taste

Directions:
In your instant pot, combine the asparagus with the stock, onion and the other ingredients, toss, put the lid on and cook on High for 12 minutes. Release the pressure naturally for 10 minutes, divide the soup into bowls and serve.

Nutrition: calories 200, fat 7.8, fiber 3.4, carbs 11.4, protein 8.2

Spinach Soup

Preparation time: 5 minutes**Cooking time:** 10 minutes**Servings:** 4

Ingredients:
- 1 pound baby spinach
- 4 cups veggie stock
- 1 red onion, sliced
- ½ teaspoon coriander, ground
- ½ teaspoon turmeric powder
- Salt and black pepper to the taste
- 1 celery stalk, chopped
- 1 carrot, chopped
- 1 tablespoon parsley, chopped

Directions:
In your instant pot, combine the spinach with the stock, onion and the other ingredients, put the lid on and cook on High for 10 minutes. Release the pressure fast for 5 minutes, divide into bowls and serve.

Nutrition: calories 192, fat 8.3, fiber 4.5, carbs 12.3, protein 4.5

Mackerel Stew

Preparation time: 5 minutes**Cooking time:** 25 minutes**Servings:** 4

Ingredients:
- 2 garlic cloves, minced
- 2 tablespoons olive oil
- 1 pound mackerel, boneless and cubed
- 1 cup canned tomatoes, chopped
- ½ teaspoon red pepper flakes, crushed
- 1 cup chicken stock
- 1 tablespoon lime juice
- 1 bunch parsley, chopped
- A pinch of salt and black pepper

Directions:
Set the instant pot on Sauté mode, add the oil, heat it up, add the garlic and the mackerel and cook for 5 minutes. Add the rest of the ingredients, toss, put the lid on and cook on High for 20 minutes. Release the pressure fast for 5 minutes, divide the stew into bowls and serve.

Nutrition: calories 300, fat 14.3, fiber 4.5, carbs 16.1, protein 11

Chili Shrimp

Preparation time: 5 minutes**Cooking time:** 8 minutes**Servings:** 4

Ingredients:
- 2 pounds shrimp, peeled and deveined
- 1 red onion, chopped
- ½ teaspoon chipotle chili powder
- 2 tablespoons olive oil
- A pinch of salt and white pepper
- ¼ cup cilantro, chopped
- 2 tablespoons lemon juice
- ½ tablespoon balsamic vinegar

Directions:
Set the instant pot on Sauté mode, add the oil, heat it up, add the onion and cook for 2 minutes. Add the shrimp and the other ingredients, toss, put the lid on and cook on High for 6 minutes. Release the pressure fast for 5 minutes, divide the mix between plates and serve.

Nutrition: calories 120, fat 4.5, fiber 3.4, carbs 12, protein 2.3

Balsamic Tuna Mix

Preparation time: 10 minutes**Cooking time:** 12 minutes**Servings:** 4

Ingredients:

- 1 pound tuna fillets, boneless and cubed
- 2 scallions, chopped
- 1 tablespoon olive oil
- 1 cup cherry tomatoes, halved
- ½ teaspoon Italian seasoning
- ½ teaspoon oregano, dried
- 2 tablespoons balsamic vinegar
- 1 garlic clove, minced
- A pinch of salt and black pepper
- 1 tablespoon chives, chopped

Directions:

Set the instant pot on Sauté mode, add the oil, heat it up, add the scallions and cook for 2 minutes. Add the tuna and the other ingredients, toss, put the lid on and cook on High for 10 minutes. Release the pressure naturally for 10 minutes, divide everything between plates and serve for lunch.

Nutrition: calories 263, fat 11.1, fiber 2.4, carbs 12.5, protein 6.32

Veggies Stew

Preparation time: 10 minutes**Cooking time:** 20 minutes**Servings:** 4

Ingredients:

- 1 yellow onion, chopped
- 2 tablespoons olive oil
- 2 zucchinis, cubed
- 2 eggplants, cubed
- 1 cup cherry tomatoes, halved
- 1 carrot, cubed
- 1 red bell pepper, roughly chopped
- 1 green bell pepper, roughly chopped
- 2 garlic cloves, minced
- 3 tablespoons tomato paste
- 16 ounces canned chickpeas, drained
- 1 teaspoon oregano, dried
- ¼ teaspoon smoked paprika
- A pinch of salt and black pepper
- 1 tablespoon cilantro, chopped

Directions:

Set the instant pot on Sauté mode, add the oil, heat it up, add the onion and the garlic and cook for 5 minutes. Add the zucchinis, eggplants and the other ingredients, toss gently, put the lid on and cook on High for 15 minutes. Release the pressure naturally for 10 minutes, divide everything into bowls and serve.

Nutrition: calories 450, fat 12, fiber 13, carbs 47, protein 34

Artichoke Soup

Preparation time: 10 minutes**Cooking time:** 20 minutes**Servings:** 4

Ingredients:
- 10 ounces canned artichoke hearts, drained and quartered
- 1 yellow onion, chopped
- 1 tablespoon olive oil
- 3 garlic cloves, minced
- 5 cups chicken stock
- ¼ tablespoon lime juice
- Salt and white pepper to the taste
- 1 tablespoon dill, chopped

Directions:
In your instant pot, combine the artichokes with the onion and the other ingredients, toss, put the lid on and cook on High for 20 minutes. Release the pressure naturally for 10 minutes, divide the soup into bowls and serve.

Nutrition: calories 200, fat 5.4, fiber 2.4, carbs 7.6, protein 3.3

Olives Stew

Preparation time: 10 minutes**Cooking time:** 15 minutes**Servings:** 4

Ingredients:
- 1 yellow onion, chopped
- 1 tablespoon avocado oil
- 1 cup cherry tomatoes, halved
- 1 cup green olives, pitted and halved
- 1 cup kalamata olives, pitted and halved
- 1 cup black olives, pitted and halved
- ½ cup chicken stock
- ½ cup tomato passata
- 1 tablespoon cilantro, chopped
- 1 tablespoon lime juice
- Salt and black pepper to the taste

Directions:
Set the instant pot on Sauté mode, add the oil, heat it up, add the onion and sauté for 5 minutes. Add the olives and the other ingredients, toss, put the lid on and cook on High for 10 minutes. Release the pressure naturally for 10 minutes, divide the stew into bowls and serve for lunch.

Nutrition: calories 235, fat 12.3, fiber 3.5, carbs 16.3, protein 10.2

Salmon and Quinoa

Preparation time: 15 minutes**Cooking time:** 30 minutes**Servings:** 4

Ingredients:
- 1 cup quinoa
- 2 cups chicken stock
- ½ teaspoon turmeric powder
- 1 pound salmon fillets, boneless and cubed
- 1 tablespoon olive oil
- 1 yellow onion, chopped
- ¼ cup lemon juice
- 2 tablespoons chives, chopped

Directions:

Set the instant pot on Sauté mode, add the oil, heat up, add the onion and cook for 5 minutes. Add quinoa, turmeric and stock, stir, put the lid and cook on High for 15 minutes. Release the pressure naturally for 10 minutes, add the salmon and the other ingredients, toss gently, put the lid on again and cook on High for 10 minutes more. Release the pressure fast for 5 minutes, divide the mix between plates and serve for lunch.

Nutrition: calories 232, fat 11, fiber 2.4, carbs 14.3, protein 12.4

Greek Eggplant and Green Beans Stew

Preparation time: 10 minutes**Cooking time:** 20 minutes**Servings:** 4

Ingredients:
- 1 pound eggplant, cubed
- 1 tablespoon olive oil
- ½ pound green beans, trimmed and halved
- 1 red onion, chopped
- ½ teaspoon smoked paprika
- ½ teaspoon chili powder
- 1 cup chicken stock
- 1 cup heavy cream
- Salt and black pepper to the taste
- 2 red bell peppers, chopped
- ¼ teaspoon allspice, ground
- 1 teaspoon oregano, dried
- 3 tablespoons Greek yogurt

Directions:

Set the instant pot on Sauté mode, add the oil, heat up, add the onion, chili powder and paprika and cook for 5 minutes. Add the eggplant, green beans and the other ingredients, toss, put the lid on and cook on High for 15 minutes. Release the pressure naturally for 10 minutes, divide everything into bowls and serve.

Nutrition: calories 256, fat 3.5, fiber 25.4, carbs 53.3, protein 8.8

Lamb and Black Beans Soup

Preparation time: 10 minutes**Cooking time:** 30 minutes**Servings:** 4

Ingredients:

- 2 tablespoon olive oil
- 1 red onion, chopped
- 1 pound lamb stew meat, cubed
- 1 cup canned black beans, drained and rinsed
- 5 cups chicken stock
- 1 bay leaf
- ½ cup tomato paste
- Salt and black pepper to the taste
- 2 carrots, chopped
- 1 tablespoon dill, chopped

Directions:

Set the instant pot on Sauté mode, add the oil, heat it up, add the onion and the meat and brown for 5 minutes. Add the rest of the ingredients, toss, put the lid on and cook on High for 25 minutes. Release the pressure naturally for 10 minutes, divide the soup into bowls and serve.

Nutrition: calories 214, fat 16.3, fiber 1.5, carbs 6.4, protein 11.8

Chicken and Peppers Soup

Preparation time: 10 minutes**Cooking time:** 30 minutes**Servings:** 4

Ingredients:

- 2 tablespoons olive oil
- 1 red onion, chopped
- 1 pound chicken breast, skinless, boneless and cubed
- 1 red bell pepper, cubed
- 1 green bell pepper, cubed
- 3 tomatoes, chopped
- 4 cups chicken stock
- 3 garlic cloves, minced
- 1 red chili pepper, chopped
- Juice of 1 lime
- Salt and black pepper to the taste
- 1 tablespoon cilantro, chopped

Directions:

Set the instant pot on Sauté mode, add the oil, heat up, add the onion and the meat and brown for 5 minutes. Add the peppers and the other ingredients, toss, put the lid on and cook on High for 25 minutes. Release the pressure naturally for 10 minutes, divide the soup into bowls and serve.

Nutrition: calories 667, fat 17.6, fiber 17.6, carbs 72.3, protein 55.4

Oregano Chicken Soup

Preparation time: 10 minutes**Cooking time:** 25 minutes**Servings:** 4

Ingredients:

- 2 pounds chicken breast, skinless, boneless and cubed
- 1 yellow onion, chopped
- 1 tablespoon olive oil
- ½ teaspoon chili powder
- Salt and black pepper to the taste
- 2 tablespoons garlic, minced
- 1 red bell pepper, chopped
- 2 tablespoons oregano, chopped
- 4 cups chicken stock
- ¼ cup lime juice

Directions:

Set the instant pot on Sauté mode, add the oil, heat up, add the onion and chili powder and cook for 5 minutes. Add the meat and brown for another 5 minutes. Add the rest of the ingredients, toss, put the lid on and cook on High for 15 minutes. Release the pressure naturally for 10 minutes, divide the soup into bowls and serve.

Nutrition: calories 312, fat 17.4, fiber 5.6, carbs 20.2, protein 15.3

Lamb and Lentils Soup

Preparation time: 10 minutes**Cooking time:** 35 minutes**Servings:** 6

Ingredients:

- 2 tablespoons olive oil
- 1 pound lamb stew meat, cubed
- 1 cup canned lentils, drained and rinsed
- 1 yellow onion, chopped
- 5 cups veggie stock
- ½ teaspoon turmeric powder
- ½ teaspoon sweet paprika
- 2 tablespoons tomato paste
- 2 garlic cloves, chopped
- 1 tablespoon cilantro, chopped
- Salt and black pepper to the taste

Directions:

Heat up a pot with the oil over medium high heat, add the chicken, onion and the garlic and brown for 10 minutes. Add the rest of the ingredients, bring the soup to a boil and simmer for 1 hour. Ladle the soup into bowls and serve for lunch.

Nutrition: calories 311, fat 13.2, fiber 4.3, carbs 17.5, protein 13.4

Sea Bass Mix

Preparation time: 5 minutes**Cooking time:** 20 minutes**Servings:** 4
Ingredients:

- 2 pounds sea bass fillets, boneless and cubed
- 1 tablespoon avocado oil
- 4 scallions, chopped
- ½ cup tomato passata
- A pinch of salt and black pepper
- 1 leek, sliced
- 2 bay leaves
- ½ cup lemon juice
- 1 tablespoon cilantro, chopped

Directions:

Set the instant pot on Sauté mode, add the oil, heat up, add the scallions and leek and sauté for 5 minutes. Add the fish and the other ingredients, toss gently, put the lid on and cook on High for 15 minutes. Release the pressure naturally for 10 minutes, divide the mix between plates and serve.

Nutrition: calories 300, fat 15, fiber 7.6, carbs 17.4, protein 22.4

Chicken and Olives Mix

Preparation time: 10 minutes**Cooking time:** 25 minutes**Servings:** 4
Ingredients:

- 1 pound chicken breasts, skinless, boneless and cubed
- 1 tablespoon olive oil
- 1 red onion, chopped
- 1 cup kalamata olives, pitted and halved
- 1 cup tomato passata
- ½ teaspoon cumin, ground
- ½ teaspoon oregano, dried
- Salt and black pepper to the taste
- ½ cup parsley, chopped
- 1 teaspoon lime juice

Directions:

Set the instant pot on Sauté mode, add the oil, heat it up, add the meat and the onion and brown for 5 minutes. Add the olives and the other ingredients, toss, put the lid on and cook on High for 20 minutes. Release the pressure naturally for 10 minutes, divide the mix between plates and serve.

Nutrition: calories 311, fat 8.4, fiber 8.3, carbs 17.4, protein 22.3

Mushrooms Soup

Preparation time: 10 minutes**Cooking time:** 30 minutes**Servings:** 4

Ingredients:
- 1 yellow onion, chopped
- 1 pound white mushrooms, sliced
- 4 cups chicken stock
- 1 cup heavy cream
- 1 tablespoon olive oil
- 2 celery stalks, chopped
- 2 garlic cloves, minced
- A pinch of salt and black pepper
- 1 tablespoon thyme, chopped
- 2 tablespoons cilantro, chopped

Directions:

Set the instant pot on Sauté mode, add the oil, heat it up, add the onion and the mushrooms and sauté for 5 minutes. Add the stock and the other ingredients, toss, put the lid on and cook on High for 25 minutes. Release the pressure naturally for 10 minutes, divide the soup into bowls and serve.

Nutrition: calories 287, fat 11.3, fiber 8.7, carbs 22.4, protein 14.4

Ginger Cod Soup

Preparation time: 10 minutes**Cooking time:** 20 minutes **Servings:** 4

Ingredients:
- 1 yellow onion, chopped
- 1 pound cod fillets, boneless and cubed
- 1 tablespoon olive oil
- 2 teaspoons rosemary, dried
- 1 and ½ teaspoons ginger, grated
- A pinch of salt and black pepper
- 1 cup cherry tomatoes, halved
- 1 carrot, chopped
- 4 cups chicken stock
- 2 tablespoons lime juice
- 1 tablespoon chives, chopped

Directions:

Set the instant pot on Sauté mode, add the oil, heat it up, add the onion, rosemary and ginger and cook for 5 minutes. Add the cod and the other ingredients, toss, put the lid on and cook on High for 15 minutes. Release the pressure naturally for 10 minutes, divide the soup into bowls and serve.

Nutrition: calories 263, fat 11.3, fiber 4.5, carbs 24.4, protein 14.4

Parsley Fish Stew

Preparation time: 10 minutes**Cooking time:** 20 minutes**Servings:** 4

Ingredients:

- 1 yellow onion, chopped
- 1 tablespoon olive oil
- 1 pound white fish fillets, boneless and cubed
- 1 cup cherry tomatoes, halved
- ½ cup tomato passata
- 1 zucchini, cubed
- Salt and black pepper to the taste
- 2 teaspoons parsley, chopped

Directions:

Set the instant pot on Sauté mode, add the oil, heat it up, add the onion and sauté for 5 minutes. Add the fish and the other ingredients, toss, put the lid on and cook on High for 15 minutes. Release the pressure naturally for 10 minutes, divide the stew into bowls and serve.

Nutrition: calories 232, fat 5.4, fiber 7.6, carbs 20.1, protein 6.5

Herbed Chicken Mix

Preparation time: 10 minutes**Cooking time:** 25 minutes**Servings:** 4

Ingredients:

- 1 pound chicken breast, skinless, boneless and cubed
- 2 tablespoons olive oil
- 4 scallions, chopped
- Salt and black pepper to the taste
- 3 garlic cloves, chopped
- 1 teaspoon basil, dried
- ½ teaspoon coriander, ground
- ½ teaspoon thyme, dried
- 1 teaspoon oregano, dried
- 1 cup canned tomatoes, chopped
- ¼ cup parsley, chopped

Directions:

Set the instant pot on Sauté mode, add the oil, heat up, add the scallions and the garlic and cook for 5 minutes. Add the meat and cook for 5 more minutes. Add the rest of the ingredients, toss, put the lid on and cook on High for 15 minutes. Release the pressure naturally for 10 minutes, divide the mix between plates and serve.

Nutrition: calories 347, fat 15.2, fiber 4.2, carbs 15.5, protein 37.7

Zucchini and Onions Stew

Preparation time: 10 minutes**Cooking time:** 25 minutes**Servings:** 4
Ingredients:

- 2 tablespoons olive oil
- 2 scallions, chopped
- 1 pound zucchinis, roughly cubed
- 3 garlic cloves, chopped
- 1 cup chicken stock
- 2 tablespoons tomato paste
- 1 teaspoon oregano, dried
- 1 pound pearl onions, peeled
- ½ teaspoon chili powder
- Salt and black pepper to the taste

Directions:
Set the instant pot on Sauté mode, add the oil, heat it up, add the scallions, garlic and pearl onions, stir and cook for 5 minutes. Add the zucchinis and the other ingredients, toss, put the lid on and cook on High for 20 minutes. Release the pressure naturally for 10 minutes, divide the stew into bowls and serve.

Nutrition: calories 221, fat 8, fiber 8, carbs 33.1, protein 8.9

Shrimp and Avocado Salad

Preparation time: 5 minutes**Cooking time:** 10 minutes**Servings:** 4
Ingredients:

- 1 pound shrimp, peeled and deveined
- 1 red onion, chopped
- 1 tablespoon olive oil
- 2 avocados, peeled, pitted and cubed
- 1 cup cherry tomatoes, halved
- ½ cup sweet chili sauce
- 1 tablespoon chives, chopped
- Salt and black pepper to the taste

Directions:
Set the instant pot on Sauté mode, add the oil, heat up, add the onion and chili sauce and sauté for 2 minutes. Add the shrimp and the other ingredients, toss, put the lid on and cook on High for 8 minutes. Release the pressure fast for 5 minutes, divide the mix into bowls and serve for lunch.

Nutrition: calories 357, fat 10.9, fiber 2.2, carbs 25.7, protein 36.6

Parsley Eggplant and Cod Mix

Preparation time: 10 minutes**Cooking time:** 20 minutes **Servings:** 4
Ingredients:
- 1 pound cod fillets, boneless and cubed
- 1 eggplant, cubed
- 1 tablespoon olive oil
- 1 tablespoon garlic, minced
- 1 red onion, sliced
- ½ cup chicken stock
- Salt and black pepper to the taste
- 3 carrots, chopped
- 3 celery stalks, chopped
- ½ cup parsley, chopped

Directions:

Set the instant pot on Sauté mode, add the oil, heat up, add the onion and the garlic and cook for 5 minutes. Add the cod and the other ingredients, toss, put the lid on and cook on High for 15 minutes. Release the pressure naturally for 10 minutes, divide the mix between plates and serve.

Nutrition: calories 364, fat 16.5, fiber 4.5, carbs 27.6, protein 33.3

Spicy Lamb Chops Mix

Preparation time: 10 minutes**Cooking time:** 30 minutes**Servings:** 4
Ingredients:
- 2 carrots, sliced
- 2 pounds lamb chops
- 1 tablespoon chili powder
- 1 tablespoon olive oil
- ½ cup veggie stock
- Salt and black pepper to the taste
- 1 red onion, sliced
- ½ teaspoon hot paprika
- 2 teaspoon peppercorns, crushed
- ½ teaspoon allspice, ground
- 1 tablespoon parsley, chopped

Directions:

In your instant pot, combine the lamb chops with the carrots and the other ingredients, toss, put the lid on and cook on High for 30 minutes. Release the pressure naturally fro 10 minutes, divide the lamb chops mix between plates and serve.

Nutrition: calories 384, fat 23.3, fiber 7.6, carbs 27.8, protein 36.4

Lamb and Green Beans

Preparation time: 10 minutes**Cooking time:** 30 minutes**Servings:** 4

Ingredients:

- 2 pounds lamb stew meat, cubed
- 1 tablespoon olive oil
- ½ pound green beans, trimmed and halved
- 1 red onion, chopped
- 1 tablespoon lemon juice
- 1 tablespoon oregano, dried
- 3 garlic cloves, minced
- A pinch of salt and black pepper
- 1 cup tomato paste
- 2 tablespoons parsley, chopped

Directions:

Set the instant pot on Sauté mode, add the oil, heat it up, add the meat and the onion and brown for 5 minutes. Add the green beans and the other ingredients, toss, put the lid on and cook on High for 25 minutes. Release the pressure naturally for 10 minutes, divide the mix between plates and serve.

Nutrition: calories 364, fat 18.5, fiber 8.5, carbs 28.7, protein 33.4

Dill Pork and Tomatoes

Preparation time: 10 minutes**Cooking time:** 30 minutes**Servings:** 4

Ingredients:

- 2 pounds pork stew meat, boneless and cubed
- 1 red onion, sliced
- ½ pound cherry tomatoes, halved
- 1 tablespoon dill, chopped
- 1 tablespoon olive oil
- 2 garlic cloves, minced
- 2 cups beef stock
- ½ teaspoon sweet paprika
- Salt and black pepper to the taste
- 2 tablespoons dill, chopped

Directions:

Set the instant pot on Sauté mode, add the oil, heat it up, add the onion and the meat and brown for 5 minutes. Add the tomatoes and the other ingredients, toss, put the lid on and cook on High for 25 minutes. Release the pressure naturally for 10 minutes, divide the mix between plates and serve.

Nutrition: calories 322, fat 17.4, fiber 7.6, carbs 26.4, protein 34.3

Tomato and Chickpeas Stew

Preparation time: 10 minutes**Cooking time:** 25 minutes **Servings:** 4

Ingredients:

- 1 cup chicken stock
- 1 cup canned chickpeas, drained and rinsed
- 1 pound cherry tomatoes, halved
- 1 tablespoon olive oil
- 2 scallions, chopped
- 1 tablespoon ginger, grated
- 1 teaspoon coriander, ground
- Salt and black pepper to the taste
- 1 cup tomato passata
- 1 tablespoon cilantro, chopped

Directions:

In your instant pot, combine the chickpeas with the stock, tomatoes and the other ingredients, toss, put the lid on and cook on High for 25 minutes. Release the pressure naturally for 10 minutes, divide the stew into bowls and serve.

Nutrition: calories 283, fat 11.9, fiber 4.5, carbs 28.8, protein 25.4

Ground Turkey Stew

Preparation time: 10 minutes**Cooking time:** 25 minutes**Servings:** 4

Ingredients:

- 2 pounds turkey meat, ground
- 2 tablespoons olive oil
- 1 red onion, sliced
- 1 cup chicken stock
- 1 cup tomato passata
- 1 red bell pepper, chopped
- 3 garlic cloves, minced
- ½ teaspoon sweet paprika
- 1 zucchini, cubed
- 1 cup cherry tomatoes, halved
- 2 carrots, peeled and cubed
- 1 tablespoon cilantro, chopped

Directions:

Set the instant pot on Sauté mode, add the oil, heat up, add the onion, garlic and the meat and brown for 5 minutes. Add the zucchini and the other ingredients, toss, put the lid on and cook on High for 20 minutes. Release the pressure naturally for 10 minutes, divide the mix into bowls and serve for lunch.

Nutrition: calories 423, fat 15.4, fiber 9.6, carbs 27.4, protein 43

Warm Peppers and Salmon Salad

Preparation time: 10 minutes**Cooking time:** 12 minutes**Servings:** 4

Ingredients:

- 1 tablespoon olive oil
- 1 pound salmon fillets, boneless and cubed
- 1 cup cherry tomatoes, halved
- 3 scallions, chopped
- 1 cup baby spinach
- 1 red bell pepper, cut into strips
- 1 green bell pepper, cut into strips
- 1 orange bell pepper, cut into strips
- ½ cup tomato sauce
- Juice of 1 lime
- Salt and black pepper to the taste
- 1 tablespoon chives, chopped

Directions:

Set the instant pot on Sauté mode, add the oil, heat it up, add the scallions and peppers and cook for 2 minutes. Add the salmon and the other ingredients, toss gently, put the lid on and cook on High for 10 minutes. Release the pressure naturally for 10 minutes, divide the salad into bowls and serve.

Nutrition: calories 277, fat 7.8, fiber 4.5, carbs 26, protein 11.2

Chives Shrimp and Kale Mix

Preparation time: 5 minutes**Cooking time:** 10 minutes**Servings:** 4

Ingredients:

- 1 pound shrimp, peeled and deveined
- 1 red onion, sliced
- 1 cup baby kale
- ½ cup tomato passata
- 2 tablespoons olive oil
- Salt and black pepper to the taste
- 1 tablespoon chives, chopped
- 1 tablespoon cilantro, chopped

Directions:

Set the instant pot on Sauté mode, add the oil, heat up, add the onion and cook for 2 minutes. Add the shrimp and the other ingredients, toss gently, put the lid on and cook on High for 8 minutes. Release the pressure fast for 5 minutes, divide the mix between plates and serve.

Nutrition: calories 245, fat 11.2, fiber 4.5, carbs 17.4, protein 12.3

Mediterranean Diet Instant Pot Side Dish Recipes

Balsamic Sweet Potatoes

Preparation time: 10 minutes**Cooking time:** 15 minutes**Servings:** 4

Ingredients:

- 4 sweet potatoes, peeled and cut into wedges
- 2 tablespoons olive oil
- 2 tablespoons balsamic vinegar
- 1 tablespoon garlic, minced
- A pinch of salt and black pepper
- 1 teaspoon chili powder
- 1 teaspoon rosemary, dried
- 1 cup water

Directions:

In a bowl, combine the potato wedges with the oil, vinegar and the other ingredients except the water and toss. Put the water in the instant pot, add the steamer basket, add the potatoes inside, put the lid on and cook on High for 15 minutes. Release the pressure naturally for 10 minutes, divide the mix between plates and serve.

Nutrition: calories 149, fat 5, fiber 3, carbs 33, protein 4

Dill Corn Mix

Preparation time: 10 minutes**Cooking time:** 10 minutes**Servings:** 2

Ingredients:

- 2 cups fresh corn
- 1 tablespoon olive oil
- 2 scallions, chopped
- 1 tablespoon dill, chopped
- ½ cup heavy cream
- ½ teaspoon turmeric powder
- A pinch of salt and black pepper
- 1 tablespoon chives, chopped

Directions:

Set the instant pot on Sauté mode, add the oil, heat it up, add the scallions and cook for 2 minutes. Add the corn and the other ingredients, toss, put the lid on and cook on Low for 8 minutes. Release the pressure naturally for 10 minutes, divide the mix between plates and serve as a side dish.

Nutrition: calories 293, fat 19, fiber 2, carbs 28, protein 6

Turmeric Broccoli Mix

Preparation time: 10 minutes**Cooking time:** 15 minutes**Servings:** 4

Ingredients:

- 1 pound broccoli florets
- 1 red onion, chopped
- ½ cup tomato passata
- 1 tablespoon avocado oil
- 2 scallions, chopped
- ½ teaspoon ginger powder
- ½ teaspoon turmeric powder
- 1 tablespoon coriander powder
- ½ teaspoon garam masala
- 1 tablespoon chives, chopped
- A pinch of salt and black pepper

Directions:

Set the instant pot on Sauté mode, add the oil, heat it up, add the onion, scallions, ginger, turmeric, coriander and garam masala and sauté for 2 minutes. Add the broccoli and the other ingredients, toss, put the lid on and cook on High for 13 minutes. Release the pressure naturally for 10 minutes, divide the mix between plates and serve as a side dish.

Nutrition: calories 168, fat 12, fiber 6, carbs 14, protein 5

Creamy Green Beans

Preparation time: 10 minutes**Cooking time:** 15 minutes**Servings:** 2

Ingredients:

- 4 scallions, chopped
- 1 tablespoon olive oil
- 1 pound green beans, trimmed and halved
- ¼ cup heavy cream
- ½ teaspoon rosemary, dried
- A pinch of salt and black pepper
- 1 teaspoon chili powder
- 1 tablespoon dill, chopped

Directions:

Set the instant pot on Sauté mode, add the oil, heat it up, add the scallions and sauté for 2 minutes. Add the green beans and the other ingredients, toss, put the lid on and cook on High for 13 minutes. Release the pressure naturally for 10 minutes, divide the mix between plates and serve.

Nutrition: calories 122, fat 7, fiber 3, carbs 10, protein 4

Cheesy Cauliflower

Preparation time: 10 minutes**Cooking time:** 15 minutes**Servings:** 4

Ingredients:

- 1 tablespoon butter, soft
- 2 ounces cream cheese, soft
- 1 pound cauliflower florets
- 2 garlic cloves, minced
- 2 scallions, chopped
- ½ cup almond milk
- A pinch of salt and black pepper
- ½ teaspoon turmeric powder
- ½ tablespoon chives, chopped
- ½ teaspoon red pepper flakes, crushed

Directions:

Set the instant pot on Sauté mode, add the butter, melt it, add the scallions and the garlic and cook for 2 minutes. Add the cauliflower, cream cheese and the other ingredients, toss, put the lid on and cook on High for 13 minutes. Release the pressure naturally for 10 minutes, divide between plates and serve.

Nutrition: calories 166, fat 13, fiber 3, carbs 9.6, protein 5

Chili Kidney Beans Mix

Preparation time: 10 minutes**Cooking time:** 25 minutes**Servings:** 4

Ingredients:

- 2 cups canned kidney beans, drained and rinsed
- 1 tablespoon avocado oil
- 2 scallions, chopped
- 1 red chili pepper, minced
- 1 teaspoon chili powder
- 1 tablespoon ginger, grated
- 2 garlic cloves, minced
- 2 tablespoons cilantro, chopped
- 1 cup cherry tomatoes, halved
- ¼ cup tomato passata
- Salt and black pepper to the taste
- 1 tablespoon cilantro, chopped

Directions:

Set the instant pot on Sauté mode, add the oil, heat it up, add the scallions, chili pepper, garlic and chili powder and sauté for 5 minutes. Add the beans, ginger and the other ingredients, toss, put the lid on and cook on High for 20 minutes. Release the pressure naturally for 10 minutes, divide the mix between plates and serve as a side dish.

Nutrition: calories 256, fat 14, fiber 5, carbs 15, protein 5

Dill Zucchini

Preparation time: 5 minutes**Cooking time:** 15 minutes**Servings:** 4

Ingredients:
- 2 zucchinis, roughly cubed
- 1 tablespoon olive oil
- 1 red onion, chopped
- ½ cup tomato passata
- ½ teaspoon coriander, ground
- ½ teaspoon rosemary, dried
- 1 tablespoon dill, chopped
- A pinch of salt and black pepper
- 1 teaspoon red pepper flakes, crushed

Directions:
Set the instant pot on Sauté mode, add the oil, heat it up, add the onion and sauté for 5 minutes. Add the zucchinis and the other ingredients, toss, put the lid on and cook on High for 10 minutes. Release the pressure fast for 5 minutes, divide the mix between plates and serve.

Nutrition: calories 230, fat 12, fiber 4, carbs 8, protein 5

Balsamic Chives Carrots

Preparation time: 10 minutes**Cooking time:** 15 minutes**Servings:** 2

Ingredients:
- 2 tablespoons butter, melted
- 2 pounds carrots, peeled and sliced
- 2 tablespoons balsamic vinegar
- A pinch of salt and black pepper
- 1 tablespoon parsley, chopped

Directions:
Set the instant pot on Sauté mode, add the butter, heat it up, add the carrots and sauté for 5 minutes. Add the rest of the ingredients, toss, put the lid on and cook on High for 10 minutes. Release the pressure naturally for 10 minutes, divide between plates and serve as a side dish.

Nutrition: calories 152, fat 4, fiber 4, carbs 12, protein 5.3

Beans and Corn Mix

Preparation time: 5 minutes**Cooking time:** 15 minutes**Servings:** 4

Ingredients:

- 1 cup fresh corn
- 1 cup canned kidney beans, drained and rinsed
- 1 cup black beans, drained and rinsed
- 1 tablespoon rosemary, chopped
- 2 tablespoons butter, soft
- ½ cup veggie stock
- 1 tablespoon chives, chopped
- A pinch of salt and white pepper

Directions:

Set the instant pot on Sauté mode, add the butter, heat up, add the corn and beans and cook for 2 minutes. Add the rest of the ingredients, toss, put the lid on and cook on High for 13 minutes. Release the pressure fast for 5 minutes, divide between plates and serve as a side dish.

Nutrition: calories 170, fat 6, fiber 3, carbs 22, protein 5

Curry Green Peas

Preparation time: 10 minutes**Cooking time:** 15 minutes**Servings:** 2

Ingredients:

- 1 tablespoon olive oil
- 2 cups green peas
- 2 scallions, chopped
- ½ teaspoon curry powder
- ½ teaspoon rosemary, dried
- 1 carrot, peeled and cubed
- ½ cup heavy cream
- 1 teaspoon red pepper flakes, crushed
- 1 teaspoon turmeric powder
- A pinch of salt and black pepper
- 1 tablespoon dill, chopped

Directions:

Set the instant pot on Sauté mode, add the oil, heat it up, add the scallions, carrot and curry powder and sauté for 3 minutes. Add the green peas and the other ingredients, toss, put the lid on and cook on High for 12 minutes. Release the pressure naturally for 10 minutes, divide the mix between plates and serve as a side dish,

Nutrition: calories 220, fat 15, fiber 4, carbs 18, protein 4

Brown Rice and Carrots Mix

Preparation time: 10 minutes**Cooking time:** 25 minutes**Servings:** 4

Ingredients:

- 1 tablespoon avocado oil
- 1 yellow onion, chopped
- 2 carrots, peeled and grated
- 1 cup brown rice
- ½ teaspoon chili powder
- ½ teaspoon cumin, ground
- 2 cups chicken stock
- 1 red bell pepper, chopped
- A pinch of salt and black pepper
- 1 tablespoon chives, chopped

Directions:

Set the instant pot on Sauté mode, add the oil, heat it up, add the onion and carrots and sauté for 5 minutes. Add the rice, stock and the other ingredients, toss, put the lid on and cook on High for 20 minutes. Release the pressure naturally for 10 minutes, divide the mix between plates and serve.

Nutrition: calories 525, fat 6.9, fiber 8.2, carbs 104, protein 10.5

Parsley Mushroom Mix

Preparation time: 10 minutes**Cooking time:** 15 minutes**Servings:** 4

Ingredients:

- 1 pound mushrooms, sliced
- 1 tablespoon olive oil
- 3 scallions, chopped
- 2 garlic cloves, minced
- ½ cup veggie stock
- ½ cup tomato passata
- ½ teaspoon rosemary, dried
- A pinch of salt and black pepper
- 1 tablespoon parsley, chopped

Directions:

Set the instant pot on Sauté mode, add the oil, heat it up, add the scallions and garlic and cook for 2 minutes. Add the mushrooms, stock and the other ingredients, toss, put the lid on and cook on High for 13 minutes. Release the pressure naturally for 10 minutes, divide the mix between plates and serve.

Nutrition: calories 260, fat 9, fiber 1, carbs 34, protein 6

Hot Potato Mix

Preparation time: 10 minutes**Cooking time:** 20 minutes**Servings:** 4

Ingredients:
- 1 pound gold potatoes, peeled and cut into wedges
- 1 tablespoon olive oil
- 1 red onion, chopped
- A pinch of salt and black pepper
- ½ cup tomato passata
- 1 teaspoon chili powder
- ½ teaspoon hot paprika
- 1 tablespoon parsley, chopped

Directions:

Set the instant pot on Sauté mode, add the oil, heat it up, add the onion and sauté for 5 minutes. Add the potatoes, passata and the other ingredients, toss, put the lid on and cook on High for 15 minutes. Release the pressure naturally for 10 minutes, divide the mix between plates and serve as a side salad.

Nutrition: calories 246, fat 5.4, fiber 3.4, carbs 12, protein 4.5

Garlic Eggplant Medley

Preparation time: 10 minutes**Cooking time:** 15 minutes**Servings:** 4

Ingredients:
- 1 pound eggplant, cubed
- 1 red onion, chopped
- 3 garlic cloves, minced
- 2 tablespoons olive oil
- 1 tablespoon rosemary, chopped
- ¼ cup tomato passata
- A pinch of salt and black pepper
- 1 tablespoon chives, chopped

Directions:

Set the instant pot on Sauté mode, add the oil, heat it up, add the onion and the garlic and cook for 3 minutes. Add the eggplants and the other ingredients, toss, put the lid on and cook on High for 12 minutes. Release the pressure naturally for 10 minutes, divide the mix between plates and serve.

Nutrition: calories 162, fat 12, fiber 3, carbs 5. protein 5

Creamy Asparagus

Preparation time: 5 minutes**Cooking time:** 10 minutes**Servings:** 4

Ingredients:

- 1 tablespoon olive oil
- 1 pound asparagus spears, trimmed and halved
- 1 cup heavy cream
- 2 tablespoons sage, chopped
- ½ teaspoon turmeric powder
- Salt and black pepper to the taste
- 1 tablespoon cilantro, chopped

Directions:

Set the instant pot on Sauté mode, add the oil, heat up, add the asparagus and cook for 2 minutes. Add the rest of the ingredients, toss, put the lid on and cook on High for 8 minutes. Release the pressure fast for 5 minutes, divide between plates and serve as a side dish.

Nutrition: calories 100, fat 10.5, fiber 1.2, carbs 2.3, protein 2.1

Eggplant and Avocado Mix

Preparation time: 5 minutes**Cooking time:** 15 minutes**Servings:** 4

Ingredients:

- 2 avocados, peeled, pitted and cubed
- ¼ cup tomatoes, crushed
- 2 eggplants, roughly cubed
- 2 tablespoons olive oil
- 2 scallions, minced
- 2 garlic cloves, minced
- ½ teaspoon turmeric powder
- 1 teaspoon sweet paprika
- 2 tablespoons lime juice
- 1 tablespoon chives, chopped
- Salt and black pepper to the taste

Directions:

Set the instant pot on Sauté mode, add the oil, heat it up, add the scallions and garlic and cook for 3 minutes. Add the avocados, eggplants and the other ingredients, toss, put the lid on and cook on High for 12 minutes. Release the pressure fast for 5 minutes, divide the mix between plates and serve as a side dish.

Nutrition: calories 123, fat 4.3, fiber 2.3, carbs 5.6, protein 2

Rosemary Potato Mix

Preparation time: 5 minutes**Cooking time:** 20 minutes**Servings:** 4

Ingredients:

- 1 pound gold potatoes, peeled and cut into wedges
- 1 tablespoon olive oil
- 1 cup tomato passata
- 2 garlic cloves, minced
- 1 tablespoon rosemary, chopped
- 2 green chilies, chopped
- 1 teaspoon chili powder
- 1 red onion, sliced
- Salt and black pepper to the taste

Directions:

Set the instant pot on Sauté mode, add the oil, heat it up, add the garlic, chilies and the onion and sauté for 5 minutes. Add the potatoes and the other ingredients, toss, put the lid on and cook on High for 15 minutes. Release the pressure fast for 5 minutes, divide the mix between plates and serve.

Nutrition: calories 121, fat 2.3, fiber 2.0, carbs 6.7, protein 2.4

Balsamic Beet

Preparation time: 10 minutes**Cooking time:** 25 minutes **Servings:** 4

Ingredients:

- 4 beets, peeled and cut into wedges
- 2 tablespoons olive oil
- 1 tablespoon balsamic vinegar
- 1 tablespoon garlic, minced
- Salt and black pepper to the taste
- 1 cup water
- 1 tablespoons chives, chopped

Directions:

In a bowl, combine the beets with the oil, vinegar and the other ingredients except the water and toss. Put the water in the instant pot, add the steamer basket, put the beets inside, put the lid on and cook on High for 25 minutes. Release the pressure naturally for 10 minutes, divide the mix between plates and serve as a side dish.

Nutrition: calories 156, fat 4.2, fiber 3.4, carbs 6.5, protein 4

Paprika Beets Mix

Preparation time: 10 minutes**Cooking time:** 25 minutes**Servings:** 4

Ingredients:
- 1 pound beets, peeled and cut into wedges
- 1 tablespoon olive oil
- 1 teaspoon sweet paprika
- ½ teaspoon coriander, ground
- ½ teaspoon rosemary, dried
- A pinch of salt and black pepper
- 1 cup water

Directions:
In a bowl, combine the beets with the oil and the other ingredients except the water and toss. Put the water in the instant pot, add the steamer basket, put the beets inside, put the lid on and cook on High for 25 minutes. Release the pressure naturally for 10 minutes, divide the mix between plates and serve.

Nutrition: calories 165, fat 3.4, fiber 4.5, carbs 11.3, protein 2.3

Zucchini and Tomato Mix

Preparation time: 10 minutes**Cooking time:** 15 minutes**Servings:** 4

Ingredients:
- 1 pound cherry tomatoes, halved
- 2 zucchinis, roughly cubed
- 2 tablespoons olive oil
- 2 garlic cloves, minced
- ¼ cup tomato passata
- A pinch of salt and black pepper
- 4 scallions, chopped
- 2 tablespoons cilantro, chopped

Directions:
Set the instant pot on Sauté mode, add the oil, heat up, add the garlic and scallions and cook for 3 minutes. Add the tomatoes and the other ingredients, toss gently, put the lid on and cook on High for 12 minutes. Release the pressure naturally for 10 minutes, divide the mix between plates and serve as a side dish.

Nutrition: calories 200, fat 4.5, fiber 3.4, carbs 6.7, protein 4

Lime Eggplant Mix

Preparation time: 10 minutes**Cooking time:** 15 minutes**Servings:** 4

Ingredients:
- 1 pound eggplant, roughly cubed
- ¼ cup tomato passata
- 3 garlic cloves, minced
- 2 tablespoons olive oil
- 1 red onion, chopped
- A pinch of salt and black pepper
- 1 tablespoon lime juice
- ¼ cup chives, chopped

Directions:
Set the instant pot on Sauté mode, add the oil, heat it up, add the garlic and onion and cook for 3 minutes. Add the eggplants and the other ingredients, toss, put the lid on and cook on High for 12 minutes. Release the pressure naturally for 10 minutes, divide the mix between plates and serve as a side dish.

Nutrition: calories 201, fat 4.5, fiber 3, carbs 5.4, protein 3

Tomato Rice Mix

Preparation time: 10 minutes**Cooking time:** 25 minutes **Servings:** 4

Ingredients:
- 1 tablespoon olive oil
- 1 red onion, chopped
- 1 cup wild rice
- 2 cups chicken stock
- 1 cup cherry tomatoes, halved
- ½ teaspoon turmeric powder
- ½ teaspoon rosemary, dried
- 1 tablespoon chives, chopped
- Salt and black pepper to the taste

Directions:
Set the instant pot on Sauté mode, add the oil, heat it up, add the onion and the turmeric and cook for 5 minutes. Add the rice, tomatoes and the other ingredients, toss, put the lid on and cook on High for 20 minutes. Release the pressure naturally for 10 minutes, divide the mix between plates and serve.

Nutrition: calories 210, fat 6.5, fiber 3.4, carbs 8.6, protein 3.4

Parsley Lentils Mix

Preparation time: 10 minutes**Cooking time:** 20 minutes**Servings:** 4

Ingredients:

- 2 cups canned lentils, drained and rinsed
- ½ cup tomato passata
- 1 yellow onion, chopped
- 2 tablespoons olive oil
- 1 teaspoon chili powder
- 1 teaspoon cumin, ground
- 1 tablespoon parsley, chopped
- Salt and black pepper to the taste

Directions:

Set the instant pot on Sauté mode, add the oil, heat it up, add the onion, chili and cumin and sauté for 5 minutes. Add the lentils, passata and the other ingredients, toss, put the lid on and cook on High for 15 minutes. Release the pressure naturally for 10 minutes, divide the mix between plates and serve as a side dish.

Nutrition: calories 199, fat 4.5, fiber 2.3, carbs 6.5, protein 3.3

Creamy Artichokes

Preparation time: 10 minutes**Cooking time:** 15 minutes **Servings:** 4

Ingredients:

- 2 tablespoons olive oil
- 3 garlic clove, minced
- 2 cups artichoke hearts, quartered
- 1 red onion, sliced
- Juice of 1 lime
- 1 cup heavy cream
- Salt and black pepper to the taste
- 1 tablespoon hives, chopped

Directions:

Set the instant pot on Sauté mode, add the oil, heat it up, add the onion and the garlic and sauté for 5 minutes. Add the artichoke hearts and the other ingredients, toss, put the lid on and cook on High for 10 minutes. Release the pressure naturally for 10 minutes, divide the mix between plates and serve.

Nutrition: calories 214, fat 5.6, fiber 3.4, carbs 6.5, protein 3.1

Cabbage and Tomato Mix

Preparation time: 10 minutes**Cooking time:** 15 minutes**Servings:** 4

Ingredients:

- 3 scallions, chopped
- 1 cup tomatoes, crushed
- 1 tablespoon olive oil
- 1 green cabbage head, shredded
- ½ tablespoon lime juice
- ½ teaspoon sweet paprika
- ½ teaspoon chili powder
- 1 tablespoon dill, chopped
- Salt and black pepper to the taste

Directions:

Set the instant pot on Sauté mode, add the oil, heat it up, add the scallions, chili powder and paprika and cook for 2 minutes. Add the cabbage, tomatoes and the other ingredients, toss, put the lid on and cook on High for 13 minutes. Release the pressure naturally for 10 minutes, divide the mix between plates and serve.

Nutrition: calories 199, fat 4.5, fiber 2.4, carbs 5.6, protein 2.2

Chili Mushroom and Tomato Mix

Preparation time: 10 minutes**Cooking time:** 15 minutes**Servings:** 4

Ingredients:

- ½ pound white mushrooms, halved
- ½ pound cherry tomatoes, halved
- 1 red chili, minced
- ½ teaspoon chili powder
- ½ cup tomato passata
- 2 tablespoons olive oil
- 2 garlic cloves, minced
- 1 tablespoon chives, chopped
- Salt and black pepper to the taste

Directions:

Set the instant pot on Sauté mode, add the oil, heat it up, add the chili and the garlic and cook for 2 minutes. Add the mushrooms and cook for 3 minutes more. Add the rest of the other ingredients, toss, put the lid on and cook on High for 12 minutes. Release the pressure naturally for 10 minutes, divide the mix between plates and serve as a side dish.

Nutrition: calories 222, fat 5.5, fiber 5.4, carbs 12.3, protein 5.6

Mint Zucchini and Olives

Preparation time: 10 minutes**Cooking time:** 20 minutes**Servings:** 4

Ingredients:

- 2 zucchinis, roughly cubed
- 1 cup kalamata olives, pitted and halved
- 1 tablespoon olive oil
- ½ cup tomato passata
- 4 scallions, chopped
- 1 tablespoon olive oil
- 1 teaspoon turmeric powder
- 1 tablespoon mint, chopped
- Salt and black pepper to the taste

Directions:

Set the instant pot on Sauté mode, add the oil, heat it up, add the scallions and turmeric and cook for 5 minutes. Add the zucchinis, olives and the other ingredients, toss, put the lid on and cook on High for 15 minutes. Release the pressure naturally for 10 minutes, divide the mix between plates and serve as a side dish.

Nutrition: calories 233, fat 8.7, fiber 4.5, carbs 14.4, protein 6.4

Rice and Kale

Preparation time: 10 minutes**Cooking time:** 25 minutes**Servings:** 4

Ingredients:

- 1 cup black rice
- 2 cups chicken stock
- 1 cup baby kale
- 3 scallions, minced
- ½ teaspoon chili powder
- ½ teaspoon rosemary, dried
- 1 tablespoon olive oil
- ½ teaspoon allspice, ground
- 2 tablespoons cilantro, chopped

Directions:

Set the instant pot on Sauté mode, add the oil, heat it up, add the scallions, chili powder, rosemary and allspice, stir and cook for 5 minutes. Add the rice, stock and the other ingredients, toss, put the lid on and cook on High for 20 minutes. Release the pressure naturally for 10 minutes, divide the mix between plates and serve.

Nutrition: calories 200, fat 6.7, fiber 3.4, carbs 15.4, protein 4.5

Kale and Olives Mix

Preparation time: 5 minutes**Cooking time:** 20 minutes**Servings:** 4

Ingredients:
- 2 tablespoons olive oil
- 3 scallions, chopped
- 1 pound kale, torn
- ½ cup black olives, pitted and halved
- ½ teaspoon chili powder
- ½ cup veggie stock
- 2 tablespoons chives, chopped

Directions:
Set the instant pot on Sauté mode, add the oil, heat it up, add the scallions and cook for 5 minutes. Add the kale and the other ingredients, toss, put the lid on and cook on High for 15 minutes. Release the pressure fast for 5 minutes, divide the mix between plates and serve as a side dish.

Nutrition: calories 188, fat 4, fiber 3, carbs 12.4, protein 4.4

Black Beans Mix

Preparation time: 10 minutes**Cooking time:** 25 minutes**Servings:** 4

Ingredients:
- 1 tablespoon olive oil
- 3 scallions, minced
- 2 cups canned black beans, rinsed and drained
- ½ cup tomato passata
- ½ teaspoon Italian seasoning
- ½ teaspoon thyme, dried
- ½ cup veggie stock
- Salt and black pepper to the taste

Directions:
Set the instant pot on Sauté mode, add the oil, heat it up, add the scallions and Italian seasoning, stir and sauté for 5 minutes. Add the beans and the remaining ingredients, toss, put the lid on and cook on High for 20 minutes. Release the pressure naturally for 10 minutes, divide the mix between plates and serve.

Nutrition: calories 224, fat 8.4, fiber 3.4, carbs 15.3, protein 6.2

Cilantro Quinoa

Preparation time: 10 minutes**Cooking time:** 20 minutes**Servings:** 4

Ingredients:
- 1 tablespoon olive oil
- 1 red onion, chopped
- 1 cup quinoa
- 2 cups chicken stock
- ½ teaspoon turmeric powder
- ½ cup cilantro, chopped
- 1 teaspoon chili paste
- Salt and black pepper to the taste

Directions:

Set the instant pot on Sauté mode, add the oil, heat it up, add the onion and turmeric and sauté for 5 minutes. Add the quinoa, stock and the other ingredients, toss, put the lid on and cook on High for 15 minutes. Release the pressure naturally for 10 minutes, divide the mix between plates and serve.

Nutrition: calories 222, fat 10.2, fiber 3.4, carbs 14.5, protein 2.4

Brussels Sprouts Salad

Preparation time: 10 minutes**Cooking time:** 20 minutes**Servings:** 4

Ingredients:
- 1 pound Brussels sprouts, trimmed and halved
- 1 tablespoon avocado oil
- 1 red chili pepper, minced
- 1 cup cherry tomatoes, halved
- 1 cup kalamata olives, pitted and halved
- 4 scallions, chopped
- 2 tablespoons balsamic vinegar
- ¼ cup veggie stock
- A pinch of salt and black pepper
- 1 tablespoon cilantro, chopped

Directions:

Set the instant pot on Sauté mode, add the oil, heat it up, add the scallions and chili pepper, stir and cook for 5 minutes Add the sprouts, tomatoes and the other ingredients, toss, put the lid on and cook on High for 15 minutes Release the pressure naturally for 10 minutes, divide the mix between plates and serve.

Nutrition: calories 175, fat 3, fiber 3, carbs 5, protein 3

Beet and Radish Mix

Preparation time: 10 minutes**Cooking time:** 14 minutes**Servings:** 4

Ingredients:

- 1 pound radishes, halved
- 2 beets, peeled and cut into wedges
- 3 scallions, chopped
- 2 tablespoons avocado oil
- ½ teaspoon sweet paprika
- ½ cup veggie stock
- 1 teaspoons balsamic vinegar
- Juice of 1 lime
- 1 tablespoon chives, minced
- Salt and black pepper to the taste

Directions:

Set the instant pot on Sauté mode, add the oil, heat it up add the scallions and paprika and cook for 2 minutes. Add the beets, radishes and the other ingredients, toss, put the lid on and cook on High for 12 minutes. Release the pressure naturally for 10 minutes, divide the mix between plates and serve.

Nutrition: calories 403, fat 30.5, fiber 10, carbs 23.5, protein 3.5

Radish and Beets Mix

Preparation time: 10 minutes**Cooking time:** 25 minutes**Servings:** 4

Ingredients:

- 1 pound beets, cooked, peeled and roughly cubed
- 2 cups radishes, halved
- 1 cup chicken stock
- 4 scallions, chopped
- 2 tablespoons olive oil
- 1 tablespoon lemon juice
- 2 tablespoons balsamic vinegar
- 3 small garlic cloves, minced
- 2 tablespoons parsley, chopped
- Salt and black pepper to the taste

Directions:

Set the instant pot on Sauté mode, add the oil, heat it up, add the scallions and sauté for 5 minutes. Add the beets and the other ingredients, toss, put the lid on and cook on High for 20 minutes. Release the pressure naturally for 10 minutes, divide the mix between plates and serve.

Nutrition: calories 268, fat 15.5, fiber 5.1, carbs 25.7, protein 9.6

Spinach and Radish Mix

Preparation time: 10 minutes**Cooking time:** 14 minutes**Servings:** 4

Ingredients:

- 2 cups radishes, halved
- 1 cup baby spinach
- 1 red onion, sliced
- 2 tablespoons olive oil
- ¼ cup veggie stock
- ½ teaspoon sweet paprika
- ½ teaspoon chili powder
- A pinch of salt and black pepper
- 2 tablespoons chives, chopped
- 2 tablespoons basil, chopped

Directions:

Set the instant pot on Sauté mode, add the oil, heat it up, add the onion, paprika and chili, stir and sauté for 4 minutes. Add the radishes, spinach and the other ingredients, toss, put the lid on and cook on High for 10 minutes. Release the pressure naturally for 10 minutes, divide the mix between plates and serve as a side dish.

Nutrition: calories 181, fat 3.4, fiber 3.2, carbs 8.6, protein 7.6

Paprika Rice Mix

Preparation time: 10 minutes**Cooking time:** 20 minutes**Servings:** 4

Ingredients:

- 1 cup black rice
- 2 cups chicken stock
- 1 teaspoon rosemary, dried
- 4 scallions, chopped
- ½ teaspoon sweet paprika
- 1 tablespoon olive oil
- Salt and black pepper to the taste
- 1 tablespoon chives, chopped

Directions:

Set your instant pot on Sauté mode, add the oil, heat it up, add the scallions and paprika and cook for 5 minutes Add the rice and the remaining ingredients, toss, put the lid on and cook on High for 15 minutes Release the pressure naturally for 10 minutes, divide the mix between plates and serve as a side dish.

Nutrition: calories 151, fat 7, fiber 6, carbs 9, protein 6

Leeks Sauté

Preparation time: 10 minutes**Cooking time:** 20 minutes**Servings:** 4

Ingredients:
- 4 leeks, sliced
- 2 garlic cloves, minced
- 1 tablespoon olive oil
- 1 tablespoon lemon juice
- ½ cup veggie stock
- A pinch of salt and black pepper
- 1 teaspoon chili powder
- 2 tablespoons chives, chopped

Directions:
Set your instant pot on Sauté mode, add oil, heat it up, add the garlic, leeks and chili powder, stir and cook for 5 minutes. Add the rest of the ingredients, toss, put the lid on and cook on High for 15 minutes. Release the pressure naturally for 10 minutes, divide the mix between plates and serve as a side dish.

Nutrition: calories 171, fat 4, fiber 5, carbs 9, protein 6

Oregano Tomato Mix

Preparation time: 10 minutes**Cooking time:** 15 minutes**Servings:** 4

Ingredients:
- 3 scallions, chopped
- 1 tablespoon olive oil
- 1 cup black olives, pitted and halved
- 1 pound cherry tomatoes, halved
- 1 tablespoon oregano, chopped
- ½ cup veggie stock
- A pinch of salt and black pepper

Directions:
Set your instant pot on Sauté mode, add the oil, heat it up, add the scallions and cook for 3 minutes. Add the tomatoes and the rest of the ingredients, put the lid on and cook on High for 12 minutes. Release the pressure naturally for 10 minutes, divide the mix between plates and serve.

Nutrition: calories 182, fat 6, fiber 3, carbs 6, protein 7

Allspice Quinoa

Preparation time: 10 minutes**Cooking time:** 20 minutes**Servings:** 4

Ingredients:
- 3 scallions, chopped
- 1 cup quinoa
- ½ teaspoon allspice, ground
- 1 tablespoon olive oil
- 2 cups chicken stock
- ½ teaspoon turmeric powder
- 1 tablespoon cilantro, chopped

Directions:
Set the instant pot on Sauté mode, add the oil, heat it up, add scallions and allspice, stir and cook for 5 minutes. Add the quinoa, stock and the rest of the ingredients, put the lid on and cook on High for 15 minutes. Release the pressure naturally for 10 minutes, divide the mix between plates and serve as a side dish.

Nutrition: calories 162, fat 6, fiber 4, carbs 6, protein 8

Basil Sprouts and Beets

Preparation time: 10 minutes**Cooking time:** 20 minutes**Servings:** 4

Ingredients:
- 1 cup Brussels sprouts, trimmed and halved
- 2 beets, peeled and cut into wedges
- 1 tablespoon olive oil
- 2 garlic cloves, minced
- ½ cup tomato passata
- 1 yellow onion, chopped
- 1 tablespoon basil, chopped

Directions:
Set your instant pot on Sauté mode, add the oil, heat it up, add the garlic and the onion and sauté for 5 minutes. Add the sprouts, beets and the rest of the ingredients, put the lid on and cook on High for 15 minutes. Release the pressure naturally for 10 minutes, divide between plates and serve as a side dish.

Nutrition: calories 200, fat 8, fiber 4, carbs 6, protein 7

Ginger Cabbage Mix

Preparation time: 10 minutes**Cooking time:** 15 minutes**Servings:** 4

Ingredients:
1. 2 tablespoons olive oil
2. 1 red onion, chopped
3. 1 green cabbage head, shredded
4. ½ teaspoon sweet paprika
5. ½ cup tomato passata
6. 1 tablespoon ginger, grated
7. 1 tablespoon thyme, chopped

Directions:

Set your instant pot on Sauté mode, add the oil, heat it up, add onion and the ginger and sauté for 5 minute Add cabbage, paprika and the other ingredients, toss, put the lid on and cook on High for 10 minutes Release the pressure naturally for 10 minutes, divide the mix between plates and serve as a side dish.

Nutrition: calories 200, fat 7, fiber 4, carbs 7, protein 6

Chives Potatoes and Beets

Preparation time: 10 minutes**Cooking time:** 25 minutes**Servings:** 4

Ingredients:
- 1 pound sweet potatoes, peeled and cut into wedges
- 2 beets, peeled and cut into wedges
- ½ cup veggie stock
- ½ teaspoon rosemary, dried
- 1 red onion, chopped
- 2 tablespoons olive oil
- 1 teaspoon sweet paprika
- 1 tablespoon chives, chopped
- A pinch of salt and black pepper

Directions:

Set the instant pot on sauté mode, add the oil, heat it up, add the onion and paprika and cook for 5 minutes. Add the potatoes, beets and the remaining ingredients, put the lid on and cook on High for 20 minutes. Release the pressure naturally for 10 minutes, divide the mix between plates and serve as a side dish.

Nutrition: calories 200, fat 8, fiber 4, carbs 6, protein 8

Almond and Sprouts Mix

Preparation time: 10 minutes**Cooking time:** 15 minutes**Servings:** 4

Ingredients:

- 2 scallions, chopped
- 1 pound Brussels sprouts, trimmed and halved
- 1 tablespoon almonds, chopped
- 1 tablespoon olive oil
- A pinch of salt and black pepper
- ½ teaspoon rosemary, dried
- ½ teaspoon turmeric powder
- ¼ cup veggie stock
- 1 tablespoon parsley, chopped

Directions:

Set the instant pot on Sauté mode, add the oil, heat it up, add the scallions and turmeric and cook for 2 minutes. Add the sprouts, almonds and the other ingredients, toss, put the lid on and cook on High for 13 minutes. Release the pressure naturally for 10 minutes, divide everything between plates and serve as a side dish.

Nutrition: calories 181, fat 7, fiber 3, carbs 6, protein 7

Rosemary Artichokes

Preparation time: 10 minutes**Cooking time:** 20 minutes**Servings:** 4

Ingredients:

- 2 tablespoons olive oil
- ½ teaspoon rosemary, dried
- ½ teaspoon cumin, ground
- 1 tablespoon lime juice
- 4 artichokes, trimmed and halved
- 1 cup water
- A pinch of salt and black pepper

Directions:

In a bowl, combine the artichokes with the olive oil and the other ingredients except the water and toss. Put the water in the instant pot, add the steamer basket, put the artichokes inside, put the lid on and cook on High for 20 minutes. Release the pressure naturally for 10 minutes, divide the artichokes between plates and serve as a side dish.

Nutrition: calories 184, fat 6, fiber 3, carbs 6, protein 6

Mint Peas

Preparation time: 10 minutes**Cooking time:** 20 minutes**Servings:** 4

Ingredients:

- 1 tablespoon olive oil
- 2 cups green peas
- 1 tablespoon mint, chopped
- 1 red onion, chopped
- 2 tablespoons avocado oil
- 1 teaspoon thyme, dried
- A pinch of salt and black pepper
- ½ cup veggie stock

Directions:

Set the instant pot on Sauté mode, add the oil, heat it up, add the onion and cook for 5 minutes. Add the peas and the remaining ingredients, toss, put the lid on and cook on High for 15 minutes. Release the pressure naturally for 10 minutes, divide the mix between plates and serve as a side dish.

Nutrition: calories 200, fat 8, fiber 3, carbs 7, protein 8

Kale and Olives Mix

Preparation time: 10 minutes**Cooking time:** 20 minutes**Servings:** 4

Ingredients:

- 2 garlic cloves, minced
- 3 scallions, chopped
- 2 tablespoons olive oil
- 1 pound kale, torn
- 1 cup kalamata olives, pitted and halved
- ½ cup tomato passata
- ½ teaspoon cumin, ground
- A pinch of salt and black pepper
- 1 tablespoon chives, chopped

Directions:

Set your instant pot on sauté mode, add the oil, heat it up, add the scallions and garlic and cook for 5 minutes. Add the kale, olives and the other ingredients, toss, put the lid on and cook on High for 15 minutes. Release the pressure naturally for 10 minutes, divide the mix between plates and serve as a side dish.

Nutrition: calories 200, fat 7, fiber 4, carbs 6, protein 5

Thyme Green Beans

Preparation time: 10 minutes**Cooking time:** 20 minutes**Servings:** 4

Ingredients:
- 1 tablespoon olive oil
- 1 pound green beans, trimmed and halved
- 1 red onion, chopped
- ½ cup tomato passata
- ½ teaspoon chili powder
- 1 tablespoon thyme, chopped
- A pinch of salt and black pepper

Directions:
Set your instant pot on Sauté mode, add the oil, heat up, add the onion and sauté for 5 minutes Add green beans, passata and the rest of the ingredients, toss, put the lid on and cook on High for 15 minutes Release the pressure naturally for 10 minutes, divide the mix between plates and serve as a side dish.

Nutrition: calories 185, fat 6, fiber 4, carbs 6, protein 8

Carrots and Peas Mix

Preparation time: 10 minutes**Cooking time:** 20 minutes**Servings:** 4

Ingredients:
- ¼ cup chicken stock
- 1 yellow onion, chopped
- 1 cup green peas
- 2 cups baby carrots, peeled
- 2 tablespoons olive oil
- A pinch of salt and black pepper
- 1 tablespoon chives, chopped
- ½ tablespoon balsamic vinegar

Directions:
Set your instant pot on Sauté mode, add the oil, heat it up, add the onion, stir and sauté for 5 minutes Add the peas, carrots and the other ingredients except the cheese, toss, put the lid on and cook on High for 15 minutes. Release the pressure naturally for 10 minutes, divide everything between plates and serve.

Nutrition: calories 200, fat 7, fiber 2, carbs 5, protein 6

Turmeric Squash Mix

Preparation time: 10 minutes**Cooking time:** 20 minutes**Servings:** 4

Ingredients:
- 1 pound butternut squash, peeled and roughly cubed
- 2 scallions, chopped
- 1 tablespoon olive oil
- ½ cup veggie stock
- 1 teaspoon turmeric powder
- A pinch of salt and black pepper
- ½ teaspoon ginger, ground
- 1 tablespoon chives, chopped

Directions:
Set the instant pot on Sauté mode, add the oil, heat up, add the scallions and ginger and cook for 5 minutes Add the squash and the other ingredients, toss, put the lid on and cook on High for 15 minutes Release the pressure naturally for 10 minutes, divide between plates and serve as a side dish.

Nutrition: calories 126, fat 4, fiber 5, carbs 8, protein 5

Spinach and Avocado Mix

Preparation time: 5 minutes**Cooking time:** 5 minutes**Servings:** 4

Ingredients:
- 1 pound baby spinach
- 1 avocado, peeled, pitted and roughly cubed
- 2 spring onions, chopped
- 1 cup cherry tomatoes, halved
- 1 tablespoon olive oil
- 1 tablespoon lime juice
- 2 tablespoons chives, chopped

Directions:
Set the instant pot on Sauté mode, add the oil, heat up, add the spring onions and the other ingredients, toss gently, put the lid on and cook on High for 5 minutes Release the pressure fast for 5 minutes, divide the mix between plates and serve as a side salad.

Nutrition: calories 175, fat 4, fiber 2, carbs 6, protein 8

Lime Potato

Preparation time: 5 minutes**Cooking time:** 20 minutes**Servings:** 4

Ingredients:
- 1 pound sweet potatoes, peeled and cut into wedges
- 1 tablespoon garlic, minced
- 1 tablespoon lime zest, grated
- Juice of 1 lime
- 2 tablespoons olive oil
- ½ cup veggie stock
- A pinch of salt and black pepper
- ¼ teaspoon sweet paprika
- 1 tablespoon chives, chopped

Directions:

Set the instant pot on Sauté mode, add the oil, heat up, add the potatoes and cook for 5 minutes. Add the garlic and the other ingredients, toss, put the lid on and cook on High for 15 minutes. Release the pressure fast for 5 minutes, divide the mix between plates and serve as a side dish.

Nutrition: calories 200, fat 5, fiber 3, carbs 6, protein 7

Tomato Salad

Preparation time: 5 minutes**Cooking time:** 12 minutes**Servings:** 4

Ingredients:
- 1 pound cherry tomatoes, halved
- 3 scallions, chopped
- 1 tablespoon lime juice
- 2 tablespoons olive oil
- A pinch of salt and black pepper
- 1 tablespoon cilantro, chopped

Directions:

In your instant pot, combine the tomatoes with the scallions, lime juice and the other ingredients, toss, put the lid on and cook on High for 12 minutes. Release the pressure fast for 5 minutes, divide the mix between plates and serve as a side salad.

Nutrition: calories 162, fat 6, fiber 2, carbs 6, protein 4

Chickpeas Mix

Preparation time: 10 minutes**Cooking time:** 20 minutes**Servings:** 4

Ingredients:
- 2 cups canned chickpeas, drained and rinsed
- 1 tablespoon olive oil
- 3 scallions, chopped
- A pinch of salt and black pepper
- 1 teaspoon rosemary, dried
- 1 teaspoon chili powder
- 1 cup veggie stock
- 2 tablespoons parsley, chopped

Directions:
Set your instant pot on Sauté mode, add the oil, heat it up, add the scallions and chili powder and sauté for 5 minutes Add the chickpeas and the rest of the ingredients except the cilantro, put the lid on and cook on High for 10 minutes Release the pressure naturally for 10 minutes, divide the mix between plates and serve as a side dish.

Nutrition: calories 152, fat 4, fiber 2, carbs 6, protein 8

Dill Red Cabbage

Preparation time: 5 minutes**Cooking time:** 20 minutes**Servings:** 4

Ingredients:
- ¼ cup veggie stock
- 1 pound red cabbage, shredded
- 1 tablespoon avocado oil
- 1 teaspoon rosemary, dried
- ½ teaspoon hot paprika
- 1 red onion, roughly chopped
- A pinch of salt and black pepper
- 1 tablespoon dill, chopped

Directions:
Set the instant pot on Sauté mode, add the oil, heat up, add the onion and cook for 5 minutes. Add the cabbage and the other ingredients, toss, put the lid on and cook on High for 15 minutes. Release the pressure fast for 5 minutes, divide the mix between plates and serve.

Nutrition: calories 200, fat 8, fiber 4, carbs 7, protein 9

108

Turmeric Baby Carrots and Onions

Preparation time: 10 minutes**Cooking time:** 20 minutes**Servings:** 4

Ingredients:

- 1 pound baby carrots, peeled
- 1 cup pearl onions, peeled
- 1 tablespoon olive oil
- Juice of 1 lime
- ½ teaspoon sweet paprika
- 2 garlic cloves, minced
- Salt and black pepper to the taste
- ½ cup veggie stock
- 1 tablespoon cilantro, chopped

Directions:

Set your instant pot on Sauté mode, add the oil, heat it up, add the onions, garlic and paprika, stir and cook for 5 minutes. Add the carrots and the rest of the ingredients, put the lid on and cook on High for 15 minutes. Release the pressure naturally for 10 minutes, divide the mix between plates and serve.

Nutrition: calories 162, fat 4, fiber 4, carbs 9, protein 7

Chickpeas and Spinach Mix

Preparation time: 10 minutes**Cooking time:** 15 minutes**Servings:** 4

Ingredients:

- 1 pound baby spinach
- 1 cup canned chickpeas, drained and rinsed
- 2 tablespoons olive oil
- 1 teaspoon sweet paprika
- 3 scallions, chopped
- ½ teaspoon chili powder
- A pinch of salt and black pepper
- ½ cup veggie stock
- 1 tablespoon chives, chopped

Directions:

Set the instant pot on Sauté mode, add the oil, heat up, add the scallions and chili powder and sauté for 5 minutes. Add chickpeas, spinach and the other ingredients, toss, put the lid on and cook on High for 10 minutes. Release the pressure naturally for 10 minutes, divide the mix between plates and serve.

Nutrition: calories 142, fat 2, fiber 4, carbs 9, protein 4

Mustard Kale Mix

Preparation time: 10 minutes**Cooking time:** 15 minutes**Servings:** 4

Ingredients:
- 1 pound baby kale
- 1 red onion, sliced
- 1 tablespoon mustard
- 2 tablespoons olive oil
- 1 tablespoon lime juice
- 1 teaspoon rosemary, dried
- ½ cup veggie stock
- Salt and black pepper to the taste

Directions:

Set the instant pot on Sauté mode, add the oil, heat it up, add the onion and rosemary and sauté for 2 minutes. Add the kale, mustard and the other ingredients, toss, put the lid on and cook on High for 13 minutes. Release the pressure naturally for 10 minutes, divide the mix between plates and serve as a side dish.

Nutrition: calories 142, fat 4, fiber 3, carbs 6, protein 10

Spinach Quinoa Mix

Preparation time: 10 minutes**Cooking time:** 20 minutes**Servings:** 4

Ingredients:
- 1 cup baby spinach
- 1 cup quinoa
- 2 cups chicken stock
- 1 yellow onion, chopped
- ½ teaspoon garam masala
- 1 teaspoon allspice, ground
- 1 tablespoon olive oil
- A pinch of salt and black pepper
- 1 tablespoon chives, chopped

Directions:

Set the instant pot on Sauté mode, add the oil, heat up, add the onion, garam masala and allspice, stir and sauté for 5 minutes. Add the quinoa, stock and the other ingredients, toss, put the lid on and cook on High for 15 minutes. Release the pressure naturally for 10 minutes, divide the mix between plates and serve as a side dish.

Nutrition: calories 132, fat 4, fiber 3, carbs 6, protein 9

Spicy Fennel Mix

Preparation time: 5 minutes**Cooking time:** 15 minutes**Servings:** 4

Ingredients:
- 2 fennel bulbs, sliced
- 1 yellow onion, minced
- 1 tablespoon olive oil
- Juice of 1 lime
- ½ teaspoon basil, dried
- ½ teaspoon hot paprika
- ½ teaspoon chili powder
- 1 tablespoon chives, chopped
- A pinch of salt and black pepper

Directions:
Set the instant pot on Sauté mode, add the oil, heat it up, add the onion and sauté for 2 minutes. Add the fennel, chili powder and the rest of the ingredients, put the lid on and cook on High for 13 minutes. Release the pressure fast for 5 minutes, divide the mix between plates and serve.

Nutrition: calories 142, fat 7, fiber 4, carbs 6, protein 8

Balsamic Spinach Mix

Preparation time: 5 minutes**Cooking time:** 8 minutes**Servings:** 4

Ingredients:
- 1 pound baby spinach
- 4 scallions, minced
- 1 tablespoon olive oil
- 1 tablespoon balsamic vinegar
- 1 carrot, peeled and sliced
- ¼ cup veggie stock
- A pinch of salt and black pepper
- 2 tablespoons chives, chopped

Directions:
Set the instant pot on Sauté mode, add the oil, heat it up, add the scallions and cook for 2 minutes. Add the spinach, vinegar and the other ingredients, toss, put the lid on and cook on High for 6 minutes. Release the pressure fast for 5 minutes, divide the mix between plates and serve.

Nutrition: calories 152, fat 7, fiber 2, carbs 7, protein 5

Orange Spinach Mix

Preparation time: 5 minutes**Cooking time:** 12 minutes**Servings:** 4

Ingredients:
- 1 pound baby spinach
- 1 tablespoon orange juice
- ½ tablespoon orange zest, grated
- 2 scallions, chopped
- 2 tablespoons olive oil
- A pinch of salt and black pepper
- 1 tablespoon cilantro, chopped

Directions:

Set the instant pot on Sauté mode, add the oil, heat it up, add the scallions and sauté for 2 minutes. Add the spinach and the other ingredients, toss, put the lid on and cook for 10 minutes. Release the pressure fast for 5 minutes, divide the mix between plates and serve.

Nutrition: calories 152, fat 4, fiber 3, carbs 4, protein 3

Italian Endives Mix

Preparation time: 10 minutes**Cooking time:** 15 minutes**Servings:** 4

Ingredients:
- 2 endives, trimmed and shredded
- 1 tablespoon olive oil
- 1 cup cherry tomatoes, halved
- 1 red onion, chopped
- ½ teaspoon Italian seasoning
- ½ teaspoon chili powder
- ½ teaspoon coriander, ground
- Salt and black pepper to the taste
- 1 tablespoon chives, chopped
- 1 teaspoon sweet paprika

Directions:

Set the instant pot on Sauté mode, add the oil, heat it up, add the onion and sauté for 5 minutes. Add the endives and the other ingredients, toss, put the lid on and cook on High for 10 minutes. Release the pressure naturally for 10 minutes, divide the mix between plates and serve.

Nutrition: calories 187, fat 7, fiber 3, carbs 5, protein 5

Rosemary Olives Mix

Preparation time: 10 minutes**Cooking time:** 15 minutes**Servings:** 4

Ingredients:
- 1 cup black olives, pitted and halved
- 1 cup green olives, pitted and halved
- 1 cup kalamata olives, pitted and halved
- ¼ cup veggie stock
- 2 tablespoons olive oil
- 2 tablespoons rosemary, chopped
- 2 tablespoons chives, chopped
- A pinch of salt and black pepper

Directions:

In the instant pot, combine the olives with the stock and the other ingredients, toss, put the lid on and cook on High for 15 minutes. Release the pressure naturally for 10 minutes, divide the mix between plates and serve.

Nutrition: calories 120, fat 4, fiber 3, carbs 8, protein 4

Corn and Spinach

Preparation time: 5 minutes**Cooking time:** 20 minutes**Servings:** 4

Ingredients:
- 2 cups baby spinach
- 3 scallions, chopped
- 1 tablespoon olive oil
- 2 garlic cloves, minced
- 2 cups fresh corn
- 2 tablespoons avocado oil
- Juice of 1 lime
- ¼ cup veggie stock
- A pinch of salt and black pepper
- 2 tablespoons chives, chopped

Directions:

Set the instant pot on Sauté mode, add the oil, heat it up, add the scallions and garlic and cook for 5 minutes. Add the spinach, the corn, lime juice and the other ingredients, toss, put the lid on and cook on High for 15 minutes. Release the pressure fast for 5 minutes, divide the mix between plates and serve.

Nutrition: calories 165, fat 4, fiber 3, carbs 7, protein 6

Mushroom and Green Beans

Preparation time: 10 minutes**Cooking time:** 20 minutes**Servings:** 4

Ingredients:
- ½ pound mushrooms, halved
- ½ pound green beans
- 1 yellow onion, chopped
- 2 tablespoons olive oil
- ¼ cup tomato passata
- 1 teaspoon chili powder
- Salt and black pepper to the taste
- 1 tablespoon balsamic vinegar
- 1 tablespoon chives, chopped

Directions:

Set the instant pot on Sauté mode, add the oil, heat it up, add the onion and the mushrooms, stir and cook for 5 minutes. Add the green beans and the other ingredients, toss, put the lid on and cook on High for 15 minutes. Release the pressure naturally for 10 minutes, divide the mix between plates and serve.

Nutrition: calories 173, fat 5, fiber 2, carbs 5, protein 6

Broccoli Salad

Preparation time: 10 minutes**Cooking time:** 15 minutes**Servings:** 4

Ingredients:
- 1 pound broccoli florets
- 2 garlic cloves, minced
- 2 tablespoons olive oil
- ½ teaspoon cumin, ground
- ½ teaspoon sweet paprika
- 1 cup cherry tomatoes, halved
- 1 tablespoon capers, drained
- A pinch of salt and black pepper
- 1 tablespoon lime juice
- 1 tablespoon chives, chopped

Directions:

Set the instant pot on Sauté mode, add the oil, heat it up, add the garlic and cook for 2 minutes. Add the broccoli, cumin and the other ingredients, toss, put the lid on and cook on High for 13 minutes. Release the pressure naturally for 10 minutes, divide the mix between plates and serve as a side salad.

Nutrition: calories 173, fat 8, fiber 2, carbs 6, protein 6

Cauliflower and Tomatoes Mix

Preparation time: 10 minutes**Cooking time:** 15 minutes**Servings:** 4

Ingredients:

- ½ pound cauliflower florets
- 1 cup cherry tomatoes, halved
- 1 tablespoon avocado oil
- 2 scallions, chopped
- ½ cup tomato passata
- A pinch of salt and black pepper
- ½ teaspoon sweet paprika
- 1 tablespoon parsley, chopped

Directions:

Set the instant pot on Sauté mode, add the oil, heat up, add the scallions and sauté for 2 minutes. Add the cauliflower, tomatoes and the other ingredients, toss, put the lid on and cook on High for 13 minutes. Release the pressure naturally for 10 minutes, divide the mix between plates and serve as a side dish.

Nutrition: calories 130, fat 5, fiber 3, carbs 6, protein 7

Tomato and Pomegranate Mix

Preparation time: 10 minutes**Cooking time:** 14 minutes**Servings:** 4

Ingredients:

- 1 pound cherry tomatoes, halved
- 2 scallions, chopped
- ½ cup black olives, pitted and halved
- ¼ cup tomato passata
- 1 cup baby spinach
- ½ cup pomegranate seeds
- 1 tablespoon olive oil
- 1 tablespoon lime juice
- 1 red chili pepper, chopped
- A pinch of salt and black pepper
- 2 tablespoons chives, chopped

Directions:

Set the instant pot on Sauté mode, add the oil, heat up, add the scallions and chili pepper and cook for 4 minutes. Add the tomatoes, spinach and the other ingredients, toss, put the lid and cook on High for 10 minutes. Release the pressure naturally for 10 minutes, divide the mix between plates and serve as a side dish.

Nutrition: calories 142, fat 4, fiber 2, carbs 4, protein 5

Broccoli Rice Mix

Preparation time: 10 minutes**Cooking time:** 25 minutes**Servings:** 4

Ingredients:
- 1 cup black rice
- 2 cups chicken stock
- 1 cup broccoli florets, chopped
- 1 yellow onion, chopped
- 1 tablespoon olive oil
- 1 teaspoon turmeric powder
- Salt and black pepper to the taste
- 1 tablespoon cilantro, chopped

Directions:
Set the instant pot on Sauté mode, add the oil, heat up, add the onion and sauté for 5 minutes. Add the rice, stock and the other ingredients, toss, put the lid on and cook on High for 20 minutes. Release the pressure naturally for 10 minutes, divide the mix between plates and serve as a side dish.

Nutrition: calories 190, fat 6, fiber 2, carbs 6, protein 7

Coriander Chickpeas

Preparation time: 10 minutes**Cooking time:** 20 minutes**Servings:** 4

Ingredients:
- 2 cups canned chickpeas, drained and rinsed
- ¼ cup tomato passata
- 1 tablespoon olive oil
- 1 red onion, sliced
- ½ teaspoon coriander, ground
- 2 tablespoons garlic, minced
- A pinch of salt and black pepper
- 1 tablespoon cilantro, chopped

Directions:
Set the instant pot on Sauté mode, add the oil, heat it up, add the onion and garlic and sauté for 5 minutes Add the chickpeas and the rest of the ingredients, put the lid on and cook on High for 15 minutes Release the pressure naturally for 10 minutes, divide the mix between plates and serve.

Nutrition: calories 161, fat 6, fiber 5, carbs 7, protein 7

Mediterranean Diet Snack and Appetizer Recipes

Balsamic Chicken Bites

Preparation time: 10 minutes**Cooking time:** 20 minutes**Servings:** 6
Ingredients:

- 1 pound chicken breasts, skinless, boneless and cut into medium cubes
- ¼ cup chicken stock
- 2 tablespoons olive oil
- ½ tablespoon honey
- 2 tablespoons balsamic vinegar
- ½ teaspoon oregano, dried
- ½ teaspoon basil, dried
- 1 tablespoon parsley, chopped

Directions:

Set the instant pot on Sauté mode, add the oil, heat up, add the chicken bites and brown for 5 minutes. Add the vinegar and the other ingredients, toss, put the lid on and cook on High for 15 minutes. Release the pressure naturally for 10 minutes, arrange the chicken bites on a platter and serve as an appetizer.

Nutrition: calories 222, fat 11.2, fiber 4.5, carbs 3.4, protein 12.6

Spicy Lentils and Walnuts Bowls

Preparation time: 10 minutes**Cooking time:** 20 minutes**Servings:** 8
Ingredients:

- 2 cups canned lentils, drained and rinsed
- 1 cup walnuts
- 1 tablespoon olive oil
- 1 tablespoon cilantro, chopped
- 1 teaspoon hot paprika
- ½ cup water
- ½ tablespoon red pepper, crushed
- A pinch of salt and black pepper
- 1 tablespoon chives, chopped

Directions:

In a bowl, combine the lentils with the walnuts, oil and the other ingredients except the water and toss. Put the water in the instant pot, add the steamer basket, put the lentils and walnuts mix inside, put the lid on and cook on High for 20 minutes. Release the pressure naturally for 10 minutes, divide the mix into bowls and serve as a snack.

Nutrition: calories 200, fat 11.2, fiber 2.4, carbs 5.3, protein 2.3

Zucchini Dip
Preparation time: 10 minutes**Cooking time:** 14 minutes**Servings:** 6

Ingredients:
- 1 cup Greek yogurt
- 1 cup zucchinis, grated
- ½ teaspoon rosemary, dried
- A pinch of salt and black pepper
- 2 scallions, chopped
- 1 tablespoon dill, chopped
- 1 cup water

Directions:
In a bowl, combine the zucchinis with the yogurt and the other ingredients except the water, stir well and divide into 6 ramekins. Put the water in the instant pot, add the trivet inside, put the ramekins in the machine, put the lid on and cook on High for 14 minutes. Release the pressure naturally for 10 minutes, and serve the dip right away.

Nutrition: calories 232, fat 9.8, fiber 2.3, carbs 5.7, protein 4.3

Lentils Spread
Preparation time: 10 minutes**Cooking time:** 25 minutes**Servings:** 6

Ingredients:
- 1 cup canned lentils, drained and rinsed
- 1 cup veggie stock
- A pinch of salt and black pepper
- 2 tablespoons olive oil
- 2 tablespoons tahini paste
- 2 tablespoons lime juice
- 2 scallions, chopped
- 2 garlic cloves, minced

Directions:
In the instant pot, combine the lentils with the stock, scallions and garlic, toss, put the lid on and cook on High for 25 minutes. Release the pressure naturally for 10 minutes, transfer the chickpeas to a blender, add the rest of the ingredients, pulse well, divide into bowls and serve.

Nutrition: calories 300, fat 12, fiber 4, carbs 12, protein 5

Garlic Turkey Strips

Preparation time: 10 minutes**Cooking time:** 20 minutes**Servings:** 6

Ingredients:
- 2 pounds turkey breast, skinless, boneless and cut into strips
- 4 garlic cloves, minced
- 2 tablespoons olive oil
- 2 tablespoons Worcestershire sauce
- ½ cup honey
- A pinch of salt and black pepper
- ½ teaspoon hot paprika

Directions:
In your instant pot, combine the turkey strips with the garlic, oil and the other ingredients, toss, put the lid on and cook on High for 20 minutes. Release the pressure naturally for 10 minutes, arrange the turkey strips on a platter and serve as an appetizer.

Nutrition: calories 234, fat 11, fiber 3, carbs 20, protein 12

Almond Dip

Preparation time: 5 minutes**Cooking time:** 12 minutes**Servings:** 4

Ingredients:
- 1 cup coconut cream
- ½ teaspoon turmeric powder
- 1 tablespoon olive oil
- 1 cup almonds, chopped
- 1 cup spring onions, chopped
- A pinch of salt and black pepper
- 1 cup water

Directions:
In a blender, combine the cream with the turmeric, almonds and the other ingredients except the water, pulse well and transfer to a ramekin. Put the water in the instant pot, add the trivet inside, put the ramekin in the trivet, put the lid on and cook on High for 12 minutes. Release the pressure fast for 5 minutes and serve as a party dip.

Nutrition: calories 132, fat 1, fiber 2, carbs 6, protein 5

Pesto Dip

Preparation time: 5 minutes**Cooking time:** 12 minutes**Servings:** 4

Ingredients:

- 2 tablespoons basil pesto
- 1 cup coconut cream
- 2 garlic cloves, minced
- 4 scallions, chopped
- 1 tablespoon lime zest, grated
- 1 tablespoon lime juice
- 1 tablespoon olive oil
- A pinch of salt and black pepper
- 1 cup water

Directions:

In a blender, combine the pesto with the garlic, cream and the other ingredients except the water, pulse well and transfer to a ramekin. Put the water in the instant pot, add the trivet inside, put the ramekin inside, put the lid on and cook on High for 12 minutes. Release the pressure fast for 5 minutes, divide into bowls and serve as a dip.

Nutrition: calories 140, fat 4, fiber 3, carbs 6, protein 6

Shrimp Bowls

Preparation time: 5 minutes**Cooking time:** 5 minutes**Servings:** 4

Ingredients:

- 2 pounds shrimp, peeled and deveined
- 1 tablespoon avocado oil
- 1 cup cherry tomatoes, halved
- 1 cup baby spinach
- 1 tablespoon balsamic vinegar
- ¼ cup veggie stock
- 1 tablespoon capers, drained
- 2 spring onions, chopped
- ½ tablespoon chives, chopped

Directions:

Set the instant pot on Sauté mode, add the oil, heat it up, add the shrimp, tomatoes and the other ingredients, toss gently, put the lid on and cook on High for 5 minutes. Release the pressure fast for 5 minutes, divide the mix into bowls and serve as an appetizer.

Nutrition: calories 170, fat 9, fiber 4, carbs 7, protein 6

Calamari Rings Bowls

Preparation time: 5 minutes**Cooking time:** 20 minutes**Servings:** 4

Ingredients:

- 1 pound calamari rings
- 2 scallions, chopped
- 1 cup baby kale
- 1 cup kalamata olives, pitted and halved
- ½ cup cherry tomatoes, halved
- ¼ cup tomato passata
- ½ teaspoon Italian seasoning
- 1 tablespoon olive oil
- 2 garlic cloves, minced
- 1 tablespoon chives, chopped

Directions:

Set the instant pot on Sauté mode, add the oil, heat up, add the scallions and cook for 2 minutes. Add the calamari, kale and the other ingredients, toss, put the lid on and cook on High for 18 minutes. Release the pressure fast for 5 minutes, divide into bowls and serve as an appetizer.

Nutrition: calories 180, fat 3, fiber 3, carbs 7, protein 9

Balsamic Tomato Bowls

Preparation time: 5 minutes**Cooking time:** 12 minutes**Servings:** 4

Ingredients:

- 1 pound cherry tomatoes, halved
- 2 scallions, chopped
- 1 cup kalamata olives, pitted and halved
- 1 tablespoon olive oil
- 1 tablespoon balsamic vinegar
- ¼ cup veggie stock
- 1 tablespoon capers, drained
- ½ cup spring onions, chopped
- ¼ cup cilantro, chopped

Directions:

Set the instant pot on Sauté mode, add the oil, heat up, add the scallions and cook for 2 minutes. Add tomatoes, olives and the other ingredients, toss, put the lid on and cook on High for 10 minutes. Release the pressure fast for 5 minutes, divide the mix into bowls and serve as an appetizer.

Nutrition: calories 150, fat 9, fiber 2, carbs 6, protein 6

Avocado Salsa

Preparation time: 5 minutes **Cooking time:** 5 minutes**Servings:** 4

Ingredients:
- 1 cup avocado, peeled, pitted and cubed
- 1 cup green olives, pitted and halved
- 1 cup cucumber, cubed
- Juice of 1 lime
- 1 tablespoon capers, drained
- 1 red onion, sliced
- 2 tablespoons balsamic vinegar
- 1 tablespoon olive oil
- 2 tablespoons chives, chopped

Directions:
In the instant pot, combine the avocado with the olives, cucumber and the other ingredients, toss, put the lid on and cook on High for 5 minutes. Release the pressure fast for 5 minutes, divide the salsa into bowls and serve.

Nutrition: calories 173, fat 9, fiber 3, carbs 5, protein 8

Kale Salsa

Preparation time: 5 minutes**Cooking time:** 15 minutes**Servings:** 4

Ingredients:
- 2 cups baby kale
- 3 scallions, chopped
- 1 tablespoon avocado oil
- 1 tablespoon lime juice
- 1 cup cherry tomatoes, halved
- A pinch of salt and black pepper
- 4 garlic cloves, minced
- 1 tablespoon chives, chopped

Directions:
Set the instant pot on Sauté mode, add the oil, heat it up, add the garlic and scallions and cook for 3 minutes. Add the kale and the other ingredients, toss, put the lid on and cook on High for 12 minutes. Release the pressure fast for 5 minutes, divide into bowls and serve.

Nutrition: calories 183, fat 9, fiber 4, carbs 7, protein 5

Shrimp and Olives Salad

Preparation time: 5 minutes**Cooking time:** 7 minutes**Servings:** 4

Ingredients:

- 1 pound shrimp, peeled and deveined
- 1 cup kalamata olives, pitted and halved
- 4 scallions, chopped
- 1 avocado, peeled, pitted and cubed
- 1 tablespoon lime juice
- ¼ cup chicken stock
- 1 tablespoon olive oil
- 2 tablespoons chives, chopped
- A pinch of salt and black pepper

Directions:

Set the instant pot on Sauté mode, add the oil, heat up, add the scallions and cook for 2 minutes. Add the shrimp, olives and the other ingredients, toss, put the lid on and cook on High for 5 minutes. Release the pressure fast for 5 minutes, divide the salad into bowls and serve as an appetizer.

Nutrition: calories 180, fat 9, fiber 2, carbs 6, protein 9

Beans Salsa

Preparation time: 10 minutes**Cooking time:** 15 minutes**Servings:** 4

Ingredients:

- 1 cup canned black beans, drained and rinsed
- 1 cup canned red kidney beans, drained and rinsed
- 1 cup kalamata olives, pitted and halved
- 1 cup tomatoes, cubed
- ½ cup veggie stock
- 1 tablespoon chili powder
- 1 tablespoon balsamic vinegar
- 2 tablespoons olive oil
- 2 garlic cloves, minced

Directions:

In your instant pot, combine the beans with the olives, tomatoes and the other ingredients, toss, put the lid on and cook on High for 15 minutes. Release the pressure naturally for 10 minutes, divide the salsa into bowls and serve.

Nutrition: calories 210, fat 7, fiber 4, carbs 6, protein 10

Smoked Salmon Salad

Preparation time: 10 minutes**Cooking time:** 10 minutes**Servings:** 4

Ingredients:
- 1 tablespoon olive oil
- 1 red onion, chopped
- 1 cup cherry tomatoes, halved
- 1 cup baby spinach
- 2 cups smoked salmon fillets, flaked
- A pinch of salt and black pepper
- ¼ cup chicken stock
- 1 tablespoon chives, chopped
- 1 tablespoon lime juice

Directions:

Set the instant pot on Sauté mode, add the oil, heat up, add the onion and sauté for 2 minutes. Add the smoked salmon, tomatoes and the other ingredients, toss, put the lid on and cook on High for 8 minutes. Release the pressure naturally for 10 minutes, divide the mix into bowls and serve.

Nutrition: calories 180, fat 9, fiber 4, carbs 6, protein 8

Chives Shrimp Mix

Preparation time: 5 minutes**Cooking time:** 6 minutes**Servings:** 4

Ingredients:
- 2 pounds shrimp, peeled and deveined
- 1 red onion, sliced
- 1 cup kalamata olives, pitted and halved
- 1 cup avocado, peeled, pitted and cubed
- Juice of 1 lime
- 1 tablespoon olive oil
- A pinch of salt and black pepper
- ¼ cup chicken stock
- 2 tablespoons chives, chopped

Directions:

In your instant pot, combine the shrimp with the onion, olives and the other ingredients, toss, put the lid on and cook on High for 6 minutes. Release the pressure fast for 5 minutes, divide everything into bowls and serve as an appetizer.

Nutrition: calories 177, fat 8, fiber 2, carbs 6, protein 7

Tomato Dip

Preparation time: 10 minutes**Cooking time:** 15 minutes**Servings:** 4

Ingredients:
- 1 pound tomatoes, cubed
- 1 red onion, chopped
- ½ cup roasted peppers, chopped
- 1 teaspoon basil, dried
- 1 teaspoon Italian seasoning
- ½ cup tomato passata
- A pinch of salt and black pepper
- ½ teaspoon chili powder
- 2 tablespoons garlic, chopped

Directions:

In your instant pot, combine the tomatoes with the onion, peppers and the other ingredients, toss, put the lid on and cook on High for 15 minutes, Release the pressure naturally for 10 minutes, blend using an immersion blender, divide the mix into bowls and serve.

Nutrition: calories 221, fat 12, fiber 4, carbs 7, protein 11

Cod Salad

Preparation time: 5 minutes**Cooking time:** 12 minutes**Servings:** 4

Ingredients:
- 1 pound cod fillets, boneless and roughly cubed
- 1 red onion, sliced
- 1 cup cherry tomatoes, halved
- 1 tablespoon olive oil
- 2 cups baby spinach
- Juice of 1 lime
- 1 cup baby kale
- ¼ cup chicken stock
- 2 garlic cloves, minced
- 1 tablespoon chives, chopped

Directions:

Set the instant pot on Sauté mode, add the oil, heat it up, add the onion and garlic and sauté for 2 minutes. Add the fish, tomatoes and the other ingredients, toss, put the lid on and cook on High for 10 minutes. Release the pressure fast for 5 minutes, divide the mix into bowls and serve as an appetizer.

Nutrition: calories 180, fat 9, fiber 3, carbs 5, protein 7

Herbed Shrimp Mix

Preparation time: 5 minutes**Cooking time:** 6 minutes**Servings:** 4

Ingredients:
- 2 pounds shrimp, peeled and deveined
- 1 red onion, sliced
- 1 tablespoon olive oil
- ¼ cup chicken stock
- 2 tablespoons balsamic vinegar
- 1 tablespoon basil, chopped
- 1 tablespoon oregano, chopped
- 1 tablespoon cilantro, chopped
- 1 tablespoon chives, chopped

Directions:
Set the instant pot on Sauté mode, add the oil, heat up, add the onion and cook for 2 minutes. Add the shrimp, vinegar and the other ingredients, toss, put the lid on and cook on High for 4 minutes. Release the pressure fast for 5 minutes, divide the mix into bowls and serve as an appetizer.

Nutrition: calories 140, fat 4, fiber 3, carbs 5, protein 4

Salmon Bites

Preparation time: 5 minutes**Cooking time:** 14 minutes**Servings:** 4

Ingredients:
- 2 pounds salmon fillets, boneless, skinless and cubed
- 1 tablespoon balsamic vinegar
- ½ cup heavy cream
- 2 tablespoons olive oil
- 2 teaspoons garlic, minced
- 2 teaspoons basil, dried
- 1 tablespoon hives, chopped

Directions:
Set your instant pot on Sauté mode, add the oil, heat it up, add the garlic and cook for 2 minutes. Add the salmon, vinegar and the other ingredients, toss, put the lid on and cook on High for 12 minutes. Release the pressure fast for 5 minutes, divide the mix into bowls and serve as an appetizer.

Nutrition: calories 176, fat 4, fiber 3, carbs 6, protein 7

Tuna Salad

Preparation time: 10 minutes**Cooking time:** 14 minutes**Servings:** 4

Ingredients:
- 1 pound tuna fillets, boneless, skinless and roughly cubed
- 1 cup cherry tomatoes, halved
- 1 cup baby spinach
- 1 red onion, sliced
- 2 tablespoons olive oil
- 1 tablespoon chives, chopped
- ¼ cup chicken stock
- 1 tablespoon cilantro, chopped
- A pinch of salt and black pepper

Directions:
Set your instant pot on Sauté mode, add the oil, heat it up, add the onions and sauté for 4 minutes Add the tuna and the ingredients, toss, put the lid on and cook on High for 10 minutes Release the pressure naturally for 10 minutes, transfer the mix bowls and serve as an appetizer.

Nutrition: calories 181, fat 4, fiber 3, carbs 7, protein 15

Chives Dip

Preparation time: 5 minutes**Cooking time:** 12 minutes**Servings:** 4

Ingredients:
- 2 cups coconut cream
- 1 red onion, chopped
- 1 tablespoon olive oil
- 3 tablespoons chives, chopped
- 1 tablespoon basil, chopped
- ½ teaspoon turmeric powder
- A pinch of salt and black pepper
- 1 teaspoon lime juice

Directions:
Set the instant pot on Sauté mode, add the oil, heat up, add the onion and turmeric and cook for 2 minutes.Add the cream, chives and the other ingredients, whisk, put the lid on and cook on High for 10 minutes.Release the pressure fast for 5 minutes, divide the dip into bowls and serve.

Nutrition: calories 201, fat 9, fiber 4, carbs 7, protein 10

Endive Salsa

Preparation time: 10 minutes**Cooking time:** 12 minutes**Servings:** 4

Ingredients:

- 2 endives, shredded
- 1 cup baby kale
- 1 cup cherry tomatoes, halved
- 1 cup kalamata olives, pitted and halved
- ½ cup heavy cream
- A pinch of salt and black pepper
- 3 garlic cloves, minced
- 1 tablespoon chives, chopped

Directions:

In your instant pot, combine the endives with the kale, tomatoes and the other ingredients, toss, put the lid on and cook on High for 12 minutes. Release the pressure naturally for 10 minutes, divide the mix into bowls and serve.

Nutrition: calories 200, fat 8, fiber 2, carbs 6, protein 8

Shrimp and Tomato Salsa

Preparation time: 5 minutes**Cooking time:** 12 minutes**Servings:** 4

Ingredients:

- 2 cups cherry tomatoes, halved
- 1 pound shrimp, peeled and deveined
- 2 tablespoons avocado oil
- 1 cup baby spinach
- 2 spring onions, chopped
- 1 teaspoon chili powder
- 1 tablespoon capers, drained
- ½ cup kalamata olives, pitted and halved
- A pinch of salt and black pepper
- 2 tablespoons lemon juice
- 2 tablespoons chives, chopped

Directions:

Set the instant pot on Sauté mode, add the oil, heat it up, add the onions and chili powder and cook for 5 minutes Add the shrimp, tomatoes and the other ingredients, toss gently, put the lid on and cook on High for 7 minutes Release the pressure fast for 5 minutes, divide the mix into bowls and serve as an appetizer.

Nutrition: calories 171, fat 3, fiber 4, carbs 7, protein 5

Mint Dip

Preparation time: 5 minutes**Cooking time:** 8 minutes**Servings:** 4

Ingredients:

- 1 cup mint, chopped
- 1 tablespoon basil pesto
- 4 scallions, minced
- 1 cup coconut ream
- 1 tablespoon lime juice
- A pinch of salt and black pepper
- 1 teaspoon turmeric powder
- 1 tablespoon chives, chopped

Directions:

In your instant pot, combine the mint with the pesto, scallions and the other ingredients, toss put the lid on and cook on High for 8 minutes. Release the pressure fast for 5 minutes, and serve the mix as a party dip.

Nutrition: calories 162, fat 3, fiber 4, carbs 7, protein 6

Rosemary Tuna Bites

Preparation time: 5 minutes**Cooking time:** 12 minutes**Servings:** 4

Ingredients:

- 2 pounds tuna fillets, boneless and roughly cubed
- 1 tablespoon olive oil
- 1 tablespoon orange juice
- ¼ cup chicken stock
- A pinch of salt and black pepper
- 1 tablespoon rosemary, chopped
- ¼ cup chives, chopped

Directions:

Set the instant pot on Sauté mode, add the oil, heat up, add the tuna, orange juice and the other ingredients, toss gently, put the lid on and cook on High for 12 minutes. Release the pressure fast for 5 minutes and serve as an appetizer.

Nutrition: calories 294, fat 18, fiber 1, carbs 21, protein 10

Balsamic Clams Bowls

Preparation time: 5 minutes**Cooking time:** 15 minutes**Servings:** 4

Ingredients:
- 1 pound clams, scrubbed
- 2 tablespoons olive oil
- 2 tablespoons balsamic vinegar
- 2 garlic cloves, minced
- A pinch of salt and black pepper
- ½ teaspoon rosemary, dried
- ½ teaspoon chili powder
- ½ cup chicken stock

Directions:
In your instant pot, combine the clams with the oil, vinegar and the other ingredients, toss, put the lid on and cook on High for 15 minutes. Release the pressure fast for 5 minutes, divide the clams into bowls and serve as an appetizer.

Nutrition: calories 162, fat 4 fiber 7, carbs 29, protein 4

Artichoke Dip

Preparation time: 10 minutes**Cooking time:** 14 minutes**Servings:** 4

Ingredients:
- 2 tablespoons avocado oil
- 1 yellow onion, chopped
- 2 cups canned artichoke hearts, drained and chopped
- 1 cup coconut cream
- 2 tablespoons chives, chopped
- ½ teaspoon basil, dried
- ½ teaspoon turmeric powder
- Salt and black pepper to the taste

Directions:
Set the instant pot on Sauté mode, add the oil, heat up, add the onion and sauté for 4 minutes. Add the artichokes and the other ingredients, toss, put the lid on and cook on High for 10 minutes. Release the pressure naturally for 10 minutes, divide the dip into bowls and serve.

Nutrition: calories 223, fat 11.2, fiber 5.34, carbs 15.5, protein 7.4

Olives Dip

Preparation time: 5 minutes**Cooking time:** 10 minutes**Servings:** 4

Ingredients:

- 1 tablespoon capers, drained
- 2 cups kalamata olives, pitted and chopped
- 1 tablespoon olive oil
- 3 scallions, hopped
- 2 tablespoons lemon juice
- 1 cup coconut cream
- ½ teaspoon chili powder

Directions:

Set the instant pot on Sauté mode, add the oil, heat up, add the scallions and cook for 2 minutes. Add the olives and the other ingredients, whisk, put the lid on and cook on High for 8 minutes. Release the pressure fast for 5 minutes, blend the mix using an immersion blender, divide into bowls and serve.

Nutrition: calories 200, fat 5.6, fiber 4.5, carbs 12.4, protein 4.6

Olives and Lentils Salsa

Preparation time: 10 minutes**Cooking time:** 15 minutes**Servings:** 4

Ingredients:

- 2 cups canned lentils, drained and rinsed
- 1 cup black olives, pitted and halved
- 1 cup kalamata olives, pitted and halved
- 1 tablespoon olive oil
- 2 scallions, chopped
- 2 tablespoons cilantro, chopped
- 2 garlic cloves, minced
- 1 teaspoon turmeric powder
- A pinch of salt and black pepper
- 1 teaspoon lemon juice
- ¼ cup tomato passata

Directions:

Set the instant pot on Sauté mode, add the oil, heat up, add the scallions and garlic and cook for 2 minutes. Add the lentils, olives and the other ingredients, toss, put the lid on and cook on High for 13 minutes. Release the pressure naturally for 10 minutes, divide the salsa into bowls and serve.

Nutrition: calories 112, fat 6.2, fiber 2, carbs 12.3, protein 3.

Turmeric Greek Dip

Preparation time: 5 minutes**Cooking time:** 8 minutes**Servings:** 4

Ingredients:

- 1 cup Greek yogurt
- 4 scallions, minced
- 1 tablespoon olive oil
- 1 teaspoon turmeric powder
- 2 tablespoons tahini paste
- 1 tablespoon lime juice
- A pinch of salt and black pepper
- 1 tablespoon cilantro, chopped
- 1 cup water

Directions:

In a bowl, combine the yogurt with the scallions and the other ingredients except the water, whisk and divide into 4 ramekins. Put the water in the instant pot, add the trivet inside, put the ramekins in the pot, put the lid on and cook on High for 8 minutes. Release the pressure fast for 5 minutes, and serve the dip right away.

Nutrition: calories 255, fat 11.4, fiber 4.5, carbs 17.4, protein 6.5

Cilantro Green Beans Salsa

Preparation time: 10 minutes**Cooking time:** 14 minutes**Servings:** 4

Ingredients:

- 1 pound green beans, trimmed and roughly chopped
- 2 scallions, minced
- 1 tablespoon olive oil
- 1 red onion, chopped
- ¼ cup tomato passata
- 1 cup cherry tomatoes, halved
- ½ cup kalamata olives, pitted and halved
- ½ cup corn
- 4 garlic cloves, minced
- 1 tablespoon cilantro, chopped
- Juice of ½ lemon
- Salt and black pepper to the taste

Directions:

Set the instant pot on Sauté mode, add the oil, heat it up, add the onion, scallions and garlic and sauté for 4 minutes. Add the green beans, passata and the other ingredients, toss, put the lid on and cook on High for 10 minutes. Release the pressure naturally for 10 minutes, divide the salsa into bowls and serve.

Nutrition: calories 274, fat 11.7, fiber 6.5, carbs 18.5, protein 16.5

Lamb Dip

Preparation time: 10 minutes**Cooking time:** 20 minutes**Servings:** 8

Ingredients:

- 1 pound lamb meat, ground
- 2 tablespoons olive oil
- 1 red onion, chopped
- ½ cup tomato passata
- 1 teaspoon chili powder
- ½ teaspoon sweet paprika
- ½ teaspoon mint, dried
- 1 tablespoon chives, chopped
- ¼ cup parsley, chopped

Directions:

Set the instant pot on Sauté mode, add the oil, heat it up, add the onion and the meat and brown for 5 minutes. Add the passata, chili powder and the other ingredients, stir, put the lid on and cook on High for 10 minutes. Divide into bowls and serve warm as a party dip.

Nutrition: calories 133, fat 9.7, fiber 1.7, carbs 6.4, protein 5.4

Zucchini and Eggplant Dip

Preparation time: 10 minutes**Cooking time:** 20 minutes**Servings:** 4

Ingredients:

- 1 pound eggplant, roughly cubed
- 2 zucchinis, cubed
- 1 red onion, chopped
- ½ teaspoon chili powder
- ½ teaspoon rosemary, dried
- 2 tablespoons olive oil
- 2 tablespoons lime juice
- ½ cup tomato passata
- 2 garlic cloves, minced
- Salt and black pepper to the taste
- 1 tablespoon chives, chopped

Directions:

Set the instant pot on Sauté mode, add the oil, heat it up, add the onion, chili powder, garlic and rosemary and sauté for 5 minutes Add the eggplants, zucchinis and the other ingredients, toss, put the lid on and cook on High for 15 minutes. Release the pressure naturally for 10 minutes, blend the mix using an immersion blender, divide the dip into bowls and serve cold.

Nutrition: calories 121, fat 4.3, fiber 1, carbs 1.4, protein 4.3

Beet Bites

Preparation time: 5 minutes**Cooking time:** 20 minutes**Servings:** 6
Ingredients:

- 1 pound beets, peeled and cubed
- 1 tablespoon avocado oil
- 2 garlic cloves, minced
- 2 tablespoons honey
- ½ tablespoon balsamic vinegar
- ½ teaspoon turmeric powder
- Salt and black pepper to the taste
- 2 tablespoons parsley, chopped

Directions:

Set the instant pot on Sauté mode, add the oil, heat it up, add the beets, garlic and the other ingredients, toss, put the lid on and cook on High for 20 minutes. Release the pressure fast for 5 minutes, arrange the beets bites on a platter and serve as an appetizer.

Nutrition: calories 209, fat 11.2, fiber 3, carbs 4.4, protein 4.8

Bulgur Salad

Preparation time: 10 minutes**Cooking time:** 20 minutes**Servings:** 4
Ingredients:

- 1 cup chicken stock
- 2 cups bulgur, cooked
- ½ cup cherry tomatoes, halved
- ½ cup black olives, pitted and halved
- ½ teaspoon cumin, ground
- ½ teaspoon turmeric powder
- 2 scallions, chopped
- 1 tablespoon olive oil
- ½ tablespoon chives, chopped
- 2 garlic cloves, minced
- A pinch of salt and black pepper
- ¼ cup parsley, chopped

Directions:

Set the instant pot on Sauté mode, add the oil, heat up, add the scallions, cumin, garlic and turmeric and cook for 5 minutes. Add the bulgur and the other ingredients, toss, put the lid on and cook on High for 15 minutes. Release the pressure naturally for 10 minutes, divide into bowls and serve as an appetizer.

Nutrition: calories 300, fat 9.6, fiber 4.6, carbs 22.6, protein 6.6

134

Yogurt Dip

Preparation time: 5 minutes**Cooking time:** 5 minutes**Servings:** 4

Ingredients:

- 2 cups Greek yogurt
- 3 scallions, minced
- 1 tablespoon olive oil
- 1 tablespoon chives, chopped
- 1 tablespoon parsley, chopped
- A pinch of salt and black pepper
- 1 cup water

Directions:

In a bowl, combine the yogurt with the scallions and the other ingredients except the water, whisk and divide into 4 small ramekins. Put the water in the instant pot, add the trivet inside, put the ramekins in the pot, put the lid on and cook on High for 5 minutes. Release the pressure fast for 5 minutes and serve the mix as a party dip.

Nutrition: calories 162, fat 3.4, fiber 2, carbs 6.4, protein 2.4

Shrimp Avocado Salsa

Preparation time: 5 minutes**Cooking time:** 5 minutes**Servings:** 4

Ingredients:

- 2 avocados, halved, pitted and roughly cubed
- 1 pound shrimp, peeled and deveined
- 1 tablespoon lime juice
- 3 scallions, chopped
- 1 tablespoon olive oil
- ½ teaspoon chili powder
- ¼ cup black olives, pitted and halved
- Salt and black pepper to the taste
- 1 tablespoon walnuts, chopped
- 1 tablespoon chives, chopped

Directions:

Set the instant pot on Sauté mode, add the oil, heat up, add the scallions, shrimp and the other ingredients, toss, put the lid on and cook on High for 5 minutes. Release the pressure fast for 5 minutes, divide the mix into small bowls and serve.

Nutrition: calories 233, fat 9, fiber 3.5, carbs 11.4, protein 5.6

Mango and Shrimp Bowls

Preparation time: 5 minutes**Cooking time:** 7 minutes**Servings:** 4

Ingredients:
- 1 pound shrimp, peeled and deveined
- 1 cup mango, peeled, and cubed
- 1 tablespoon capers, drained
- ½ cup kalamata olives, pitted and halved
- 1 tablespoon olive oil
- 4 scallions, chopped
- ¼ cup chicken stock
- ½ teaspoon turmeric powder
- 1 tablespoon chives, chopped

Directions:
Set the instant pot on Sauté mode, add the oil heat up, add the scallions and cook for 2 minutes. Add the shrimp and the other ingredients, toss, put the lid on and cook on High for 5 minutes. Release the pressure fast for 5 minutes, divide the mix into small bowls and serve as an appetizer.

Nutrition: calories 30, fat 1, fiber 0, carbs 4, protein 2

Creamy Mozzarella Dip

Preparation time: 5 minutes**Cooking time:** 10 minutes**Servings:** 6

Ingredients:
- 1 cup mozzarella, shredded
- 1 cup heavy cream
- 1 tablespoon chives, chopped
- 1 teaspoon mustard
- 1 tablespoon olive oil
- 1 tablespoon lime juice
- Salt and black pepper to the taste
- 1 cup water

Directions:
In a bowl, combine the mozzarella with the cream and the other ingredients except the water, whisk well and divide into 4 ramekins. Put the water in the instant pot, add the trivet inside, put the ramekins in the pot, put the lid on and cook on High for 10 minutes. Release the pressure fast for 5 minutes and serve the mix as a party dip.

Nutrition: calories 187, fat 12.4, fiber 2.1, carbs 4.5, protein 8.2

136

Cucumber and Tuna Bowls

Preparation time: 5 minutes**Cooking time:** 10 minutes**Servings:** 4

Ingredients:

- 1 cup cucumber, cubed
- 1 pound tuna, skinless and cubed
- 1 tablespoon olive oil
- ¼ cup chicken stock
- 4 scallions, chopped
- 1 tablespoon lime juice
- 1 tablespoon balsamic vinegar
- 1 cup baby spinach
- 1 avocado, peeled, pitted, halved and sliced
- Salt and black pepper to the taste
- 1 tablespoon chives, chopped

Directions:

Set the instant pot on Sauté mode, add the oil, heat up, add the scallions and cook for 2 minutes. Add the tuna, cucumber and the other ingredients, toss, put the lid on and cook on High for 8 minutes. Release the pressure fast for 5 minutes, divide the mix into bowls and serve.

Nutrition: calories 200, fat 6, fiber 3.4, carbs 7.6, protein 3.5

Stuffed Mushrooms

Preparation time: 5 minutes**Cooking time:** 14 minutes**Servings:** 4

Ingredients:

- 1 pound baby Bella mushroom caps
- 4 scallions, chopped
- Cooking spray
- ¼ teaspoon chili powder
- ½ cup feta cheese, crumbled
- ½ cup kalamata olives, chopped
- ¼ cup rosemary, chopped
- Salt and black pepper to the taste
- 1 cup water

Directions:

In a bowl, combine the scallions with the chili powder and the other ingredients except the mushroom caps and the water, stir and stuff the mushroom caps with this mix. Put the water in the instant pot, add the trivet inside, arrange the stuffed mushrooms into the pot, put the lid on and cook on High for 14 minutes. Release the pressure fast for 5 minutes, arrange the stuffed mushrooms on a platter and serve as an appetizer.

Nutrition: calories 136, fat 8.6, fiber 4.8, carbs 5.6, protein 5.1

Cabbage Slaw

Preparation time: 5 minutes**Cooking time:** 12 minutes**Servings:** 4

Ingredients:
- 1 pound red cabbage, shredded
- 1 cup Greek yogurt
- 4 scallions, chopped
- 2 spring onions, chopped
- 1 tablespoon olive oil
- 1 cup basil, chopped
- 1 tablespoon balsamic vinegar
- 1 tablespoon lime juice
- 1 tablespoon chives, chopped
- Salt and black pepper to the taste

Directions:

Set the instant pot on Sauté mode, add the oil, heat up, add the scallions and the spring onions and cook for 2 minutes. Add the cabbage, yogurt and the other ingredients, toss, put the lid on and cook on High for 10 minutes. Release the pressure fast for 5 minutes, divide the slaw into bowls and serve as an appetizer..

Nutrition: calories 160, fat 13.7, fiber 5.5, carbs 10.1, protein 2.2

Pineapple Salsa

Preparation time: 5 minutes**Cooking time:** 5 minutes**Servings:** 4

Ingredients:
- 1 cup black olives, pitted and halved
- 1 cup baby spinach
- 1 cup cucumber, cubed
- 1 cup tomatoes, cubed
- 2 scallions, chopped
- 1 cup pineapple, peeled and cubed
- ½ cup Greek yogurt
- ¼ cup chives, chopped

Directions:

In your instant pot, combine the spinach with the pineapple, olives and the other ingredients, toss, put the lid on and cook on High for 5 minutes. Release the pressure fast for 5 minutes, divide the salsa into bowls and serve.

Nutrition: calories 62, fat 4.7, fiber 1.3, carbs 3.9, protein 2.3

Spinach and Cabbage Bowls
Preparation time: 5 minutes**Cooking time:** 12 minutes**Servings:** 4

Ingredients:
- 1 pound baby spinach
- 1 cup red cabbage, shredded
- 2 shallots, chopped
- 1 tablespoon olive oil
- 1 tablespoon lime juice
- 2 tablespoons mint, chopped
- ¾ cup kalamata olives, pitted and halved
- ½ Greek yogurt
- Salt and black pepper to the taste

Directions:
In your instant pot, combine the spinach with the cabbage, shallots, oil and the other ingredients, toss, put the lid on and cook on High for 12 minutes. Release the pressure fast for 5 minutes, divide the mix into bowls and serve as an appetizer.

Nutrition: calories 204, fat 11.5, fiber 3.1, carbs 4.2, protein 5.9

Mushroom Dip
Preparation time: 10 minutes**Cooking time:** 15 minutes**Servings:** 4

Ingredients:
- 2 cups mushrooms, sliced
- 4 scallions, chopped
- 1 tablespoon olive oil
- 3 garlic cloves, minced
- 1 cup heavy cream
- ¾ cup basil, chopped
- A pinch of salt and black pepper

Directions:
Set the instant pot on Sauté mode, add the oil, heat up, add the scallions and mushrooms and cook for 5 minutes. Add the rest of the ingredients, toss, put the lid on and cook on High for 10 minutes. Release the pressure naturally for 10 minutes and serve as a party dip.

Nutrition: calories 186, fat 12.4, fiber 0.9, carbs 2.6, protein 1.5

Chili Dip

Preparation time: 5 minutes**Cooking time:** 12 minutes**Servings:** 4

Ingredients:

- 1 cup Greek yogurt
- 1 green chili, minced
- 1 red chili, minced
- 1 tablespoon lime juice
- 4 scallions, chopped
- 1 tablespoon chives, chopped
- Salt and black pepper to the taste
- 1 cup cilantro, chopped
- 1 cup water

Directions:

In a blender, combine the yogurt with the chilies, lime juice and the other ingredients except the water, pulse well and divide into 4 small ramekins. Put the water in the instant pot, add the trivet inside, put the ramekins inside, put the lid on and cook on High for 12 minutes. Release the pressure fast for 5 minutes and serve cold as a party dip.

Nutrition: calories 200, fat 14.5, fiber 3.8, carbs 8.1, protein 7.6

Zucchini and Tomato Salsa

Preparation time: 5 minutes**Cooking time:** 10 minutes**Servings:** 4

Ingredients:

- 1 pound cherry tomatoes, halved
- 1 cup zucchinis, cubed
- 2 scallions, chopped
- 2 tablespoons chives, chopped
- 1 tablespoon balsamic vinegar
- 1 tablespoon basil, chopped
- ½ cup heavy cream
- Salt and black pepper to the taste
- 2 tablespoons avocado oil

Directions:

Set the instant pot on Sauté mode, add the oil, heat up, add the scallions and cook for 2 minutes. Add tomatoes, zucchinis and the other ingredients, toss, put the lid on and cook on High for 8 minutes. Release the pressure fast for 5 minutes, divide the mix into small bowls and serve as an appetizer.

Nutrition: calories 220, fat 11.5, fiber 4.8, carbs 8.9, protein 5.6

Chickpeas Salsa

Preparation time: 5 minutes**Cooking time:** 15 minutes**Servings:** 4
Ingredients:

- 2 tablespoons olive oil
- 1 red onion, sliced
- 1 tablespoon lime zest, grated
- 1 cup zucchini, cubed
- 1 cup canned chickpeas, drained and rinsed
- ½ cup kalamata olives, pitted and halved
- 1 cup red chard, chopped
- ½ cup veggie stock
- Salt and black pepper to the taste
- 1 tablespoon chives, chopped

Directions:

Set the instant pot on Sauté mode, add the oil, heat it up, add the onion and lime zest and cook for 5 minutes. Add the chickpeas, olives and the other ingredients, toss, put the lid on and cook on High for 10 minutes. Release the pressure fast for 5 minutes, divide the mix into bowls and serve as an appetizer.

Nutrition: calories 224, fat 5.1, fiber 1, carbs 9.9, protein 15.1

Coconut and Ginger Dip

Preparation time: 5 minutes**Cooking time:** 10 minutes**Servings:** 4
Ingredients:

- 2 tablespoons ginger, grated
- 2 cups coconut cream
- ½ teaspoon turmeric powder
- ½ teaspoon chili powder
- 3 tablespoons chives, chopped
- 2 tablespoons olive oil
- 2 scallions, chopped
- A pinch of salt and white pepper

Directions:

Set the in the instant pot on Sauté mode, add the oil heat up, add the scallions and ginger and cook for 4 minutes. Add the cream and the other ingredients, whisk, put the lid on and cook on High for 6 minutes. Release the pressure fast for 5 minutes, divide into bowls and serve the mix as a party dip.

Nutrition: calories 213, fat 4.9, fiber 4.1, carbs 8.8, protein 17.8

Mediterranean Diet Instant Pot Seafood Recipes

Lemon Cod
Preparation time: 10 minutes**Cooking time:** 12 minutes**Servings:** 4

Ingredients:
- 1 pound cod fillets, boneless and cubed
- 2 scallions, chopped
- ½ teaspoon turmeric powder
- 1 tablespoon lemon juice
- ½ cup chicken stock
- 1 tablespoon rosemary, chopped
- A pinch of salt and black pepper
- 1 tablespoon chives, chopped

Directions:
In your instant pot, combine cod with the turmeric, scallions and the other ingredients, toss gently, put the lid on and cook on High for 12 minutes. Release the pressure naturally for 10 minutes, divide the mix into bowls and serve.

Nutrition: calories 198, fat 7, fiber 2, carbs 6, protein 7

Sage Tuna Mix
Preparation time: 10 minutes**Cooking time:** 14 minutes**Servings:** 4

Ingredients:
- 2 tablespoons avocado oil
- 1 pound tuna fillets, boneless and cut into strips
- 2 scallions, chopped
- 1 tablespoon sage, chopped
- ½ teaspoon chili powder
- ½ cup chicken stock
- A pinch of salt and black pepper

Directions:
Set your instant pot on Sauté mode, add the oil, heat it up, add the scallions and chili powder and sauté for 2 minutes. Add the fish and the rest of the ingredients, put the lid on and cook on High for 12 minutes. Release the pressure naturally for 10 minutes, divide the mix into bowls and serve.

Nutrition: calories 221, fat 8, fiber 3, carbs 6, protein 7

Shrimp and Onions Mix

Preparation time: 5 minutes**Cooking time:** 12 minutes**Servings:** 4

Ingredients:
- 1 pound shrimp, peeled and deveined
- 1 tablespoon olive oil
- 2 red onions, sliced
- 3 garlic cloves, crushed
- 1 cup chicken stock
- A pinch of salt and black pepper

Directions:
Set the instant pot on Sauté mode, add the oil, heat it up, add the onions and sauté for 2 minutes. Add the shrimp and the rest of the ingredients, put the lid on and cook on High for 10 minutes. Release the pressure fast for 5 minutes, divide the mix into bowls and serve.

Nutrition: calories 235, fat 8, fiber 4, carbs 7, protein 9

Paprika Crab Mix

Preparation time: 10 minutes**Cooking time:** 10 minutes**Servings:** 4

Ingredients:
- 1 tablespoon avocado oil
- 2 scallions, chopped
- 1 pound crab meat
- ½ teaspoon rosemary, dried
- ½ teaspoon cumin, ground
- ¼ cup chicken stock
- 1 teaspoon sweet paprika
- A pinch of salt and black pepper

Directions:
Set the instant pot on Sauté mode, add the oil, heat it up, add the scallions, rosemary and cumin and cook for 2 minutes. Add the crab meat, paprika and the rest of the ingredients, put the lid on and cook on High for 8 minutes. Release the pressure naturally for 10 minutes, divide everything into bowls and serve.

Nutrition: calories 211, fat 8, fiber 4, carbs 8, protein 8

Spicy Shrimp and Kale

Preparation time: 10 minutes**Cooking time:** 10 minutes**Servings:** 4

Ingredients:

- 1 pound shrimp, peeled and deveined
- ½ cup chicken stock
- 1 cup baby kale
- ½ teaspoon chili powder
- 1 green chili, minced
- ½ teaspoon red pepper flakes, crushed
- 2 tablespoons avocado oil
- A pinch of salt and black pepper
- 1 tablespoon cilantro, chopped

Directions:

Set the instant pot on Sauté mode, add the oil, heat it up, add the green chili, chili powder and pepper flakes and cook for 2 minutes. Add the shrimp and the rest of the ingredients, put the lid on and cook on High for 8 minutes. Release the pressure naturally for 10 minutes, transfer the mix to bowls and serve.

Nutrition: calories 193, fat 7, fiber 3, carbs 6, protein 6

Tuna and Green Beans

Preparation time: 5 minutes**Cooking time:** 12 minutes**Servings:** 4

Ingredients:

- 1 pound tuna fillets, boneless and roughly cubed
- 1 cup green beans, trimmed and halved
- 1 red onion, chopped
- 2 tablespoons olive oil
- ½ teaspoon sweet paprika
- ½ teaspoon ginger, ground
- Juice of 1 lime
- 4 garlic cloves, minced
- A pinch of salt and black pepper

Directions:

Set the instant pot on Sauté mode, add the oil, heat it up, add the onion, garlic and ginger and sauté for 2 minutes. Add the tuna, green beans and the other ingredients, put the lid on and cook on High for 10 minutes. Release the pressure fast for 5 minutes, divide the mix into bowls and serve.

Nutrition: calories 200, fat 11, fiber 4, carbs 5, protein 12

Turmeric Cod

Preparation time: 10 minutes**Cooking time:** 12 minutes**Servings:** 4

Ingredients:

- 1 pound cod fillets, boneless
- 1 teaspoon turmeric powder
- 1 tablespoon olive oil
- 2 spring onions, chopped
- ½ cup chicken stock
- 1 teaspoon oregano, dried
- 1 tablespoon chives, chopped

Directions:

Set the instant pot on Sauté mode, add the oil, heat up, add the spring onions and turmeric and cook for 2 minutes. Add the cod and the other ingredients, put the lid on and cook on High for 10 minutes. Release the pressure naturally for 10 minutes, divide the mix between plates and serve.

Nutrition: calories 200, fat 12, fiber 3, carbs 7, protein 9

Salmon and Mango Mix

Preparation time: 5 minutes**Cooking time:** 15 minutes**Servings:** 4

Ingredients:

- 1 pound salmon fillets, boneless and roughly cubed
- 1 cup mango, peeled and cubed
- ¼ cup chicken stock
- 3 scallions, chopped
- Juice of 1 lime
- 1 tablespoon olive oil
- A pinch of salt and black pepper
- ¼ teaspoon coriander, ground
- ½ teaspoon basil, dried
- 1 tablespoon cilantro, chopped

Directions:

Set the instant pot on Sauté mode, add the oil, heat it up, add the scallions, coriander and basil and sauté for 2 minutes. Add the salmon, mango and the rest of the ingredients, put the lid on and cook on High for 13 minutes. Release the pressure fast for 5 minutes, divide the mix into bowls and serve.

Nutrition: calories 232, fat 10, fiber 4, carbs 6, protein 9

Salmon and Peas

Preparation time: 6 minutes**Cooking time:** 15 minutes**Servings:** 4

Ingredients:
- 1 pound salmon fillets, boneless
- 3 scallions, minced
- ½ teaspoon ginger, ground
- ½ teaspoon garam masala
- 1 cup fresh peas
- 1 tablespoon olive oil
- 1 tablespoon olive oil
- ½ cup chicken stock
- 1 tablespoon dill, chopped
- Salt and black pepper to the taste

Directions:

Set your instant pot on Sauté mode, add the oil, heat it up, add the scallions, ginger and garam masala, toss and cook for 3 minutes. Add the salmon, peas and the rest of the ingredients, put the lid on and cook on High for 12 minutes. Release the pressure naturally for 10 minutes, divide the mix into between plates and serve.

Nutrition: calories 182, fat 7, fiber 3, carbs 6, protein 9

Lemon Shrimp and Corn

Preparation time: 5 minutes**Cooking time:** 12 minutes**Servings:** 4

Ingredients:
- 1 pound shrimp, peeled and deveined
- 1 tablespoon avocado oil
- 2 spring onions, chopped
- 1 cup corn
- ½ teaspoon red pepper flakes, crushed
- ½ tablespoon lemon juice
- 1 tablespoon chives, chopped
- ¼ cup chicken stock
- A pinch of salt and black pepper

Directions:

Set the instant pot on Sauté mode, add the oil, heat up, add the spring onions and pepper flakes and cook for 4 minutes. Add the shrimp, corn and the other ingredients, toss, put the lid on and cook on High for 8 minutes. Release the pressure fast for 5 minutes, divide the mix into bowls and serve.

Nutrition: calories 210, fat 8, fiber 3, carbs 6, protein 14

146

Ginger Sea Bass

Preparation time: 5 minutes**Cooking time:** 15 minutes**Servings:** 4

Ingredients:
- 1 pound sea bass fillets, boneless
- 1 tablespoon ginger, grated
- 1 red onion, chopped
- ½ teaspoon garam masala
- ½ teaspoon turmeric powder
- ½ teaspoon basil, dried
- 2 tablespoons avocado oil
- Salt and black pepper to the taste
- Juice of 1lime
- 1 tablespoon chives, chopped

Directions:

Set the instant pot on sauté mode, add the oil, heat it up, add the onion, ginger, garam masala and turmeric and sauté for 3 minutes. Add the sea bass fillets and the rest of the ingredients, put the lid on and cook on High for 12 minutes. Release the pressure fast for 5 minutes, divide the mix between plates and serve.

Nutrition: calories 200, fat 12, fiber 3, carbs 6, protein 11

Mackerel and Tomatoes Mix

Preparation time: 5 minutes**Cooking time:** 15 minutes**Servings:** 4

Ingredients:
- 1 pound mackerel fillets, boneless
- 1 cup cherry tomatoes, halved
- ½ teaspoon rosemary, dried
- ¼ cup tomato passata
- ½ teaspoon oregano, dried
- 2 scallions, minced
- 2 garlic cloves, minced
- 1 tablespoon olive oil
- Salt and black pepper to the taste

Directions:

Set the instant pot on Sauté mode, add the oil, heat it up, add the scallions, garlic and oregano and cook for 3 minutes. Add the fish and the rest of the ingredients, put the lid on and cook on High for 12 minutes. Release the pressure fast for 5 minutes, divide everything between plates and serve.

Nutrition: calories 132, fat 9, fiber 2, carbs 5, protein 11

Curry Tuna Mix

Preparation time: 10 minutes**Cooking time:** 14 minutes**Servings:** 4

Ingredients:
- 1 pound tuna fillets, boneless and roughly cubed
- 1 red onion, chopped
- 2 tablespoons avocado oil
- ½ cup coconut cream
- 1 tablespoon yellow curry paste
- 1 tablespoon ginger, grated
- A pinch of salt and black pepper
- 2 tablespoons cilantro, chopped

Directions:
Set your instant pot on Sauté mode, add the oil, heat it up, add the onion, ginger and curry paste, stir and cook for 2 minutes. Add the fish and the rest of the ingredients, put the lid on and cook on High for 12 minutes. Release the pressure naturally for 10 minutes, divide the mix into bowls and serve.

Nutrition: calories 200, fat 12, fiber 2, carbs 6, protein 11

Parsley Shrimp Mix

Preparation time: 5 minutes**Cooking time:** 12 minutes**Servings:** 4

Ingredients:
- 2 pounds shrimp, peeled and deveined
- 3 scallions, chopped
- 2 tablespoons olive oil
- Juice of 1 lime
- 1 teaspoon sweet paprika
- Salt and black pepper to the taste
- 1 tablespoon parsley, chopped

Directions:
Set the instant pot on Sauté mode, add the oil, heat it up, add the scallions and paprika and cook for 5 minutes. Add the shrimp and the rest of the ingredients, put the lid on and cook on High for 7 minutes. Release the pressure fast for 5 minutes, divide the mix into bowls and serve.

Nutrition: calories 200, fat 12, fiber 2, carbs 6, protein 9

Pesto Tuna Mix

Preparation time: 10 minutes**Cooking time:** 12 minutes**Servings:** 4

Ingredients:
- 1 pound tuna fillets, boneless and roughly cubed
- 2 tablespoons basil pesto
- 1 tablespoon olive oil
- 4 scallions, chopped
- ½ teaspoon chili powder
- 1 tablespoon chives, chopped
- ½ cup fish stock
- A pinch of salt and black pepper

Directions:
Set the instant pot on Sauté mode, add the oil, heat it up, add the scallions, chili powder and pesto, stir and cook for 5 minutes. Add the tuna and the other ingredients, toss, put the lid on and cook on High for 7 minutes. Release the pressure naturally for 10 minutes, divide the mix into bowls and serve.

Nutrition: calories 211, fat 13, fiber 2, carbs 7, protein 11

Orange Shrimp Mix

Preparation time: 5 minutes**Cooking time:** 6 minutes**Servings:** 4

Ingredients:
- 1 pound shrimp, peeled and deveined
- 1 tablespoon avocado oil
- 2 scallions, chopped
- Juice of 1 orange
- 2 tablespoons chives, chopped
- A pinch of salt and black pepper

Directions:
In your instant pot, combine the shrimp with the orange juice, scallions and the other ingredients, toss, put the lid on and cook on High for 6 minutes. Release the pressure fast for 5 minutes, divide the mix into bowls and serve.

Nutrition: calories 200, fat 12, fiber 4, carbs 6, protein 8

Garlic Mackerel

Preparation time: 5 minutes**Cooking time:** 14 minutes**Servings:** 4

Ingredients:

- 2 pounds mackerel fillets, boneless
- 2 tablespoons olive oil
- ½ teaspoon sweet paprika
- ½ teaspoon oregano, dried
- ½ teaspoon rosemary, dried
- 4 garlic cloves, minced
- ½ cup chicken stock
- A pinch of salt and black pepper
- 1 tablespoon cilantro, chopped

Directions:

In your instant pot, combine the mackerel fillets with the paprika, oregano and the rest of the ingredients, put the lid on and cook on High for 14 minutes. Release the pressure fast for 5 minutes, divide the mix between plates and serve.

Nutrition: calories 232, fat 7, fiber 3, carbs 7, protein 9

Shrimp and Brussels Sprouts

Preparation time: 5 minutes**Cooking time:** 15 minutes**Servings:** 4

Ingredients:

- 2 pounds shrimp, peeled and deveined
- 1 cup Brussels sprouts, trimmed and halved
- 1 red onion, chopped
- 2 tablespoons avocado oil
- Juice of 1 lime
- ½ teaspoon garlic powder
- A pinch of salt and black pepper
- ¼ cup chicken stock
- 1 tablespoon cilantro, chopped

Directions:

Set the instant pot on Sauté mode, add the oil, heat it up, add the onion, garlic powder and sprouts and cook for 5 minutes. Add the fish and the other ingredients, put the lid on and cook on High for 10 minutes. Release the pressure fast for 5 minutes, divide the mix between plates and serve.

Nutrition: calories 232, fat 9, fiber 2, carbs 6, protein 8

Tuna, Corn and Spinach

Preparation time: 10 minutes**Cooking time:** 15 minutes**Servings:** 4

Ingredients:

- 1 pound tuna fillets, boneless and roughly cubed
- 1 cup corn
- 1 cup baby spinach
- 3 scallions, chopped
- 1 tablespoon olive oil
- ½ teaspoon sweet paprika
- ½ teaspoon chili powder
- ½ cup chicken stock
- A pinch of salt and black pepper
- 1 tablespoon cilantro, chopped

Directions:

Set the instant pot on Sauté mode, add the oil, heat it up, add the scallions, paprika and chili powder and cook for 3 minutes. Add the fish and the rest of the ingredients, put the lid on and cook on High for 12 minutes. Release the pressure naturally for 10 minutes, divide the mix between plates and serve.

Nutrition: calories 200, fat 13, fiber 3, carbs 6, protein 11

Shrimp, Tomatoes and Avocado Mix

Preparation time: 5 minutes**Cooking time:** 8 minutes**Servings:** 4

Ingredients:

- 1 pound shrimp, peeled and deveined
- 1 cup avocado, peeled, pitted and cubed
- 3 scallions, minced
- Juice of 1 lime
- 1 tablespoon olive oil
- ½ teaspoon hot paprika
- 2 tablespoons chili pepper, minced
- A pinch of salt and black pepper
- 1 tablespoon chives, chopped

Directions:

In your instant pot, mix the shrimp with the avocado, scallions and other ingredients, toss, put the lid on and cook on High for 8 minutes. Release the pressure fast for 5 minutes, divide the mix into bowls and serve.

Nutrition: calories 200, fat 12, fiber 2, carbs 6, protein 9

Salmon and Asparagus

Preparation time: 10 minutes**Cooking time:** 12 minutes**Servings:** 4

Ingredients:

- 1 pound salmon fillets, boneless
- ¼ pound asparagus spears, trimmed
- 2 garlic cloves, minced
- 1 tablespoon avocado oil
- 1 tablespoon lime juice
- 1 red onion, chopped
- A pinch of salt and black pepper
- 2 tablespoons chives, chopped

Directions:

Set the instant pot on Sauté mode, add the oil, heat it up, add the garlic and the onion and sauté for 2 minutes. Add the salmon, asparagus and the rest of the ingredients, put the lid on and cook on High for 10 minutes. Release the pressure naturally for 10 minutes, divide the whole mix between plates and serve.

Nutrition: calories 200, fat 12, fiber 2, carbs 5, protein 6

Cod and Tomato Sauce

Preparation time: 10 minutes**Cooking time:** 15 minutes**Servings:** 4

Ingredients:

- 1 tablespoon olive oil
- 1 pound cod fillets, boneless and cubed
- 3 scallions, chopped
- 2 garlic cloves, minced
- 1 teaspoon lemon juice
- 1 tablespoon cilantro, chopped
- ½ teaspoon sweet paprika
- 1 cup tomato passata
- ½ teaspoon chili powder
- A pinch of salt and black pepper

Directions:

Set the instant pot on Sauté mode, add the oil, heat it up, add the scallions, garlic, chili powder and paprika and cook for 2 minutes. Add the fish, tomato passata and the other ingredients, toss, put the lid on and cook on High for 13 minutes. Release the pressure naturally for 10 minutes, divide the mix between plates and serve.

Nutrition: calories 192, fat 9, fiber 2, carbs 8, protein 7

Cod and Shallots

Preparation time: 10 minutes**Cooking time:** 14minutes**Servings:** 4

Ingredients:

- 1 pound cod fillets, skinless, boneless
- ½ cup shallots, chopped
- 1 tablespoon lime juice
- ½ teaspoon rosemary, dried
- ½ teaspoon cumin, ground
- 1 tablespoon olive oil
- ½ teaspoon turmeric powder
- ½ teaspoon chili powder
- ½ cup chicken stock
- A pinch of salt and black pepper
- 1 tablespoon chives, chopped

Directions:

Set the instant pot on Sauté mode, add the oil, heat it up, add the shallots and cook for 2 minutes. Add the fish, lime juice and the other ingredients, toss , put the lid on and cook on High for 12 minutes. Release the pressure naturally for 10 minutes, divide the mix between plates and serve.

Nutrition: calories 210, fat 9, fiber 2, carbs 6, protein 7

Balsamic Salmon

Preparation time: 5 minutes**Cooking time:** 15 minutes**Servings:** 4

Ingredients:

- 4 salmon fillets, boneless
- 3 garlic cloves, minced
- 1 tablespoon avocado oil
- ¼ cup chicken stock
- 2 tablespoons balsamic vinegar
- ½ teaspoon rosemary, dried
- 2 tablespoons parsley, chopped
- A pinch of salt and black pepper

Directions:

Set the instant pot on Sauté mode, add the oil, heat it up, add the garlic and rosemary and cook for 3 minutes. Add the fish, vinegar and the rest of the ingredients, toss, put the lid on and cook on High for 12 minutes. Release the pressure fast for 5 minutes, divide the mix between plates and serve.

Nutrition: calories 200, fat 10, fiber 2, carbs 5, protein 9

Lemon Trout Mix
Preparation time: 10 minutes**Cooking time:** 14 minutes**Servings:** 4

Ingredients:
- 1 pound trout fillets, boneless
- 3 scallions, minced
- 2 tablespoons avocado oil
- 2 tablespoons garlic, minced
- 2 tablespoons lemon juice
- 1 teaspoon lemon zest, grated
- A pinch of salt and black pepper

Directions:
Set the instant pot on Sauté mode, add the oil, heat it up, add the scallions and the garlic and sauté for 2 minutes. Add the trout, lemon juice and the remaining ingredients, put the lid on and cook on High for 12 minutes. Release the pressure naturally for 10 minutes, divide everything into bowls and serve.

Nutrition: calories 200, fat 13, fiber 3, carbs 6, protein 11

Turmeric Mussels
Preparation time: 10 minutes**Cooking time:** 14 minutes**Servings:** 4

Ingredients:
- 1 pound mussels, scrubbed
- 1 tablespoon olive oil
- 1 teaspoon turmeric powder
- ½ cup chicken stock
- A pinch of salt and black pepper
- 1 tablespoon lemon juice

Directions:
In your instant pot, combine mussels with the oil, turmeric and the other ingredients, toss, put the lid on and cook on High for 14 minutes. Release the pressure naturally for 10 minutes, divide the mix into bowls and serve.

Nutrition: calories 198, fat 7, fiber 2, carbs 6, protein 7

Cod with Cherry Tomatoes
Preparation time: 10 minutes**Cooking time:** 12 minutes**Servings:** 4

Ingredients:
- 2 tablespoons olive oil
- 1 pound cod fillets, boneless
- 2 cups cherry tomatoes, halved
- 2 scallions, chopped
- 2 garlic cloves, minced
- ¼ cup tomato passata
- A pinch of salt and black pepper
- ¼ cup chives, chopped

Directions:
Set your instant pot on Sauté mode, add the oil, heat it up, add the scallions and garlic and cook for 2 minutes. Add the fish, tomatoes and the rest of the ingredients, put the lid o and cook on High for 10 minutes. Release the pressure naturally for 10 minutes, divide the mix between plates and serve.

Nutrition: calories 221, fat 8, fiber 3, carbs 6, protein 7

Salmon with Spinach and Pineapple
Preparation time: 5 minutes**Cooking time:** 15 minutes**Servings:** 4

Ingredients:
- 1 pounds salmon fillets, boneless, skinless and cubed
- 1 cup pineapple, peeled and cubed
- 1 cup baby spinach
- 1 tablespoon avocado oil
- 3 scallions, chopped
- 3 garlic cloves, crushed
- 2 tablespoons dill, chopped
- ½ cup chicken stock
- A pinch of salt and black pepper

Directions:
Set the instant pot on Sauté mode, add the oil, heat it up, add the scallions and garlic and cook for 2 minutes. Add the salmon, pineapple and the rest of the ingredients, put the lid on and cook on High for 13 minutes. Release the pressure fast for 5 minutes, divide the mix between plates and serve.

Nutrition: calories 235, fat 8, fiber 4, carbs 7, protein 9

Paprika Crab and Avocado
Preparation time: 10 minutes**Cooking time:** 12 minutes**Servings:** 4

Ingredients:
- 1 tablespoon olive oil
- 1 pound crab meat
- 1 cup avocado, peeled, pitted and cubed
- ¼ cup shallots, chopped
- 1 tablespoon lime juice
- 1 cup chicken stock
- 1 teaspoon sweet paprika
- A pinch of salt and black pepper

Directions:
Set the instant pot on Sauté mode, add the oil, heat it up, add the shallots and the paprika and cook for 2 minutes. Add the crab meat, avocado and the rest of the ingredients, put the lid on and cook on High for 10 minutes. Release the pressure naturally for 10 minutes, divide everything into bowls and serve.

Nutrition: calories 211, fat 8, fiber 4, carbs 8, protein 8

Chives Crab
Preparation time: 10 minutes**Cooking time:** 10 minutes**Servings:** 4

Ingredients:
- 1 pound crab meat
- ¼ cup tomato passata
- 2 scallions, chopped
- 1 tablespoon olive oil
- ½ teaspoon rosemary, dried
- 1 tablespoon smoked paprika
- A pinch of salt and black pepper
- 2 tablespoons chives, chopped

Directions:
Set the instant pot on Sauté mode, add the oil, heat it up, add the scallions, rosemary and paprika and cook for 2 minutes. Add the crab and the rest of the ingredients, put the lid on and cook on High for 8 minutes. Release the pressure naturally for 10 minutes, transfer the mix to bowls and serve.

Nutrition: calories 193, fat 7, fiber 3, carbs 6, protein 6

Lime Calamari and Eggplant
Preparation time: 5 minutes**Cooking time:** 20 minutes**Servings:** 4

Ingredients:
- 1 pound calamari rings
- 2 tablespoons olive oil
- Juice of 1 lime
- 1 eggplant, cubed
- 1 red onion, chopped
- 4 garlic cloves, minced
- 1 tablespoon coriander, chopped
- 1 tablespoon chives, chopped
- A pinch of salt and black pepper

Directions:
Set the instant pot on Sauté mode, add the oil, heat it up, add the onion, garlic and calamari and cook for 5 minutes. Add the eggplant and the other ingredients, put the lid on and cook on High for 15 minutes. Release the pressure fast for 5 minutes, divide the mix into bowls and serve.

Nutrition: calories 200, fat 11, fiber 4, carbs 5, protein 12

Mackerel and Sweet Potatoes
Preparation time: 10 minutes**Cooking time:** 20 minutes**Servings:** 4

Ingredients:
- 1 pound mackerel fillets, boneless
- 2 sweet potatoes, peeled and roughly cubed
- 1 tablespoon avocado oil
- ½ teaspoon turmeric powder
- ½ teaspoon Italian seasoning
- 2 spring onions, chopped
- 1 cup chicken stock
- 1 tablespoon cilantro, chopped

Directions:
In your instant pot, combine mackerel with the sweet potatoes, oil, turmeric and the other ingredients, put the lid on and cook on High for 20 minutes Release the pressure naturally for 10 minutes, divide the mix between plates and serve.

Nutrition: calories 200, fat 12, fiber 3, carbs 7, protein 9

Coconut Tuna and Zucchinis

Preparation time: 5 minutes**Cooking time:** 15 minutes**Servings:** 4

Ingredients:

- 1 pound tuna fillets, boneless, skinless and cubed
- 1 tablespoon avocado oil
- 1 cup coconut cream
- ½ teaspoon garam masala
- ½ teaspoon rosemary, dried
- ½ teaspoon cumin, ground
- 2 zucchinis, cubed
- A pinch of salt and black pepper
- 4 scallions, minced
- 1 tablespoon cilantro, chopped

Directions:

Set the instant pot on Sauté mode, add the oil, heat it up, add the scallions and cook for 2 minutes. Add the tuna, coconut cream and the rest of the ingredients, put the lid on and cook on High for 13 minutes. Release the pressure fast for 5 minutes, divide the mix into bowls and serve.

Nutrition: calories 232, fat 10, fiber 4, carbs 6, protein 9

Tuna and Peas

Preparation time: 10 minutes**Cooking time:** 14 minutes**Servings:** 4

Ingredients:

- 1 pound tuna fillets, boneless and cubed
- 2 tablespoons avocado oil
- 1 tablespoon lemon juice
- ½ cup tomato passata
- 1 cup fresh peas
- ½ teaspoon oregano, dried
- 1 teaspoon sweet paprika
- Salt and black pepper to the taste

Directions:

Set your instant pot on Sauté mode, add the oil, heat it up, add the tuna and cook for 2 minutes. Add the peas, passata and the rest of the ingredients, put the lid on and cook on High for 12 minutes. Release the pressure naturally for 10 minutes, divide the mix into bowls and serve.

Nutrition: calories 182, fat 7, fiber 3, carbs 6, protein 9

Chili Cod

Preparation time: 10 minutes**Cooking time:** 15 minutes**Servings:** 4

Ingredients:
- 1 pound cod fillets, skinless, boneless and cubed
- 2 scallions, minced
- 1 cup tomato passata
- ½ teaspoon Italian seasoning
- ½ teaspoon rosemary, dried
- 2 green chilies, chopped
- A pinch of salt and black pepper
- 1 tablespoon chives, chopped

Directions:
In your instant pot, combine the cod fillets with scallions, passata, Italian seasoning and the other ingredients, toss, put the lid on and cook on High for 15 minutes. Release the pressure naturally for 10 minutes, divide the mix between plates and serve.

Nutrition: calories 210, fat 8, fiber 3, carbs 6, protein 14

Honey Shrimp

Preparation time: 5 minutes**Cooking time:** 7 minutes**Servings:** 4

Ingredients:
- 1 pound shrimp, peeled and deveined
- 2 tablespoons avocado oil
- 2 tablespoons honey
- 1 teaspoon Italian seasoning
- ½ teaspoon rosemary, dried
- Salt and black pepper to the taste
- Juice of 1 lime
- 1 tablespoon chives, chopped

Directions:
Set the instant pot on sauté mode, add the oil, heat it up, add the shrimp, honey, seasoning and the other ingredients, toss, put the lid on and cook on High for 7 minutes. Release the pressure fast for 5 minutes, divide the mix into bowls and serve.

Nutrition: calories 200, fat 12, fiber 3, carbs 6, protein 11

Basil Tuna

Preparation time: 5 minutes**Cooking time:** 14 minutes**Servings:** 4
Ingredients:

- 1 pound tuna fillets, boneless
- ¼ cup chicken stock
- 1 tablespoon basil, chopped
- 1 tablespoon olive oil
- 1 red onion, sliced
- 1 tablespoon lime juice
- 2 garlic cloves, minced
- Salt and black pepper to the taste

Directions:

Set the instant pot on Sauté mode, add the oil, heat it up, add the onion and garlic and sauté for 2 minutes. Add the fish and the rest of the ingredients, put the lid on and cook on High for 14 minutes. Release the pressure fast for 5 minutes, divide everything between plates and serve.

Nutrition: calories 132, fat 9, fiber 2, carbs 5, protein 11

Curry Tuna

Preparation time: 10 minutes**Cooking time:** 14 minutes**Servings:** 4
Ingredients:

- 1 pound tuna fillets, boneless and cubed
- ½ teaspoon curry powder
- ½ teaspoon chili powder
- ½ teaspoon oregano, dried
- 1 red onion, chopped
- 2 tablespoons olive oil
- ½ cup coconut cream
- A pinch of salt and black pepper
- 2 tablespoons cilantro, chopped

Directions:

Set your instant pot on Sauté mode, add the oil, heat it up, add the onion, curry powder and chili powder, stir and sauté for 2 minutes. Add the tuna and the rest of the ingredients, put the lid on and cook on High for 12 minutes. Release the pressure naturally for 10 minutes, divide the mix into bowls and serve.

Nutrition: calories 200, fat 12, fiber 2, carbs 6, protein 11

Hot Cod and Mushrooms

Preparation time: 10 minutes**Cooking time:** 15 minutes**Servings:** 4

Ingredients:

- 4 cod fillets, boneless
- 4 scallions, minced
- 2 cups mushrooms, halved
- 2 tablespoons avocado oil
- Juice of 1 lime
- 1 tablespoon rosemary, dried
- 1 teaspoon turmeric powder
- Salt and black pepper to the taste
- 1 tablespoon chives, minced

Directions:

Set the instant pot on Sauté mode, add the oil, heat it up, add the scallions and mushrooms and cook for 5 minutes. Add the fish and the rest of the ingredients, put the lid on and cook on High for 10 minutes. Release the pressure naturally for 10 minutes, divide the mix between plates and serve.

Nutrition: calories 200, fat 12, fiber 2, carbs 6, protein 9

Trout and Okra Mix

Preparation time: 10 minutes**Cooking time:** 12 minutes**Servings:** 4

Ingredients:

- 4 trout fillets, boneless
- 1 tablespoon avocado oil
- 1 cup okra, halved
- 4 scallions, chopped
- ½ teaspoon Italian seasoning
- ½ teaspoon basil, dried
- ½ teaspoon sweet paprika
- ½ cup fish stock
- A pinch of salt and black pepper

Directions:

Set the instant pot on Sauté mode, add the oil, heat it up, add the scallions and Italian seasoning, stir and cook for 2 minutes. Add the fish and the other ingredients, toss, put the lid on and cook on High for 10 minutes. Release the pressure naturally for 10 minutes, divide the whole mix between plates and serve.

Nutrition: calories 211, fat 13, fiber 2, carbs 7, protein 11

Coriander Mackerel

Preparation time: 5 minutes**Cooking time:** 15 minutes**Servings:** 4

Ingredients:
- 1 pound mackerel fillets, boneless
- 2 scallions, chopped
- 1 tablespoon olive oil
- 2 scallions, chopped
- Juice of 1 lemon
- ½ cup chicken stock
- 2 tablespoons coriander, chopped
- A pinch of salt and black pepper

Directions:
In your instant pot, combine the mackerel with the scallions, oil and the other ingredients, put the lid on and cook on High for 15 minutes. Release the pressure fast for 5 minutes, divide the mix between plates and serve.

Nutrition: calories 200, fat 12, fiber 4, carbs 6, protein 8

Shrimp and Tomato Sauce

Preparation time: 5 minutes**Cooking time:** 8 minutes**Servings:** 4

Ingredients:
- 2 pounds shrimp, peeled and deveined
- 1 cup tomato passata
- ½ teaspoon rosemary, dried
- ½ teaspoon garam masala
- ½ cup chicken stock
- A pinch of salt and black pepper
- 1 tablespoon parsley, chopped

Directions:
In your instant pot, combine the shrimp with the passata, rosemary and the other ingredients, toss, put the lid on and cook on High for 8 minutes. Release the pressure fast for 5 minutes, divide the mix into bowls and serve.

Nutrition: calories 232, fat 7, fiber 3, carbs 7, protein 9

Cod and Quinoa

Preparation time: 5 minutes**Cooking time:** 20 minutes**Servings:** 4

Ingredients:

- 1 pound cod fillets, boneless and cubed
- 1 cup quinoa
- 2 cups chicken stock
- 1 tablespoon olive oil
- 1 red onion, chopped
- ½ teaspoon rosemary, dried
- ½ teaspoon sweet paprika
- A pinch of salt and black pepper
- 1 tablespoon cilantro, chopped

Directions:

Set the instant pot on Sauté mode, add the oil, heat it up, add the onion and paprika and cook for 4 minutes. Add the fish, quinoa and the other ingredients, toss gently, put the lid on and cook on High for 16 minutes. Release the pressure fast for 5 minutes, divide the mix between plates and serve.

Nutrition: calories 232, fat 9, fiber 2, carbs 6, protein 8

Shrimp, Quinoa and Spinach

Preparation time: 5 minutes**Cooking time:** 12 minutes**Servings:** 4

Ingredients:

- 1 pound shrimp, peeled and deveined
- Juice of 1 lime
- 1 cup quinoa, cooked
- ½ cup chicken stock
- 1 cup baby spinach
- 1 red onion, sliced
- 1 tablespoon olive oil
- ½ teaspoon sweet paprika
- ½ teaspoon chili powder
- A pinch of salt and black pepper
- 1 tablespoon parsley, chopped

Directions:

Set the instant pot on Sauté mode, add the oil, heat it up, add the onion, paprika and chili powder, stir and cook for 2 minutes. Add the shrimp, quinoa and the rest of the ingredients, put the lid on and cook on High for 10 minutes. Release the pressure fast for 5 minutes, divide the mix into bowls and serve.

Nutrition: calories 200, fat 13, fiber 3, carbs 6, protein 11

Parsley Mussels and Sauce

Preparation time: 5 minutes**Cooking time:** 14 minutes**Servings:** 4

Ingredients:

- 1 pound mussels, debearded
- 3 scallions, minced
- Juice of 1 lime
- 1 cup tomato passata
- 1 tablespoon olive oil
- ½ teaspoon hot paprika
- A pinch of salt and black pepper
- 1 tablespoon parsley, chopped

Directions:

In your instant pot, combine the mussels with the scallions, lime juice and the other ingredients, toss, put the lid on and cook on High for 15 minutes. Release the pressure fast for 5 minutes, divide the mix into bowls and serve.

Nutrition: calories 200, fat 12, fiber 2, carbs 6, protein 9

Shrimp and Veggie Salad

Preparation time: 10 minutes**Cooking time:** 10 minutes**Servings:** 4

Ingredients:

- 1 pound shrimp, peeled and deveined
- 3 spring onions, chopped
- ¼ cup chicken stock
- 1 tablespoon lime juice
- 1 zucchini, cubed
- 1 eggplant, cubed
- 1 cup cherry tomatoes, halved
- ½ cup black olives, pitted and halved
- 1 cup baby spinach
- 1 tablespoon avocado oil
- A pinch of salt and black pepper
- 2 tablespoons chives, chopped

Directions:

Set the instant pot on Sauté mode, add the oil, heat it up, add the spring onions and sauté for 2 minutes. Add the shrimp, zucchini, eggplant and the rest of the ingredients, put the lid on and cook on High for 8 minutes. Release the pressure naturally for 10 minutes, divide the salad into bowls and serve.

Nutrition: calories 200, fat 12, fiber 2, carbs 5, protein 6

Creamy Shrimp

Preparation time: 5 minutes**Cooking time:** 8 minutes**Servings:** 4

Ingredients:

- 1 pound shrimp, peeled and deveined
- 1 yellow onion, chopped
- 1 tablespoon avocado oil
- 1 cup coconut cream
- ½ teaspoon turmeric powder
- ½ teaspoon chili powder
- ½ tablespoon rosemary, chopped
- A pinch of salt and black pepper
- 1 tablespoon chives, chopped

Directions:

Set the instant pot on Sauté mode, add the oil, heat it up, add the onion, stir and sauté for 2 minutes. Add the shrimp, coconut cream and the other ingredients, toss , put the lid on and cook on High for 6 minutes. Release the pressure fast for 5 minutes, divide the mix into bowls and serve.

Nutrition: calories 210, fat 9, fiber 2, carbs 6, protein 7

Salmon and Pine Nuts Mix

Preparation time: 10 minutes**Cooking time:** 15 minutes**Servings:** 4

Ingredients:

- 4 salmon fillets, boneless
- 1 red onion, sliced
- 1 tablespoon olive oil
- 1 tablespoon pine nuts, toasted
- 2 tablespoons basil pesto
- Juice of 1 lime
- 2 tablespoons parsley, chopped
- A pinch of salt and black pepper

Directions:

Set the instant pot on Sauté mode, add the oil, heat it up, add the onion, pine nuts and pesto and sauté for 3 minutes. Add the fish and the rest of the ingredients, toss, put the lid on and cook on High for 12 minutes. Release the pressure naturally for 10 minutes, divide the mix between plates and serve.

Nutrition: calories 200, fat 10, fiber 2, carbs 5, protein 9

Smoked Salmon Mix

Preparation time: 5 minutes**Cooking time:** 10 minutes**Servings:** 4

Ingredients:
- 2 cups smoked salmon, boneless and flaked
- 1 cup baby spinach
- 1 cup cherry tomatoes, halved
- 1 tablespoon balsamic vinegar
- 2 tablespoons olive oil
- 2 tablespoons garlic, minced
- ½ cup tomato passata
- A pinch of salt and black pepper

Directions:
Set the instant pot on Sauté mode, add the oil, heat it up, add the garlic, fish, spinach and the other ingredients, toss, put the lid on and cook on High for 10 minutes. Release the pressure fast for 5 minutes, divide everything into bowls and serve.

Nutrition: calories 200, fat 13, fiber 3, carbs 6, protein 11

Creole Shrimp

Preparation time: 5 minutes**Cooking time:** 10 minutes**Servings:** 4

Ingredients:
- 4 scallions, chopped
- 2 tablespoons avocado oil
- 1 tablespoon lime juice
- 1 pound shrimp, peeled and deveined
- 1 tablespoon Creole seasoning
- ½ cup chicken stock
- 1 tablespoon chives, chopped

Directions:
Set your instant pot on Sauté mode, add the oil, heat it up, add the scallions and sauté for 4 minutes. Add the shrimp and the rest of the ingredients, toss, put the lid on and cook on High for 6 minutes. Release the pressure fast for 5 minutes, divide the mix into bowls and serve.

Nutrition: calories 211, fat 12, fiber 3, carbs 6, protein 7

Mediterranean Diet Instant Pot Poultry Recipes

Lime Chicken and Zucchini
Preparation time: 10 minutes**Cooking time:** 20 minutes**Servings:** 4
Ingredients:
- 2 pounds chicken breast, skinless, boneless and cubed
- 2 tablespoons olive oil
- 2 zucchinis, cubed
- 1 red onion, chopped
- ½ cup tomato passata
- 4 garlic cloves, minced
- 1 tablespoon lime juice
- 1 tablespoon chives, chopped
- A pinch of salt and black pepper

Directions:
Set the instant pot on Sauté mode, add the oil, heat it up, add the onion and garlic and cook for 5 minutes. Add the chicken and brown for 5 more minutes. Add the other ingredients, toss, put the lid on and cook on High for 10 minutes. Release the pressure naturally for 10 minutes, divide everything between plates and serve.

Nutrition: calories 263, fat 12, fiber 3, carbs 6, protein 14

Pesto Chicken and Okra
Preparation time: 10 minutes**Cooking time:** 25 minutes**Servings:** 4
Ingredients:
- 1 pound chicken breasts, skinless, boneless and cubed
- 1 cup okra, halved
- 1 tablespoon basil pesto
- 1 tablespoon lime juice
- 2 tablespoons olive oil
- ½ teaspoon oregano, dried
- 1 teaspoon chili powder
- A pinch of salt and black pepper
- 1 cup chicken stock

Directions:
Set the instant pot on Sauté mode, add the oil, heat it up, add the meat, oregano and chili powder and brown for 5 minutes. Add the pesto and the other ingredients, toss, put the lid on and cook on High for 20 minutes. Release the pressure naturally for 10 minutes, divide everything between plates and serve.

Nutrition: calories 162, fat 8, fiber 2, carbs 5, protein 9

Mustard Turkey

Preparation time: 10 minutes**Cooking time:** 25 minutes**Servings:** 4

Ingredients:

- 2 tablespoons olive oil
- 3 scallions minced
- 1 tablespoon mustard
- 1 tablespoon lime zest, grated
- 1 pound turkey breast, skinless, boneless and cubed
- ¾ cup chicken stock
- 1 tablespoon lime juice
- A pinch of salt and black pepper
- 1 tablespoon cilantro, chopped

Directions:

Set your instant pot on sauté mode, add the oil, heat it up, add the scallions, lime juice and zest and cook for 5 minutes. Add the meat and brown for 5 more minutes. Add the other ingredients, toss well, put the lid on and cook on High for 15 minutes. Release the pressure naturally for 10 minutes, divide the mix between plates and serve.

Nutrition: calories 200, fat 9, fiber 2, carbs 5, protein 10

Orange Chicken and Mango

Preparation time: 10 minutes**Cooking time:** 25 minutes**Servings:** 4

Ingredients:

- 1 pound chicken breast, skinless, boneless and roughly cubed
- 1 cup mango, peeled and cubed
- 2 tablespoons avocado oil
- 4 scallions, minced
- 1 tablespoon orange zest, grated
- 1 cup orange juice
- 1 tablespoon chives, chopped
- A pinch of salt and black pepper

Directions:

Set the instant pot on Sauté mode, add the oil, heat it up, add the scallions and the meat and brown for 10 minutes. Add the mango, orange juice and the rest of the ingredients, toss, put the lid on and cook on High for 15 minutes. Release the pressure naturally for 10 minutes, divide the mix into bowls and serve.

Nutrition: calories 200, fat 7, fiber 2, carbs 6, protein 11

Turkey and Turnips

Preparation time: 10 minutes**Cooking time:** 25 minutes**Servings:** 4

Ingredients:

- 1 pound turkey breasts, skinless, boneless and cubed
- 2 turnips, roughly cubed
- 2 tablespoons avocado oil
- 1 tablespoon balsamic vinegar
- 1 red onion, chopped
- 1 teaspoon sweet paprika
- 1 cup chicken stock
- ½ cup chives, chopped

Directions:

Set your instant pot on Sauté mode, add the oil, heat it up, add the onion, the meat and paprika and brown for 10 minutes. Add the turnips and the rest of the ingredients, toss, put the lid on and cook on High for 15 minutes. Release the pressure naturally for 10 minutes, divide the mix between plates and serve.

Nutrition: calories 210, fat 8, fiber 2, carbs 6, protein 11

Italian Chicken Thighs

Preparation time: 10 minutes**Cooking time:** 20 minutes**Servings:** 4

Ingredients:

- 2 pounds chicken thighs, boneless
- 1 teaspoon Italian seasoning
- ½ teaspoon rosemary, dried
- ½ teaspoon turmeric powder
- 2 tablespoons olive oil
- ½ cup chicken stock
- 1 yellow onion, chopped
- ½ teaspoon chili powder
- A pinch of salt and black pepper
- 1 tablespoon chives, chopped

Directions:

Set your instant pot on Sauté mode, add the oil, heat it up, add the onion, chili powder, Italian seasoning and the meat and brown for 5 minutes Add the rosemary and the other ingredients, toss, put the lid on and cook on High for 15 minutes Release the pressure naturally for 10 minutes, divide between plates and serve with a side salad.

Nutrition: calories 220, fat 8, fiber 2, carbs 5, protein 11

Chicken and Black Beans

Preparation time: 10 minutes**Cooking time:** 25 minutes**Servings:** 4

Ingredients:

- 1 pound chicken breasts, skinless, boneless and roughly cubed
- 2 cups canned black beans, drained and rinsed
- 1 red onion, chopped
- 1 cup tomato passata
- 2 tablespoons olive oil
- Salt and black pepper to the taste
- ½ teaspoon sweet paprika
- 1 tablespoon cilantro, chopped

Directions:

Set the instant pot on Sauté mode, add the oil, heat it up, add the onion and paprika and cook for 5 minutes Add the meat and brown for another 5 minutes Add the black beans and the other ingredients, toss, put the lid on and cook on High for 15 minutes Release the pressure naturally for 10 minutes, divide the mix between plates and serve.

Nutrition: calories 192, fat 12, fiber 3, carbs 5, protein 12

Coriander Turkey and Tomatoes

Preparation time: 10 minutes**Cooking time:** 25 minutes**Servings:** 4

Ingredients:

- 1 pound turkey breasts, skinless, boneless and cubed
- 1 cup cherry tomatoes, halved
- 4 scallions, minced
- 2 tablespoons olive oil
- ½ teaspoon coriander, ground
- ½ teaspoon turmeric powder
- 1 tablespoon lime zest, grated
- 1 cup lime juice
- 1 tablespoon chives, chopped
- ¼ cup chicken stock

Directions:

Set the instant pot on Sauté mode, add the oil, heat it up, add the scallions, turmeric and lime zest and cook for 5 minutes. Add the meat and brown for 5 minutes more. Add the rest of the ingredients, put the lid on and cook on High for 15 minutes. Release the pressure naturally for 10 minutes, divide the mix between plates and serve.

Nutrition: calories 200, fat 7, fiber 1, carbs 5, protein 12

Garlic Chicken and Cauliflower

Preparation time: 10 minutes**Cooking time:** 25 minutes**Servings:** 4

Ingredients:

- 1 pound chicken breast, skinless, boneless and cubed
- 1 tablespoon olive oil
- 2 tablespoons garlic, minced
- 3 scallions, chopped
- ½ teaspoon oregano, dried
- A pinch of salt and black pepper
- 1 cup chicken stock
- 1 cup cauliflower florets
- 1 tablespoon parsley, chopped

Directions:

Set the instant pot on Sauté mode, add the oil, heat it up, add the scallions, garlic and oregano and cook for 5 minutes. Add the meat and brown for 5 minutes more. Add the stock and the rest of the ingredients, toss, put the lid on and cook on High for 15 minutes. Release the pressure naturally for 10 minutes, divide the mix between plates and serve.

Nutrition: calories 231, fat 7, fiber 2, carbs 6, protein 12

Chicken and Eggplant Mix

Preparation time: 10 minutes**Cooking time:** 25 minutes**Servings:** 4

Ingredients:

- 1 pound chicken breast, skinless, boneless and cubed
- 2 eggplants, cubed
- 2 tablespoons olive oil
- 1 yellow onion, chopped
- 1 teaspoon coriander, ground
- ½ teaspoon sweet paprika
- ½ teaspoon chili powder
- ½ teaspoon cumin, ground
- A pinch of salt and black pepper
- ½ cup tomato passata
- 1 tablespoon chives, chopped

Directions:

Set your instant pot on Sauté mode, add the oil, heat it up, add the onion, paprika, chili powder and cumin and cook for 5 minutes. Add the meat and brown for 5 minutes more. Add the eggplant and the rest of the ingredients, toss, put the lid on and cook on High for 15 minutes. Release the pressure naturally for 10 minutes, divide everything between plates and serve.

Nutrition: calories 252, fat 12, fiber 4, carbs 7, protein 13

Turkey and Green Beans Mix

Preparation time: 10 minutes**Cooking time:** 25 minutes**Servings:** 4

Ingredients:

- 1 pound turkey breasts, skinless, boneless and cubed
- 1 cup green beans, trimmed and halved
- Juice of 1 lime
- 1 red onion, chopped
- 2 tablespoons olive oil
- A pinch of salt and black pepper
- 2 garlic cloves, minced
- 1 cup tomato passata
- 1 tablespoon chives, chopped

Directions:

Set the instant pot on Sauté mode, add the oil, heat it up, add the onion, garlic and the meat and brown for 10 minutes. Add the rest of the ingredients, toss, put the lid on and cook on High for 15 minutes. Release the pressure naturally for 10 minutes, divide everything between plates and serve.

Nutrition: calories 221, fat 14, fiber 3, carbs 7, protein 14

Turkey and Veggies

Preparation time: 10 minutes**Cooking time:** 25 minutes**Servings:** 4

Ingredients:

- 1 pound turkey breast, skinless, boneless and cut into strips
- 2 tablespoons avocado oil
- 1 yellow onion, chopped
- 1 eggplant, cubed
- 1 cup green beans, trimmed and halved
- 1 cup cherry tomatoes, halved
- 2 tablespoons balsamic vinegar
- 1 cup chicken stock
- A handful cilantro, chopped
- A pinch of salt and black pepper

Directions:

Set your instant pot on Sauté mode, add the oil, heat it up, add the onion and the meat and cook for 10 minutes. Add the eggplant, green beans and the rest of the ingredients, put the lid on and cook on High for 15 minutes. Release the pressure naturally for 10 minutes, divide the mix between plates and serve.

Nutrition: calories 263, fat 14, fiber 1, carbs 8, protein 12

Chicken and Peppers

Preparation time: 10 minutes**Cooking time:** 25 minutes**Servings:** 4

Ingredients:

- 1 pound chicken breast, skinless, boneless and cubed
- 1 red bell pepper, cut into strips
- 1 green bell pepper, cut into strips
- 2 tablespoons olive oil
- 1 tablespoon ginger, grated
- 1 cup tomato passata
- A pinch of salt and black pepper
- 1 tablespoon chili powder
- 1 tablespoon cilantro, chopped

Directions:

Set your instant pot on Sauté mode, add the oil, heat it up, add the peppers and the meat and brown for 10 minutes. Add the rest of the ingredients, put the lid on and cook on High for 15 minutes. Release the pressure naturally for 10 minutes, divide everything between plates and serve.

Nutrition: calories 263, fat 12, fiber 3, carbs 6, protein 14

Turkey with Plums and Tomatoes

Preparation time: 10 minutes**Cooking time:** 25 minutes**Servings:** 4

Ingredients:

- 1 pound turkey breast, skinless, boneless and sliced
- 1 cup plums, stoned and halved
- 1 cup cherry tomatoes, halved
- 2 tablespoons avocado oil
- 1 cup chicken stock
- 1 teaspoon garam masala
- ½ teaspoon turmeric powder
- 1 tablespoon olive oil
- 1 tablespoon rosemary, chopped
- A pinch of salt and black pepper

Directions:

In your instant pot, combine the turkey slices with the plums, tomatoes and the other ingredients, put the lid on and cook on High for 25 minutes. Release the pressure naturally for 10 minutes, divide the mix between plates and serve.

Nutrition: calories 253, fat 13, fiber 2, carbs 7, protein 16

Turkey with Ginger Carrots

Preparation time: 10 minutes**Cooking time:** 20 minutes**Servings:** 4

Ingredients:

- 1 pound turkey breast, skinless, boneless and cubed
- 1 tablespoon ginger, grated
- 1 tablespoon olive oil
- 1 tablespoon balsamic vinegar
- 3 scallions, chopped
- 1 cup baby carrots, peeled
- ¼ cup chives, chopped
- A pinch of salt and black pepper
- ¼ cup chicken stock
- 1 tablespoon rosemary, chopped

Directions:

Set your instant pot on Sauté mode, add the oil, heat it up, add the scallions, ginger and the meat and brown for 5 minutes. Add the vinegar, carrots and the rest of the ingredients, toss, put the lid on and cook on High for 15 minutes. Release the pressure naturally for 10 minutes, divide everything between plates and serve.

Nutrition: calories 234, fat 14, fiber 4, carbs 7, protein 15

Turkey and Yams Mix

Preparation time: 10 minutes**Cooking time:** 25 minutes**Servings:** 4

Ingredients:

- 1 pound turkey breast, skinless, boneless and sliced
- 2 yams, peeled and cubed
- 1 yellow onion, chopped
- 2 tablespoons avocado oil
- 1 tablespoon rosemary, chopped
- ½ teaspoon cumin, ground
- ½ teaspoon chili powder
- 3 garlic cloves, minced
- 1 cup chicken stock
- A pinch of salt and black pepper
- 1 tablespoon cilantro, chopped

Directions:

Set pot on Sauté mode, add the oil, heat it up, add the onion, cumin, chili powder and the garlic and cook for 5 minutes. Add the meat and brown for another 5 minutes. Add the rest of the ingredients, put the lid on and cook on High for 15 minutes. Release the pressure naturally for 10 minutes, divide the mix between plates and serve.

Nutrition: calories 263, fat 13, fiber 2, carbs 7, protein 15

Chicken and Scallions

Preparation time: 5 minutes**Cooking time:** 20 minutes**Servings:** 4

Ingredients:

- 1 pound chicken breasts, skinless, boneless and cubed
- 2 tablespoons olive oil
- 2 garlic cloves, minced
- ½ teaspoon coriander, dried
- ½ teaspoon sweet paprika
- ½ teaspoon cumin , ground
- 6 scallions, chopped
- 1 asparagus bunch, trimmed and steamed
- 1 cup chicken stock
- 1 tablespoon cilantro, chopped
- A pinch of salt and black pepper

Directions:

Set the instant pot on Sauté mode, add the oil, heat it up, add the scallions, garlic and the meat and brown for 10 minutes. Add the coriander, paprika and the other ingredients, toss, put the lid on and cook on High for 19 minutes. Release the pressure fast for 5 minutes, divide everything between plates and serve.

Nutrition: calories 200, fat 13, fiber 2, carbs 5, protein 16

Mustard Chicken

Preparation time: 5 minutes**Cooking time:** 25 minutes**Servings:** 4

Ingredients:

- 1 pound chicken breast, skinless, boneless and cubed
- 2 tablespoons mustard
- 1 tablespoon garlic, minced
- 1 tablespoon lime juice
- 2 tablespoons olive oil
- ½ teaspoon mustard seeds, crushed
- 1 cup chicken stock
- A pinch of salt and black pepper
- 1 tablespoon chives, chopped

Directions:

Set the instant pot on Sauté mode, add the oil, heat it up, add the garlic and mustard seeds and cook for 5 minutes. Add the meat and brown for 5 minutes more. Add the other ingredients, toss, put the lid on and cook on High for 15 minutes. Release the pressure fast for 5 minutes, divide the mix between plates and serve.

Nutrition: calories 200, fat 12, fiber 2, carbs 6, protein 15

Chicken with Broccoli

Preparation time: 10 minutes**Cooking time:** 25 minutes**Servings:** 4

Ingredients:

- 1 pound chicken breast, skinless, boneless and cubed
- 2 tablespoons olive oil
- 1 cup broccoli florets
- ½ teaspoon chili powder
- ½ teaspoon oregano, dried
- 1 yellow onion, sliced
- 3 garlic cloves, minced
- A pinch of salt and black pepper
- 1 cup chicken stock
- 1 tablespoon cilantro, chopped

Directions:

Set the instant pot on Sauté mode, add the oil, heat it up, add the onion, garlic and the meat and brown for 10 minutes Add the broccoli and the rest of the ingredients, toss, put the lid on and cook on High for 15 minutes Release the pressure naturally for 10 minutes, divide the mix between plates and serve.

Nutrition: calories 253, fat 14, fiber 2, carbs 7, protein 16

Rosemary Chicken

Preparation time: 10 minutes**Cooking time:** 25 minutes**Servings:** 4

Ingredients:

- 2 pounds chicken breast, skinless, boneless and roughly cubed
- 1 tablespoon avocado oil
- 1 teaspoon sweet paprika
- 1 tablespoon rosemary, chopped
- 1 red onion, chopped
- ½ teaspoon cumin, dried
- ½ teaspoon fennel seeds, crushed
- 1 cup chicken stock
- A pinch of salt and black pepper
- 1 tablespoon chives, chopped

Directions:

Set the instant pot on Sauté mode, add the oil, heat it up, add the onion, cumin, fennel and the meat and brown for 10 minutes. Add the stock and the remaining ingredients, toss, put the lid on and cook on High for 15 minutes. Release the pressure naturally for 10 minutes, divide the mix between plates and serve.

Nutrition: calories 273, fat 13, fiber 3, carbs 7, protein 17

Turkey with Endives

Preparation time: 10 minutes**Cooking time:** 25 minutes**Servings:** 4

Ingredients:

- 1 pound chicken breast, skinless, boneless and sliced
- 2 endives, shredded
- 3 scallions, chopped
- 1 tablespoon lemon juice
- ½ teaspoon basil, dried
- 2 tablespoons olive oil
- 1 teaspoon black peppercorns, crushed
- 1 cup chicken stock
- 1 tablespoon cilantro, chopped

Directions:

Set the instant pot on Sauté mode, add the oil, heat it up, add the scallions, peppercorns and the meat and brown for 10 minutes. Add the endives and the other ingredients, toss, put the lid on and cook on High for 15 minutes. Release the pressure naturally for 10 minutes, divide the mix between plates and serve.

Nutrition: calories 276, fat 15, fiber 3, carbs 7, protein 16

Balsamic Turkey and Passata

Preparation time: 10 minutes**Cooking time:** 25 minutes**Servings:** 4

Ingredients:

- 1 pound turkey breast, skinless, boneless and sliced
- 4 scallions, chopped
- 2 garlic cloves, minced
- 2 tablespoons olive oil
- 1 tablespoon balsamic vinegar
- A pinch of salt and black pepper
- 1 tablespoon chives, chopped
- ½ cup tomato passata

Directions:

Set your instant pot on Sauté mode, add the oil, heat it up, add the scallions and the meat and brown for 10 minutes. Add the passata, vinegar and the rest of the ingredients, put the lid on and cook on High for 15 minutes. Release the pressure naturally for 10 minutes, divide the mix between plates and serve.

Nutrition: calories 252, fat 15, fiber 2, carbs 6, protein 15

Turkey and Blackberries Mix

Preparation time: 10 minutes**Cooking time:** 25 minutes**Servings:** 4

Ingredients:

- 1 pound turkey breasts, skinless, boneless and cubed
- 1 cup blackberries
- 2 spring onions, chopped
- 2 tablespoons olive oil
- 1 tablespoon oregano, chopped
- ½ teaspoon chili powder
- 1 avocado, peeled, pitted and roughly cubed
- 1 tablespoons lemon zest, grated
- 1 tablespoon lemon juice
- A pinch of salt and black pepper
- 1 tablespoon chives, chopped

Directions:

Set the instant pot on Sauté mode, add the oil, heat it up, add the spring onions, chili powder and the meat and brown for 10 minutes. Add the berries and the rest of the ingredients, put the lid on and cook on High for 15 minutes. Release the pressure naturally for 10 minutes, divide everything between plates and serve.

Nutrition: calories 234, fat 12, fiber 3, carbs 5, protein 7

Turkey with Paprika Olives

Preparation time: 10 minutes**Cooking time:** 25 minutes**Servings:** 4

Ingredients:

- 1 pound turkey breast, skinless, boneless and sliced
- 1 cup kalamata olives, pitted and halved
- 1 tablespoon avocado oil
- 4 scallions, minced
- 1 cup black olives, pitted and halved
- 1 cup chicken stock
- 1 teaspoon sweet paprika
- A pinch of salt and black pepper
- 1 tablespoon parsley, chopped

Directions:

Set the instant pot on Sauté mode, add the oil, heat it up, add the scallions and the meat and brown for 10 minutes. Add the olives and the rest of the ingredients, toss, put the lid on and cook on High for 15 minutes. Release the pressure naturally for 10 minutes, divide everything between plates and serve.

Nutrition: calories 263, fat 14, fiber 3, carbs 7, protein 16

Parsley Chicken

Preparation time: 10 minutes**Cooking time:** 20 minutes**Servings:** 4

Ingredients:

- 1 pound chicken thighs, boneless and skinless
- 2 tablespoons avocado oil
- 2 tablespoons parsley, chopped
- ½ teaspoon turmeric powder
- ½ teaspoon cumin, ground
- ½ cup chicken stock
- A pinch of salt and black pepper

Directions:

Set your instant pot on Sauté mode, add the oil, heat it up, add the meat and brown for 5 minutes. Add the turmeric and the rest of the ingredients, put the lid on and cook on High for 15 minutes. Release the pressure naturally for 10 minutes, divide the mix between plates and serve.

Nutrition: calories 263, fat 12, fiber 2, carbs 7, protein 18

Turkey and Basil Salsa

Preparation time: 10 minutes**Cooking time:** 25 minutes**Servings:** 4

Ingredients:

- 1 pound turkey breasts, skinless, boneless and cubed
- A pinch of salt and black pepper
- 2 scallions, chopped
- 1 tablespoon avocado oil
- 1 teaspoon coriander, dried
- 1 cup tomatoes, cubed
- 1 cup avocado, peeled, pitted and cubed
- ½ cup black olives, pitted and halved
- ¼ cup chicken stock
- 2 tablespoons basil, chopped
- 1 tablespoon balsamic vinegar

Directions:

Set the instant pot on Sauté mode, add the oil, heat it up, add the scallions and the meat and brown for 10 minutes. Add the tomatoes, avocado and the other ingredients, toss, put the lid on and cook on High for 15 minutes. Release the pressure naturally for 10 minutes, divide the mix between plates and serve.

Nutrition: calories 201, fat 7, fiber 3, carbs 6, protein 8

Turkey with Fennel

Preparation time: 10 minutes**Cooking time:** 25 minutes**Servings:** 4

Ingredients:

- 1 cup fennel, sliced
- 2 tablespoons avocado oil
- 3 scallions, chopped
- 1 tablespoon lime juice
- 1 pound turkey breast, skinless, boneless and cubed
- 1 yellow onion, chopped
- 2 garlic cloves, minced
- 1 tablespoon chili powder
- 1 cup chicken stock
- A pinch of salt and black pepper
- 1 tablespoon chives, chopped

Directions:

Set the instant pot on Sauté mode, add the oil, heat it up, add the scallions, onion, garlic and the meat and brown for 10 minutes. Add the chili powder, fennel and the rest of the ingredients, toss, put the lid on and cook on High for 15 minutes. Release the pressure naturally for 10 minutes, divide the mix between plates and serve.

Nutrition: calories 263, fat 12, fiber 3, carbs 7, protein 15

Creamy Turkey

Preparation time: 10 minutes**Cooking time:** 25 minutes**Servings:** 4

Ingredients:

- 3 scallions, chopped
- 2 tablespoons olive oil
- 2 garlic cloves, minced
- 1 tablespoon Italian seasoning
- 1 pound turkey breasts, skinless, boneless and cubed
- 1 cup coconut cream
- 1 tablespoon cumin, ground
- A pinch of salt and black pepper
- 2 tablespoons cilantro, chopped

Directions:

Set your instant pot on Sauté mode, add the oil, heat it up, add the scallions, garlic and the Italian seasoning and cook for 5 minutes. Add the meat and brown for another 5 minutes. Add the rest of the ingredients, toss, put the lid on and cook on High for 15 minutes. Release the pressure naturally for 10 minutes, divide everything into bowls and serve.

Nutrition: calories 214, fat 14, fiber 2, carbs 6, protein 15

Coriander Turkey and Kidney Beans

Preparation time: 10 minutes**Cooking time:** 25 minutes**Servings:** 4

Ingredients:
- 1 pound turkey breasts, skinless, boneless and cubed
- 1 tablespoon avocado oil
- 1 cup canned red kidney beans, drained and rinsed
- 3 scallions, chopped
- 1 tablespoon coriander, chopped
- ½ teaspoon chili powder
- 1 cup chicken stock
- 1 tablespoon chives, chopped

Directions:

Set your instant pot on Sauté mode, add the oil, heat it up, add the scallions, chili powder and the meat and brown for 10 minutes. Add the stock and the rest of the ingredients, put the lid on and cook on High for 15 minutes. Release the pressure naturally for 10 minutes, divide the mix between plates and serve.

Nutrition: calories 231, fat 12, fiber 4, carbs 7, protein 15

Paprika Duck Mix

Preparation time: 10 minutes**Cooking time:** 30 minutes**Servings:** 4

Ingredients:
- 2 pounds duck breast, skinless, boneless and cubed
- 2 tablespoons avocado oil
- 2 garlic cloves, minced
- 1 tablespoon sweet paprika
- 1 tablespoon cilantro, chopped
- 1 cup chicken stock
- 1 teaspoon coriander, ground

Directions:

Set your instant pot on Sauté mode, add the oil, heat it up, add the garlic and the meat and brown for 10 minutes. Add the stock and the rest of the ingredients, put the lid on and cook on High for 20 minutes. Release the pressure naturally for 10 minutes, divide everything between plates and serve.

Nutrition: calories 263, fat 12, fiber 5, carbs 7, protein 16

Dill Chicken

Preparation time: 10 minutes**Cooking time:** 25 minutes**Servings:** 4
Ingredients:

- 2 tablespoons avocado oil
- 2 pound chicken breasts, skinless, boneless and roughly cubed
- ½ cup scallions, chopped
- ½ cup tomato passata
- ½ teaspoon basil, dried
- 1 teaspoon garam masala
- A pinch of salt and black pepper
- 1 cup chicken stock
- 1 tablespoon dill, chopped

Directions:

Set your instant pot on Sauté mode, add the oil, heat it up, add the scallions, the meat and basil and cook for 10 minutes Add the passata and the rest of the ingredients, toss, put the lid on and cook on High for 15 minutes Release the pressure naturally for 10 minutes, divide the mix into bowls and serve.

Nutrition: calories 242, fat 14, fiber 3, carbs 7, protein 14

Turkey and Rice

Preparation time: 10 minutes**Cooking time:** 25 minutes**Servings:** 4
Ingredients:

- 2 pounds turkey breasts, skinless, boneless and cubed
- 2 tablespoons olive oil
- 1 yellow onion, chopped
- 1 cup wild rice
- 2 cups chicken stock
- ½ teaspoon chili powder
- ½ teaspoon turmeric powder
- 2 tablespoons green onions, chopped
- A pinch of salt and black pepper

Directions:

Set the instant pot on Sauté mode, add the oil, heat it up, add the onion, chili powder and the turmeric and cook for 5 minutes. Add the meat and brown fro another 5 minutes. Add the rest of the ingredients, toss, put the lid on and cook on High for 15 minutes. Release the pressure naturally for 10 minutes, divide everything between plates and serve.

Nutrition: calories 232, fat 12, fiber 2, carbs 6, protein 15

Spicy Chicken Wings

Preparation time: 10 minutes**Cooking time:** 25 minutes**Servings:** 4

Ingredients:

- 1 pound chicken wings, halved
- 1 teaspoon hot paprika
- 1 red chili pepper, chopped
- 2 tablespoons olive oil
- 1 red onion, sliced
- 1 cup chicken stock
- 1 tablespoon cilantro, chopped
- A pinch of salt and black pepper

Directions:

Set the instant pot on Sauté mode, add the oil, heat it up, onion, chili pepper and the meat and brown for 10 minutes. Add the stock and the rest of the ingredients, toss, put the lid on and cook on High for 15 minutes. Release the pressure naturally for 10 minutes, divide the mix between plates and serve.

Nutrition: calories 263, fat 14, fiber 4, carbs 6, protein 18

Chicken with Mushrooms and Tomatoes

Preparation time: 10 minutes**Cooking time:** 25 minutes**Servings:** 4

Ingredients:

- 1 pound chicken breast, skinless, boneless and sliced
- 3 scallions, chopped
- 1 cup cherry tomatoes, halved
- 1 cup mushrooms, halved
- 2 tablespoons lemon juice
- 1 tablespoon olive oil
- ½ cup chicken stock
- 1 teaspoon chili powder
- ¼ cup chives, chopped

Directions:

Set the instant pot on Sauté mode, add the oil, heat it up, add the scallions and the mushrooms and cook for 5 minutes Add the meat and brown for another 5 minutes Add the remaining ingredients, toss, put the lid on and cook on High for 15 minutes Release the pressure naturally for 10 minutes, divide everything between plates and serve.

Nutrition: calories 262, fat 16, fiber 2, carbs 8, protein 16

Turkey with Basil Lemon Sauce

Preparation time: 10 minutes**Cooking time:** 25 minutes**Servings:** 4

Ingredients:

- 1 tablespoon olive oil
- Juice of 1 lemon
- 1 tablespoon basil, chopped
- 1 pound turkey breast, skinless, boneless and roughly cubed
- 1 yellow onion, chopped
- 2 tablespoons olive oil
- ½ cup chicken stock
- 1 tablespoon cilantro, chopped
- A pinch of salt and black pepper

Directions:

Set the instant pot on Sauté mode, add the oil, heat it up, add the onion, lemon juice and basil, stir and cook for 5 minutes. Add the meat and the rest of the ingredients, put the lid on and cook on High for 20 minutes. Release the pressure naturally for 10 minutes, divide everything between plates and serve.

Nutrition: calories 283, fat 16, fiber 2, carbs 6, protein 17

Chicken and Lentils

Preparation time: 10 minutes**Cooking time:** 25 minutes**Servings:** 4

Ingredients:

- 2 tablespoons avocado oil
- 2 pounds chicken breast, boneless, skinless and roughly cubed
- 1 cup canned lentils, drained and rinsed
- ½ cup tomato passata
- ½ teaspoon cumin, ground
- 1 cup chicken stock
- A pinch of salt and black pepper
- 1 tablespoon cilantro, chopped

Directions:

Set your instant pot on Sauté mode, add the oil, heat it up, add the meat and brown for 10 minutes. Add the lentils and the rest of the ingredients, put the lid on and cook on High for 15 minutes. Release the pressure naturally for 10 minutes, divide the mix between plates and serve.

Nutrition: calories 291, fat 17, fiber 3, carbs 7, protein 16

Duck with Tomatoes and Leeks

Preparation time: 10 minutes**Cooking time:** 25 minutes**Servings:** 4

Ingredients:

- 2 pounds duck breast, skinless, boneless and cubed
- 2 tablespoons olive oil
- 2 leeks, sliced
- 1 red onion, chopped
- ½ teaspoon cumin, ground
- ½ teaspoon coriander, ground
- 1 green chili, chopped
- A pinch of salt and black pepper
- 1 cup chicken stock
- ½ teaspoon sweet paprika
- 1 tablespoon parsley, chopped

Directions:

Set your instant pot on Sauté mode, add the oil, heat it up, add the meat, onion and leeks and cook for 10 minutes. Add the stock, paprika and the rest of the ingredients, put the lid on and cook on High for 15 minutes. Release the pressure naturally for 10 minutes, divide everything between plates and serve.

Nutrition: calories 226, fat 9, fiber 1, carbs 6, protein 12

Turmeric Duck and Sauce

Preparation time: 10 minutes**Cooking time:** 25 minutes**Servings:** 4

Ingredients:

- 1 yellow onion, chopped
- 2 garlic cloves, minced
- 1 tablespoon lime juice
- 1 tablespoon lime zest, grated
- 2 tablespoons olive oil
- 1 pound duck breast, skinless, boneless and cubed
- 1 teaspoon turmeric powder
- 1 cup chicken stock
- A pinch of salt and black pepper
- 1 tablespoon oregano, chopped

Directions:

Set your instant pot on Sauté mode, add the oil, heat it up, add the onion, garlic, lime juice and lime zest and cook for 5 minutes. Add the meat and cook for 5 minutes more. Add the rest of the ingredients, put the lid on and cook on High for 15 minutes. Release the pressure naturally for 10 minutes, divide the mix between plates and serve.

Nutrition: calories 283, fat 11, fiber 2, carbs 8, protein 15

Chicken and Green Beans Rice

Preparation time: 10 minutes**Cooking time:** 25 minutes**Servings:** 4

Ingredients:
- 1 pound chicken breasts, skinless, boneless and cubed
- 1 cup green beans, halved
- 1 cup wild rice
- 2 cups chicken stock
- 1 yellow onion, chopped
- 1 tablespoon olive oil
- A pinch of salt and black pepper
- 1 teaspoon sweet paprika
- ½ teaspoon coriander, ground
- 1 tablespoon cilantro, chopped

Directions:

Set the instant pot on Sauté mode, add the oil, heat it up, add the onion, paprika, coriander and the meat and brown for 10 minutes. Add the rice and the remaining ingredients, put the lid on and cook on High for 15 minutes. Release the pressure naturally for 10 minutes, divide the mix between plates and serve.

Nutrition: calories 221, fat 12, fiber 2, carbs 5, protein 17

Chicken and Chard Mix

Preparation time: 10 minutes**Cooking time:** 25 minutes**Servings:** 4

Ingredients:
- 1 tablespoon avocado oil
- 1 cup red chard, torn
- 1 red onion, chopped
- 2 garlic cloves, minced
- 1 tablespoon balsamic vinegar
- 1 pound chicken breast, skinless, boneless and cubed
- 1 teaspoon sweet paprika
- A pinch of salt and black pepper
- 1 cup chicken stock
- ½ tablespoon cilantro, chopped

Directions:

Set the instant pot on sauté mode, add the oil, heat it up, add the onion, garlic and the meat and brown for 10 minutes. Add the stock and the rest of the ingredients, put the lid on and cook on High for 15 minutes. Release the pressure naturally for 10 minutes, divide the mix between plates and serve.

Nutrition: calories 227, fat 12, fiber 3, carbs 7, protein 18

186

Creamy Duck

Preparation time: 10 minutes**Cooking time:** 20 minutes**Servings:** 4

Ingredients:

- 1 pound duck breasts, boneless, skinless and cubed
- 1 tablespoon olive oil
- 1 teaspoon turmeric powder
- ½ teaspoon coriander, ground
- 1 yellow onion, chopped
- 1 cup heavy cream
- A pinch of salt and black pepper
- 1 tablespoon parsley, chopped

Directions:

Set the instant pot on Sauté mode, add the oil, heat it up, add the onion, turmeric, coriander and the meat and brown for 10 minutes. Add the rest of the ingredients, put the lid on and cook on High for 10 minutes. Release the pressure naturally for 10 minutes, divide everything between plates, and serve.

Nutrition: calories 293, fat 15, fiber 4, carbs 6, protein 14

Chicken and Tomato Chickpeas

Preparation time: 10 minutes**Cooking time:** 25 minutes**Servings:** 4

Ingredients:

- 1 pound chicken breasts, skinless, boneless and cubed
- 1 tablespoon avocado oil
- 1 cup canned chickpeas, drained and rinsed
- 1 cup tomato passata
- 3 scallions, chopped
- A pinch of salt and black pepper
- 1 teaspoon chili powder
- ½ teaspoon sweet paprika
- 1 tablespoon cilantro, chopped

Directions:

Set the instant pot on Sauté mode, add the oil, heat up, add the scallions, chili powder, paprika and the meat and brown for 10 minutes. Add the rest of the ingredients, toss, put the lid on and cook on High for 15 minutes Release the pressure naturally for 10 minutes, divide the mix between plates and serve.

Nutrition: calories 223, fat 9, fiber 2, carbs 4, protein 11

Turkey and Squash

Preparation time: 10 minutes**Cooking time:** 25 minutes**Servings:** 4
Ingredients:

- 1 pound turkey breasts, skinless, boneless and roughly cubed
- 1 cup butternut squash, peeled and roughly cubed
- 1 teaspoon turmeric powder
- 2 scallions, chopped
- 1 tablespoon olive oil
- ½ teaspoon garam masala
- 1 cup chicken stock
- 1 tablespoon cilantro, chopped

Directions:

Set instant pot on Sauté mode, add the oil, heat it up, add the scallions, masala and the meat and brown for 10 minutes. Add the squash and the rest of the ingredients, toss, put the lid on and cook on High for 15 minutes. Release the pressure naturally for 10 minutes, divide the mix between plates and serve.

Nutrition: calories 210, fat 11, fiber 2, carbs 7, protein 14

Turkey Strips with Pomegranate and Spinach

Preparation time: 10 minutes**Cooking time:** 30 minutes**Servings:** 4
Ingredients:

- 1 pound turkey breast, skinless, boneless and cut into strips
- 1 cup baby spinach
- 2 garlic cloves, minced
- 1 green chili pepper, minced
- 1 cup pomegranate seeds
- 4 scallions, chopped
- 2 tablespoons olive oil
- 1 cup tomato passata
- 1 tablespoon sweet paprika
- A pinch of salt and black pepper
- 1 tablespoon cilantro, chopped

Directions:

Set the instant pot on Sauté mode, add the oil, heat it up, add the garlic, chili pepper, scallions and the meat and brown for 10 minutes. Add the pomegranate seeds and the rest of the ingredients, put the lid on and cook on High for 20 minutes. Release the pressure naturally for 10 minutes, divide everything into bowls and serve.

Nutrition: calories 263, fat 8, fiber 2, carbs 7, protein 12

Turkey and Kale

Preparation time: 10 minutes**Cooking time:** 25 minutes**Servings:** 4

Ingredients:

- 1 pound turkey breasts, skinless, boneless and cubed
- 1 cup baby kale
- 2 tablespoons olive oil
- 2 garlic cloves, minced
- 2 scallions, chopped
- 1 cup tomato sauce
- 1 tablespoon basil, chopped
- 1 teaspoon chili powder

Directions:

Set the instant pot on Sauté mode, add the oil, heat up, add the garlic, scallions and the meta and brown for 10 minutes. Add the kale and the other ingredients, toss, put the lid on and cook on High for 15 minutes. Release the pressure naturally for 10 minutes, divide everything between plates and serve.

Nutrition: calories 220, fat 8, fiber 2, carbs 7, protein 15

Chicken and Chili Peppers

Preparation time: 10 minutes**Cooking time:** 25 minutes**Servings:** 4

Ingredients:

- 1 pound chicken breasts, skinless, boneless and cubed
- 1 cup roasted red peppers, cut into strips
- 1 teaspoon chili powder
- ½ teaspoon rosemary, dried
- 2 tablespoon olive oil
- ¼ cup sweet chili sauce
- A pinch of cayenne pepper
- 1 cup chicken stock
- 1 tablespoon cilantro, chopped

Directions:

Set the instant pot on Sauté mode, add the oil, heat it up, add the meat, chili powder and rosemary and brown for 10 minutes. Add the chili sauce, peppers and the other ingredients, put the lid on and cook on High for 15 minutes. Release the pressure naturally for 10 minutes, divide everything between plates and serve.

Nutrition: calories 282, fat 12, fiber 2, carbs 6, protein 18

Yogurt Turkey Mix

Preparation time: 10 minutes**Cooking time:** 25 minutes**Servings:** 4

Ingredients:
- 1 pound turkey breasts, skinless, boneless and halved
- 2 cups Greek yogurt
- 4 scallions, chopped
- 2 garlic cloves, minced
- 2 tablespoons olive oil
- A pinch of salt and black pepper
- ½ teaspoon garam masala
- ¼ cup chives, chopped

Directions:

Set the instant pot on Sauté mode, add the oil, heat up, add the scallions, garlic, masala and the meat and brown for 10 minutes. Add the rest of the ingredients, toss, put the lid on and cook on High for 15 minutes. Release the pressure naturally for 10 minutes, divide everything between plates and serve.

Nutrition: calories 285, fat 16, fiber 4, carbs 8, protein 18

Lime Duck

Preparation time: 10 minutes**Cooking time:** 25 minutes**Servings:** 4

Ingredients:
- 1 pound duck breasts, skinless, boneless and cubed
- 1 tablespoon lime zest, grated
- 3 scallions, chopped
- 1 tablespoon olive oil
- 1 cup chicken stock
- A pinch of salt and black pepper
- 2 tablespoons lime juice
- 1 tablespoon chives, chopped

Directions:

Set your instant pot on Sauté mode, add the oil, heat it up, add the scallions, lime zest and the meat and brown for 10 minutes. Add the stock and the rest of the ingredients, put the lid on and cook on High for 15 minutes. Release the pressure naturally for 10 minutes, divide everything into bowls and serve.

Nutrition: calories 292, fat 17, fiber 2, carbs 7, protein 16

Chicken Wings with Peppers and Tomatoes

Preparation time: 10 minutes**Cooking time:** 25 minutes**Servings:** 4

Ingredients:
- 1 pound chicken wings, halved
- 1 cup cherry tomatoes, halved
- 1 cup red bell peppers, cut into strips
- 1 cup chicken stock
- ½ teaspoon sweet paprika
- ½ teaspoon cumin, ground
- A pinch of salt and black pepper
- 3 scallions, chopped
- 2 tablespoons avocado oil
- ¼ cup cilantro, chopped

Directions:

Set the instant pot on Sauté mode, add the oil, heat up, add the scallions, paprika, cumin and the meat and brown for 10 minutes. Add the bell peppers and the other ingredients, toss, put the lid on and cook on High for 15 minutes. Release the pressure naturally for 10 minutes, divide everything between plates and serve.

Nutrition: calories 224, fat 11, fiber 2, carbs 9, protein 11

Cayenne Chicken

Preparation time: 10 minutes**Cooking time:** 25 minutes**Servings:** 4

Ingredients:
- 2 pounds chicken breast, skinless, boneless and cubed
- 1 cup scallions, minced
- 2 garlic cloves, minced
- 1 tablespoon avocado oil
- A pinch of salt and black pepper
- 1 teaspoon cayenne pepper
- 1 cup chicken stock
- 1 tablespoon parsley, chopped

Directions:

Set your instant pot on Sauté mode, add the oil, heat it up, add the meat, scallions and garlic and cook for 10 minutes. Add the cayenne and the rest of the ingredients, put the lid on and cook on High for 15 minutes. Release the pressure naturally for 10 minutes, divide everything between plates and serve.

Nutrition: calories 229, fat 9, fiber 4, carbs 7, protein 16

Herbed Turkey
Preparation time: 10 minutes**Cooking time:** 25 minutes**Servings:** 4

Ingredients:
- 2 pounds turkey breast, skinless, boneless and cubed
- 2 tablespoons olive oil
- 3 scallions, chopped
- 1 tablespoon oregano, chopped
- 1 tablespoon basil, chopped
- 1 tablespoon parsley, chopped
- ½ cup chicken stock
- A pinch of salt and black pepper
- 1 teaspoon sweet paprika

Directions:
Set the instant pot on Sauté mode, add the oil, heat up, add the scallions and the meat and brown for 10 minutes. Add the rest of the ingredients, toss, put the lid on and cook on High for 15 minutes. Release the pressure naturally for 10 minutes, divide the mix between plates and serve.

Nutrition: calories 183, fat 2.5, fiber 1.2, carbs 1.5, protein 13.4

Allspice Chicken Mix
Preparation time: 10 minutes**Cooking time:** 25 minutes**Servings:** 4

Ingredients:
- 2 pounds chicken breasts, skinless, boneless and cubed
- 1 red onion, chopped
- ½ teaspoon Italian seasoning
- 2 tablespoons avocado oil
- ½ teaspoon cumin, ground
- 1 teaspoon allspice, ground
- 2 tablespoons tomato paste
- 1 cup chicken stock

Directions:
Set your instant pot on Sauté mode, add the oil, heat it up, add the onion, Italian seasoning and the meat and brown for 10 minutes. Add the rest of the ingredients, put the lid on and cook on High for 15 minutes Release the pressure naturally for 10 minutes, divide the mix between plates and serve.

Nutrition: calories 238, fat 9.7, fiber 1, carbs 2.9, protein 33.3

Coconut Chicken

Preparation time: 10 minutes**Cooking time:** 20 minutes**Servings:** 4

Ingredients:

- 2 pounds chicken breast, skinless, boneless and cubed
- 3 spring onions, chopped
- 2 tablespoons olive oil
- 1 tablespoon balsamic vinegar
- A pinch of salt and black pepper
- 1 cup coconut cream
- ½ teaspoon garam masala
- ½ teaspoon turmeric powder
- 1 tablespoon oregano, chopped
- 1 tablespoon chives, chopped

Directions:

Set your instant pot on Sauté mode, add the oil, heat it up, add the onions, turmeric, masala and the chicken and brown for 10 minutes. Add the cream and the rest of the ingredients, put the lid on and cook on High for 10 minutes Release the pressure naturally for 10 minutes, divide everything between plates and serve.

Nutrition: calories 256, fat 12.6, fiber 0.6, carbs 1.2, protein 33.2

Cumin Duck

Preparation time: 10 minutes**Cooking time:** 25 minutes**Servings:** 4

Ingredients:

- 2 pounds duck breasts, skinless, boneless and cubed
- 2 tablespoons avocado oil
- 1 teaspoon cumin, ground
- 1 teaspoon lime zest, grated
- 3 scallions, chopped
- A pinch of salt and black pepper
- 1 tablespoon chili powder
- ½ cup chicken stock
- 2 tablespoons chives, chopped

Directions:

Set the instant pot on Sauté mode, add the oil, heat up, add the scallions, chili powder and cumin and cook for 5 minutes Add the meat and brown for 5 minutes more Add the rest of the ingredients, toss, put the lid on and cook on High for 15 minutes Release the pressure naturally for 10 minutes, divide the mix between plates and serve.

Nutrition: calories 364, fat 23.2, fiber 2.3, carbs 5.1, protein 35.4

Chicken Meatballs and Sauce

Preparation time: 10 minutes**Cooking time:** 25 minutes**Servings:** 4

Ingredients:

- 1 pound chicken breasts, skinless, boneless and ground
- 2 eggs, whisked
- 1 tablespoon chives, chopped
- A pinch of salt and black pepper
- 1 tablespoon almond flour
- 1 tablespoon lemon juice
- 2 tablespoons olive oil
- 2 tablespoons oregano, chopped
- 1 cup tomato passata

Directions:

In a bowl, combine the meat with the eggs, chives, flour, salt and pepper, stir and shape medium meatballs out of this mix. Set the instant pot on Sauté mode, add the oil, heat it up, add the meatballs and brown them for 10 minutes. Add the rest of the ingredients, toss, put the lid on and cook on High for 15 minutes. Release the pressure naturally for 10 minutes, divide the mix between plates and serve.

Nutrition: calories 300, fat 15.8, fiber 2, carbs 5.2, protein 33.9

Turkey and Bulgur Mix

Preparation time: 10 minutes**Cooking time:** 25 minutes**Servings:** 4

Ingredients:

- 1 pound turkey breast, skinless, boneless and cubed
- A pinch of salt and black pepper
- 2 scallions, chopped
- ½ cup bulgur
- 1 cup chicken stock
- 3 garlic cloves, minced
- 1 teaspoon turmeric powder
- 1 tablespoon chives, chopped

Directions:

In your instant pot, combine the turkey with the scallions, bulgur and the other ingredients, toss, put the lid on and cook on High for 25 minutes. Release the pressure naturally for 10 minutes, divide the mix into bowls and serve.

Nutrition: calories 360, fat 22.1, fiber 1.4, carbs 4.3, protein 34.5

Duck and Eggplant Mix

Preparation time: 10 minutes**Cooking time:** 20 minutes**Servings:** 4

Ingredients:

- 2 pounds duck breasts, skinless, boneless and cubed
- 1 red onion, chopped
- 1 tablespoon avocado oil
- ½ teaspoon smoked paprika
- ½ teaspoon rosemary, dried
- A pinch of salt and black pepper
- 2 eggplants, roughly cubed
- 1 cup tomato passata
- 1 tablespoon cilantro, chopped

Directions:

Set the instant pot on Sauté mode, add the oil, heat up, add the onion, paprika and the meat and brown for 5 minutes. Add the rest of the ingredients, toss, put the lid on and cook on High for 15 minutes. Release the pressure naturally for 10 minutes, divide between plates and serve.

Nutrition: calories 362, fat 16.1, fiber 4.4, carbs 5.4, protein 36.4

Turkey and Sprouts

Preparation time: 10 minutes**Cooking time:** 25 minutes**Servings:** 4

Ingredients:

- 2 pounds turkey breasts, skinless, boneless and cubed
- 2 tablespoons olive oil
- 1 cup Brussels sprouts, trimmed and halved
- 4 garlic cloves, minced
- 1 tablespoon lime juice
- A pinch of salt and black pepper
- 1 cup tomato passata
- 1 tablespoon parsley, chopped

Directions:

Set the instant pot on Sauté mode, add the oil, heat up, add the garlic and the meat and brown for 10 minutes. Add the sprouts and the other ingredients, toss, put the lid on and cook on High for 15 minutes. Release the pressure naturally for 10 minutes, divide everything between plates and serve.

Nutrition: calories 243, fat 9, fiber 1.6, carbs 5.4, protein 34.1

Smoked Chicken and Spring Onions

Preparation time: 10 minutes**Cooking time:** 25 minutes**Servings:** 4

Ingredients:

- 2 pounds chicken breast, skinless, boneless and cubed
- 1 teaspoon smoked paprika
- 2 scallions, chopped
- 4 spring onions, chopped
- 2 tablespoons avocado oil
- 1 cup tomato passata
- 1 tablespoon parsley, chopped
- A pinch of salt and black pepper

Directions:

Set your instant pot on Sauté mode, add the oil, heat it up, add the scallions, spring onions, the meat and paprika and brown for 10 minutes. Add the rest of the ingredients, put the lid on and cook on High for 15 minutes. Release the pressure naturally for 10 minutes between plates, divide the mix between plates and serve.

Nutrition: calories 222, fat 6.7, fiber 1.6, carbs 4.8, protein 34.4

Chicken and Cabbage Mix

Preparation time: 10 minutes**Cooking time:** 25 minutes**Servings:** 4

Ingredients:

- 1 pound chicken breasts, skinless, boneless and cubed
- 1 cup red cabbage, shredded
- 2 tablespoons olive oil
- 1 red onion, chopped
- 2 tablespoons balsamic vinegar
- A pinch of salt and black pepper
- 1 tablespoon olive oil
- 1 tablespoon sweet paprika
- 1 cup chicken stock
- 1 tablespoon cilantro, chopped

Directions:

Set your instant pot on Sauté mode, add the oil, heat it up, add the onion, the meat and paprika and cook for 10 minutes. Add the rest of the ingredients, put the lid on and cook on High for 15 minutes. Release the pressure naturally for 10 minutes, divide between plates and serve.

Nutrition: calories 264, fat 13.2, fiber 0.7, carbs 1.9, protein 33.2

Duck and Mango Mix

Preparation time: 10 minutes**Cooking time:** 25 minutes**Servings:** 4

Ingredients:

- 2 pounds duck breast, skinless, boneless and cubed
- 1 tablespoon avocado oil
- 1 cup mango, peeled, and cubed
- 1 tablespoon lime juice
- 1 tablespoon basil, chopped
- 1 teaspoon chili powder
- ½ cup veggie stock
- 2 tablespoons cilantro, chopped
- A pinch of salt and black pepper

Directions:

Set the instant pot on Sauté mode, add the oil, heat it up, add the meat and chili powder and cook for 10 minutes. Add the rest of the ingredients, toss, put the lid on and cook on High for 15 minutes. Release the pressure naturally for 10 minutes, divide the mix between plates and serve.

Nutrition: calories 249, fat 6.6, fiber 2.5, carbs 4.5, protein 37.3

Chicken and Artichokes

Preparation time: 10 minutes**Cooking time:** 25 minutes**Servings:** 4

Ingredients:

- 1 pound chicken breast, skinless, boneless and cubed
- 1 red onion, chopped
- 1 cup canned artichoke hearts, drained and quartered
- 1 tablespoon lime juice
- 1 teaspoon turmeric powder
- A pinch of salt and black pepper
- 1 cup chicken stock
- 2 tablespoons chives, chopped

Directions:

Set your instant pot on Sauté mode, add the oil, heat it up, add the onion, the meat and turmeric and brown for 10 minutes. Add the rest of the ingredients, toss, put the lid on and cook on High for 15 minutes. Release the pressure naturally for 10 minutes, divide the mix between plates and serve.

Nutrition: calories 288, fat 9.5, fiber 2.1, carbs 5.6, protein 38.6

Turkey with Broccoli Millet

Preparation time: 10 minutes**Cooking time:** 30 minutes**Servings:** 4
Ingredients:

- 1 pound turkey breast, skinless, boneless and cubed
- 1 cup broccoli florets
- 1 cup millet
- 2 cups chicken stock
- 1 red onion, chopped
- 1 teaspoon Italian seasoning
- A pinch of salt and black pepper
- 1 tablespoon cilantro, chopped

Directions:

In your instant pot, combine the meat with the broccoli, millet and the other ingredients, toss, put the lid on and cook on High for 30 minutes. Release the pressure naturally for 10 minutes, divide the mix between plates and serve.

Nutrition: calories 217, fat 10.1, fiber 1.8, carbs 5.9, protein 25.4

Turkey with Spinach

Preparation time: 10 minutes**Cooking time:** 25 minutes**Servings:** 4
Ingredients:

- 2 pounds turkey breasts, skinless, boneless and cubed
- 1 red onion, chopped
- 1 cup baby spinach
- 2 tablespoons balsamic vinegar
- 2 tablespoons avocado oil
- 1 cup chicken stock
- 2 tablespoons tomato puree
- ½ teaspoon rosemary, dried
- ½ teaspoon chili powder
- A pinch of salt and black pepper

Directions:

Set the instant pot on Sauté mode, add the oil, heat up, add the onion, the meat, rosemary and chili powder and cook for 10 minutes. Add the rest of the ingredients, toss, put the lid on and cook on High for 15 minutes. Release the pressure naturally for 10 minutes, divide everything between plates and serve.

Nutrition: calories 392, fat 11.6, fiber 0.3, carbs 1.1, protein 24.2

Duck and Zucchini
Preparation time: 10 minutes**Cooking time:** 25 minutes**Servings:** 4

Ingredients:
- 1 pound duck breast, skinless, boneless and cubed
- 1 tablespoon avocado oil
- 1 red onion, chopped
- A pinch of salt and black pepper
- 2 zucchinis, roughly cubed
- 3 garlic cloves, minced
- 1 tablespoon balsamic vinegar
- ½ teaspoon sweet paprika
- 1 tablespoon chives, chopped

Directions:
Set the instant pot on Sauté mode, add the oil, heat it up, add the onion, garlic, the meat and paprika and brown for 10 minutes. Add the rest of the ingredients, put the lid on and cook on High for 15 minutes. Release the pressure naturally for 10 minutes, divide the mix between plates and serve.

Nutrition: calories 249, fat 9.7, fiber 1.9, carbs 5.3, protein 34.3

Ginger Chicken Mix
Preparation time: 10 minutes**Cooking time:** 25 minutes**Servings:** 4

Ingredients:
- 2 pounds chicken breasts, skinless, boneless and cubed
- 1 red onion, chopped
- 2 tablespoons olive oil
- 1 tablespoon balsamic vinegar
- 1 tablespoon ginger, grated
- A pinch of salt and black pepper
- 1 cup chicken stock
- 1 tablespoon cilantro, chopped

Directions:
Set the instant pot on Sauté mode, add the oil, heat it up, add the onion, ginger and the meat and brown for 10 minutes. Add the rest of the ingredients, put the lid on and cook on High for 15 minutes. Release the pressure naturally for 10 minutes, divide the mix between plates and serve.

Nutrition: calories 269, fat 12.6, fiber 1.7, carbs 4.4, protein 33.9

Thyme Turkey

Preparation time: 10 minutes**Cooking time:** 25 minutes**Servings:** 4

Ingredients:
- 2 pounds turkey breasts, skinless, boneless and cubed
- 1 yellow onion, chopped
- 2 tablespoons olive oil
- ½ teaspoon rosemary, dried
- ½ teaspoon sweet paprika
- 1 cup tomato passata
- A pinch of salt and black pepper
- 1 tablespoon thyme, chopped

Directions:
Set the instant pot on Sauté mode, add the oil, heat up, add the onion, rosemary, paprika and the meat and cook for 10 minutes. Add the rest of the ingredients, toss, put the lid on and cook on High for 15 minutes. Release the pressure fast for 5 minutes, divide the mix between plates and serve.

Nutrition: calories 241, fat 8.6, fiber 1.5, carbs 5.6, protein 34.1

Duck and Swiss Chard

Preparation time: 10 minutes**Cooking time:** 25 minutes**Servings:** 4

Ingredients:
- 2 duck breasts, boneless and skin scored
- 1 cup Swiss chard, torn
- 2 scallions, chopped
- 2 garlic cloves, minced
- Juice of 1 lime
- 1 tablespoon avocado oil
- 1 cup tomato passata
- 1 tablespoon chives, chopped

Directions:
Set the instant pot on Sauté mode, add the oil, heat it up, add the duck breasts skin side down and cook for 5 minutes. Add the chard and the rest of the ingredients, put the lid on and cook on High for 20 minutes. Release the pressure naturally for 10 minutes, divide the mix between plates and serve.

Nutrition: calories 260, fat 7.7, fiber 3.4, carbs 4.5, protein 34.5

Turkey and Chervil Sauce

Preparation time: 10 minutes**Cooking time:** 25 minutes**Servings:** 4

Ingredients:
- 2 pounds turkey breasts, skinless, boneless and sliced
- 2 tablespoons olive oil
- 1 cup chicken stock
- 1 red onion, chopped
- 1 tablespoon balsamic vinegar
- A pinch of salt and black pepper
- 1 tablespoon chervil, chopped

Directions:

Set your instant pot on Sauté mode, add the onion and the meat and brown for 10 minutes. Add the stock and the rest of the ingredients, put the lid on and cook on High for 15 minutes. Release the pressure naturally for 10 minutes, divide the mix between plates and serve.

Nutrition: calories 277, fat 15, fiber 0.3, carbs 0.9, protein 33.2

Turkey and Avocado Dill Sauce

Preparation time: 10 minutes**Cooking time:** 25 minutes**Servings:** 4

Ingredients:
- 2 pounds turkey breast, skinless, boneless and cubed
- 1 tablespoon olive oil
- 1 avocado, peeled, pitted and cubed
- 1 tablespoon lemon juice
- 1 tablespoon dill, chopped
- 1 cup chicken stock
- 1 tablespoon smoked paprika
- A pinch of salt and black pepper

Directions:

In a blender, combine the avocado with the oil, lemon juice and the other ingredients except the turkey and pulse well. Set the instant pot on Sauté mode, add the avocado sauce, heat it up, add the meat, toss, put the lid on and cook on High for 25 minutes. Release the pressure naturally for 10 minutes, divide the mix between plates and serve.

Nutrition: calories 230, fat 9.2, fiber 0.8, carbs 1.6, protein 33.8

Mediterranean Diet Instant Pot Meat Recipes

Lamb and Onions

Preparation time: 10 minutes**Cooking time:** 40 minutes**Servings:** 4

Ingredients:
- 2 pound lamb chops
- 2 tablespoons avocado oil
- 1 cup veggie stock
- ½ teaspoon turmeric powder
- ½ teaspoon rosemary, dried
- 1 yellow onion, sliced
- 1 red onion, sliced
- Salt and black pepper to the taste
- 2 tablespoons chives, chopped

Directions:

Set the instant pot on Sauté mode, add the oil, heat up, add the onions, turmeric and rosemary and sauté for 10 minutes. Add the lamb chops and brown for 5 minutes. Add the rest of the ingredients, toss, put the lid on and cook on High for 25 minutes. Release the pressure naturally for 10 minutes, divide everything between plates and serve.

Nutrition: calories 254, fat 12, fiber 2, carbs 6, protein 16

Thyme Lamb Mix

Preparation time: 10 minutes**Cooking time:** 40 minutes**Servings:** 4

Ingredients:
- 2 pounds lamb stew meat, roughly cubed
- 2 tablespoons avocado oil
- 1 tablespoon lime juice
- 1 tablespoon thyme, chopped
- 1 cup scallions, chopped
- ½ cup veggie stock
- 2 garlic cloves, minced
- ½ teaspoon chili powder
- A pinch of salt and black pepper

Directions:

Set the instant pot on Sauté mode, add the oil, heat up, add the scallions, garlic and the meat and brown for 10 minutes. Add the other ingredients, toss, put the lid on and cook on High for 30 minutes. Release the pressure naturally for 10 minutes, divide everything between plates and serve.

Nutrition: calories 243, fat 15, fiber 3, carbs 6, protein 20

Coconut Beef

Preparation time: 10 minutes**Cooking time:** 40 minutes**Servings:** 4

Ingredients:

- 2 pounds beef stew meat, cubed
- 2 tablespoons avocado oil
- 1 cup coconut cream
- 1 red onion, chopped
- 1 teaspoon chili powder
- ½ teaspoon garam masala
- ½ teaspoon rosemary, dried
- 2 garlic cloves, minced
- 1 tablespoon parsley, chopped
- A pinch of salt and black pepper

Directions:

Set your instant pot on Sauté mode, add the oil, heat it up, add the onion, chili powder, masala, rosemary and the meat and brown for 10 minutes. Add the rest of the ingredients, put the lid on and cook on High for 30 minutes. Release the pressure naturally for 10 minutes, divide everything between plates and serve.

Nutrition: calories 263, fat 14, fiber 3, carbs 6, protein 16

Italian Beef and Artichokes

Preparation time: 10 minutes**Cooking time:** 35 minutes**Servings:** 4

Ingredients:

- 2 pounds beef stew meat, cubed
- 1 cup canned artichoke hearts, drained and quartered
- 1 red onion, chopped
- 1 teaspoon Italian seasoning
- ½ teaspoon turmeric powder
- 2 tablespoons avocado oil
- 2 garlic cloves, minced
- 1 cup tomato passata
- A pinch of salt and black pepper

Directions:

Set your instant pot on Sauté mode, add oil, heat it up, add the onion, seasoning, turmeric, garlic and the meat and brown for 10 minutes. Add the rest of the ingredients, put the lid on and cook on High for 25 minutes. Release the pressure naturally for 10 minutes, divide the mix between plates and serve.

Nutrition: calories 264, fat 14, fiber 4, carbs 7, protein 15

Lamb and Tomatoes

Preparation time: 10 minutes**Cooking time:** 40 minutes**Servings:** 4

Ingredients:

- 2 pounds lamb meat, roughly cubed
- 1 cup cherry tomatoes, halved
- 2 scallions, chopped
- 2 tablespoons avocado oil
- 2 garlic cloves, minced
- 1 tablespoon chives, chopped
- 1 teaspoon cumin, ground
- A pinch of salt and black pepper
- 1 cup beef stock

Directions:

Set your instant pot on Sauté mode, add the oil, heat it up, add the scallions, garlic, cumin and the meat and brown for 10 minutes. Add the rest of the ingredients, put the lid on and cook on High for 30 minutes. Release the pressure naturally for 10 minutes, divide the mix between plates and serve.

Nutrition: calories 263, fat 12, fiber 4, carbs 6, protein 16

Basil Beef

Preparation time: 10 minutes**Cooking time:** 40 minutes**Servings:** 4

Ingredients:

- 2 pounds beef stew meat, cubed
- 1 tablespoon avocado oil
- 1 red onion, chopped
- 1 tablespoon basil, chopped
- 1 tablespoon lime juice
- 1 cup beef stock
- A pinch of salt and black pepper
- ½ teaspoon chili powder
- 2 garlic cloves, minced

Directions:

Set your instant pot on Sauté mode, add the oil, heat it up, add the onion, the meat, garlic and chili powder and brown for 10 minutes. Add the rest of the ingredients, put the lid on and cook on High for 30 minutes. Release the pressure naturally for 10 minutes, divide the mix between plates and serve right away.

Nutrition: calories 263, fat 14, fiber 4, carbs 6, protein 18

Cumin Beef and Green Beans

Preparation time: 10 minutes**Cooking time:** 40 minutes**Servings:** 4

Ingredients:
- 2 pounds beef roast, cubed
- 1 cup green beans, trimmed and halved
- 1 tablespoon shallots, chopped
- 1 tablespoon lime juice
- 1 tablespoon avocado oil
- ½ teaspoon cumin, ground
- ½ teaspoon rosemary, dried
- A pinch of salt and black pepper
- 1 cup beef stock
- 1 tablespoon parsley, chopped

Directions:
Set the instant pot on Sauté mode, add the oil, heat it up, add the shallots, cumin, rosemary and the meat and brown for 10 minutes. Add the rest of the ingredients, put the lid on and cook on High for 30 minutes. Release the pressure naturally for 10 minutes, divide the mix between plates and serve.

Nutrition: calories 264, fat 14, fiber 4, carbs 6, protein 17

Garlic Lamb

Preparation time: 10 minutes**Cooking time:** 40 minutes**Servings:** 4

Ingredients:
- 2 tablespoons olive oil
- 2 pounds lamb stew meat, cubed
- 1 red onion, chopped
- 2 tablespoons garlic, minced
- 1 cup beef stock
- 1 tablespoon parsley, chopped
- A pinch of salt and black pepper

Directions:
Set the instant pot on Sauté mode, add the oil, heat it up, add the onion, garlic and the meat and brown for 10 minutes. Add the rest of the ingredients, put the lid on and cook on High for 30 minutes. Release the pressure naturally for 10 minutes, divide the mix between plates and serve.

Nutrition: calories 263, fat 14, fiber 3, carbs 7, protein 20

Beef and Tomato Sauce

Preparation time: 10 minutes**Cooking time:** 40 minutes**Servings:** 4

Ingredients:

- 1 tablespoon avocado oil
- 2 pounds beef stew meat, cubed
- 1 red onion, sliced
- ½ teaspoon red pepper flakes, crushed
- A pinch of salt and black pepper
- 1 cup tomato passata
- 2 garlic cloves, minced
- A pinch of salt and black pepper
- ¼ tablespoon chives, chopped

Directions:

Set your instant pot on Sauté mode, add the oil, heat it up, add the onion, pepper flakes, garlic and the meat and brown for 10 minutes. Add the rest of the ingredients, put the lid on and cook on High for 30 minutes. Release the pressure naturally for 10 minutes, divide the mix between plates and serve.

Nutrition: calories 263, fat 14, fiber 5, carbs 7, protein 15

Mint Lamb and Carrots

Preparation time: 10 minutes**Cooking time:** 40 minutes**Servings:** 4

Ingredients:

- 2 pounds lamb stew meat, roughly cubed
- 1 tablespoon avocado oil
- 1 tablespoon mint, chopped
- 1 tablespoon balsamic vinegar
- 2 cups baby carrots, peeled
- 1 red onion, chopped
- 1 cup beef stock
- ½ teaspoon chili powder
- A pinch of salt and black pepper

Directions:

Set your instant pot on Sauté mode, add the oil, heat it up, add the onion, chili powder and the meat and brown for 10 minutes. Add the rest of the ingredients, toss, put the lid on and cook on High for 30 minutes. Release the pressure naturally for 10 minutes, divide everything between plates and serve.

Nutrition: calories 253, fat 14, fiber 3, carbs 7, protein 17

Lamb and Eggplant Mix

Preparation time: 10 minutes**Cooking time:** 40 minutes**Servings:** 4

Ingredients:

- 2 tablespoons olive oil
- 1 pound lamb stew meat, cubed
- 2 eggplants, cubed
- 1 tablespoon oregano, chopped
- 1 cup beef stock
- ½ teaspoon sweet paprika
- 1 red onion, chopped
- ½ teaspoon rosemary, dried
- A pinch of salt and black pepper
- 2 tablespoons chives, chopped

Directions:

Set your instant pot on Sauté mode, add the oil, heat it up, add the onion, rosemary, paprika and the meat and brown for 10 minutes. Add the rest of the ingredients, toss, put the lid on and cook on High for 30 minutes. Release the pressure naturally for 10 minutes, divide the mix between plates and serve.

Nutrition: calories 276, fat 14, fiber 3, carbs 7, protein 20

Lamb and Asparagus

Preparation time: 10 minutes**Cooking time:** 35 minutes**Servings:** 4

Ingredients:

- 2 pounds lamb chops
- 2 tablespoons avocado oil
- 8 asparagus spears, trimmed and halved
- 1 red onion, chopped
- 1 cup beef stock
- ½ teaspoon mint, dried
- 2 teaspoons sweet paprika
- 1 tablespoon chives, chopped

Directions:

Set your instant pot on Sauté mode, add the oil, heat it up, add the onion, mint, paprika and the meat and brown for 10 minutes. Add the stock, toss, toss, put the lid on and cook on High for 20 minutes. Release the pressure naturally for 10 minutes, set the pot on Sauté mode again, add the asparagus and chives, toss, cook for 5 minutes more, divide the mix between plates and serve.

Nutrition: calories 287, fat 16, fiber 4, carbs 6, protein 20

Lamb and Mushrooms

Preparation time: 10 minutes**Cooking time:** 30 minutes**Servings:** 4

Ingredients:

- 2 pounds lamb stew meat, cubed
- 1 red onion, chopped
- 1 cup white mushrooms, halved
- 1 tablespoon lemon juice
- 1 tablespoon lemon zest, grated
- 2 tablespoon olive oil
- 3 garlic cloves, chopped
- ½ teaspoon coriander, ground
- A pinch of salt and black pepper
- 1 cup beef stock
- 1 tablespoon cilantro, chopped

Directions:

Set the instant pot on Sauté mode, add the oil, heat it up, add the onion, garlic, coriander and the mushrooms and sauté for 5 minutes. Add the meat and cook for another 5 minutes. Add the rest of the ingredients, toss, put the lid on and cook on High for 20 minutes more. Release the pressure naturally for 10 minutes, divide the mix between plates and serve.

Nutrition: calories 264, fat 8, fiber 3, carbs 6, protein 17

Pork and Olives

Preparation time: 10 minutes**Cooking time:** 30 minutes**Servings:** 4

Ingredients:

- 2 pounds pork stew meat, cubed
- 2 tablespoons olive oil
- 3 garlic cloves, minced
- 1 cup kalamata olives, pitted and halved
- 3 scallions, chopped
- 1 teaspoon sweet paprika
- 1 cup beef stock
- A pinch of salt and black pepper
- 1 tablespoon chives, chopped

Directions:

Set your instant pot on Sauté mode, add the oil, heat it up, add the scallions, garlic, paprika and the meat and brown for 10 minutes. Add the rest of the ingredients, put the lid on and cook on High for 20 minutes. Release the pressure naturally for 10 minutes, divide between plates and serve.

Nutrition: calories 275, fat 13, fiber 4, carbs 7, protein 20

Spiced Lamb

Preparation time: 10 minutes**Cooking time:** 30 minutes**Servings:** 4

Ingredients:

- 1 pound lamb stew meat , roughly cubed
- ½ teaspoon allspice, ground
- ½ teaspoon nutmeg, ground
- ½ teaspoon sweet paprika
- ½ teaspoon rosemary, dried
- 2 tablespoons olive oil
- 1 yellow onion, chopped
- ½ teaspoon chili powder
- 4 garlic cloves, minced
- 1 cup beef stock
- A pinch of salt and black pepper

Directions:

Set your instant pot on Sauté mode, add the oil, heat it up, add the onion, the garlic and the meat and brown for 5 minutes. Add the allspice, nutmeg and the remaining ingredients, toss, put the lid on and cook on High for 25 minutes. Release the pressure naturally for 10 minutes, divide the mix between plates and serve with a side salad.

Nutrition: calories 263, fat 12, fiber 4, carbs 7, protein 12

Beef and Endives

Preparation time: 10 minutes**Cooking time:** 40 minutes**Servings:** 4

Ingredients:

- 2 pounds beef stew meat, roughly cubed
- 2 endives, shredded
- 1 tablespoon lemon juice
- 2 tablespoons avocado oil
- 1 yellow onion, chopped
- 4 garlic cloves, minced
- 1 cup tomato passata
- A pinch of salt and black pepper
- 1 tablespoon chives, chopped

Directions:

Set your instant pot on Sauté mode, add the oil, heat it up, add the onion, garlic and the meat and brown for 10 minutes. Add the rest of the ingredients, put the lid on and cook on High for 30 minutes. Release the pressure naturally for 10 minutes, divide the mix between plates and serve.

Nutrition: calories 263, fat 12, fiber 3, carbs 7, protein 10

Creamy Coconut Lamb

Preparation time: 10 minutes**Cooking time:** 40 minutes**Servings:** 4

Ingredients:

- 2 pounds lamb shoulder, cubed
- 2 tablespoons avocado oil
- 1 cup coconut cream
- 1 tablespoon yellow curry paste
- 1 teaspoon turmeric powder
- 1 yellow onion, chopped
- A pinch of salt and black pepper
- 1 tablespoon chives, chopped

Directions:

Set your instant pot on Sauté mode, add the oil, heat it up, add the onion, turmeric, curry paste and the meat and brown for 10 minutes. Add the rest of the ingredients, put the lid on and cook on High for 30 minutes. Release the pressure naturally for 10 minutes, divide the mix into bowls and serve.

Nutrition: calories 233, fat 7, fiber 2, carbs 6, protein 12

Lamb with Capers

Preparation time: 10 minutes**Cooking time:** 30 minutes**Servings:** 4

Ingredients:

- 2 pounds lamb chops
- 3 scallions, chopped
- 2 tablespoons avocado oil
- 1 teaspoon cumin, ground
- 1 tablespoon capers, drained
- 1 teaspoon sweet paprika
- ½ cup beef stock
- A pinch of salt and black pepper
- 2 tablespoons parsley, chopped

Directions:

Set your instant pot on Sauté mode, add the oil, heat it up, add the scallions, cumin, paprika and the meat and brown for 10 minutes. Add the rest of the ingredients, put the lid on and cook on High for 20 minutes. Release the pressure naturally for 10 minutes, divide the mix between plates and serve.

Nutrition: calories 235, fat 12, fiber 5, carbs 7, protein 10

Paprika Lamb and Berries

Preparation time: 10 minutes**Cooking time:** 30 minutes**Servings:** 4

Ingredients:

- 2 pounds lamb shoulder, cubed
- 1 tablespoon lime juice
- ½ teaspoon sweet paprika
- 1 cup blueberries
- 2 tablespoons olive oil
- 1 teaspoon cumin, ground
- 1 cup beef stock
- A pinch of salt and black pepper

Directions:

Set the instant pot on Sauté mode, add the oil, heat it up, add the meat and brown for 10 minutes. Add the berries and the rest of the ingredients, toss, put the lid on and cook on High for 20 minutes. Release the pressure naturally for 10 minutes, divide the mix between plates and serve.

Nutrition: calories 211, fat 9, fiber 2, carbs 6, protein 12

Lamb and Savoy Cabbage

Preparation time: 10 minutes**Cooking time:** 30 minutes**Servings:** 4

Ingredients:

- 2 pounds lamb shoulder, cubed
- 1 cup Savoy cabbage, shredded
- 1 cup beef stock
- 1 red onion, chopped
- 2 tablespoons olive oil
- ½ teaspoon curry powder
- 1 teaspoon sweet paprika
- ½ teaspoon garam masala
- 2 tablespoons tomato paste
- A pinch of salt and black pepper
- 1 tablespoon cilantro, chopped

Directions:

Set your instant pot on Sauté mode, add the oil, heat it up, add the onion, curry powder, paprika, garam masala and the meat and brown for 10 minutes. Add the rest of the ingredients, put the lid on and cook on High for 20 minutes. Release the pressure naturally for 10 minutes, divide everything between plates and serve.

Nutrition: calories 254, fat 12, fiber 3, carbs 6, protein 16

Beef and Chickpeas

Preparation time: 10 minutes**Cooking time:** 30 minutes**Servings:** 4
Ingredients:

- 2 pounds beef stew meat, cubed
- 1 cup canned chickpeas, drained and rinsed
- 2 tablespoons olive oil
- 1 yellow onion, chopped
- ½ teaspoon rosemary, dried
- ½ teaspoon cumin , ground
- ¼ cup tomato sauce
- A pinch of salt and black pepper
- 1 tablespoon cilantro, chopped

Directions:

Set the instant pot on Sauté mode, add the oil, heat it up, add the onion, rosemary, cumin and the meat and brown for 10 minutes. Add the rest of the ingredients, toss, put the lid on and cook on High for 20 minutes. Release the pressure naturally for 10 minutes, divide the mix between plates and serve.

Nutrition: calories 232, fat 10, fiber 5, carbs 7, protein 11

Chives Lamb Mix

Preparation time: 10 minutes**Cooking time:** 30 minutes**Servings:** 4
Ingredients:

- 2 pounds lamb stew meat, cubed
- 2 tablespoons avocado oil
- 2 tablespoons chives, chopped
- 1 yellow onion, chopped
- 1 tablespoon balsamic vinegar
- ½ teaspoon chili powder
- A pinch of salt and black pepper
- 1 cup beef stock

Directions:

Set the instant pot on Sauté mode, add the oil, heat it up, add the onion, chili powder and the meat and brown fro 10 minutes. Add the rest of the ingredients, toss, put the lid on and cook on High for 20 minutes. Release the pressure naturally for 10 minutes, divide the mix into bowls and serve.

Nutrition: calories 243, fat 11, fiber 4, carbs 6, protein 10

Beef and Tomatoes

Preparation time: 10 minutes**Cooking time:** 30 minutes**Servings:** 4
Ingredients:

- 2 pounds beef stew meat, cubed
- 2 tablespoons avocado oil
- 1 cup cherry tomatoes, halved
- 1 yellow onion, chopped
- ¼ cup tomato passata
- 3 garlic cloves, minced
- A pinch of salt and black pepper
- 1 tablespoon parsley, chopped

Directions:

Set your instant pot on Sauté mode, add the oil, heat it up, add the onion, garlic and the meat and brown for 10 minutes. Add the passata and the rest of the ingredients, put the lid on and cook on High for 20 minutes. Release the pressure naturally for 10 minutes, divide the mix between plates and serve.

Nutrition: calories 232, fat 12, fiber 4, carbs 6, protein 9

Lamb and Rosemary Sweet Potatoes

Preparation time: 10 minutes**Cooking time:** 40 minutes**Servings:** 4
Ingredients:

- 2 pounds lamb stew meat, roughly cubed
- 2 sweet potatoes, peeled and cut into wedges
- 2 tablespoons avocado oil
- 1 red onion, chopped
- 1 cup tomato passata
- 1 tablespoon garlic, minced
- A pinch of salt and black pepper
- 2 tablespoons cilantro, chopped

Directions:

Set your instant pot on Sauté mode, add the oil, heat it up, add the onion, garlic and the meat and brown for 10 minutes. Add the sweet potatoes and the rest of the ingredients, put the lid on and cook on High for 30 minutes. Release the pressure naturally for 10 minutes, divide the mix between plates and serve.

Nutrition: calories 274, fat 9, fiber 5, carbs 6, protein 12

Lamb and Peas

Preparation time: 10 minutes**Cooking time:** 30 minutes**Servings:** 4
Ingredients:

- 4 lamb chops
- 1 cup fresh peas
- 1 tablespoon lime juice
- 2 scallions, chopped
- 1 cup tomato passata
- 2 tablespoons avocado oil
- A pinch of salt and black pepper
- 1 teaspoon chili powder
- 1 tablespoon dill, chopped

Directions:

Set your instant pot on Sauté mode, add the oil, heat it up, add the scallions, chili powder and lamb chops and brown for 10 minutes. Add the peas and the rest of the ingredients, put the lid on and cook on High for 20 minutes. Release the pressure naturally for 10 minutes, divide everything between plates and serve.

Nutrition: calories 232, fat 9, fiber 3, carbs 6, protein 10

Balsamic Beef

Preparation time: 10 minutes**Cooking time:** 30 minutes**Servings:** 4
Ingredients:

- 2 pounds beef roast, sliced
- 2 tablespoons balsamic vinegar
- 2 tablespoons olive oil
- 1 red onion, sliced
- ½ teaspoon chili powder
- ½ teaspoon Italian seasoning
- A pinch of salt and black pepper
- 1 tablespoon rosemary, chopped
- ½ cup beef stock

Directions:

Set your instant pot on Sauté mode, add the oil, heat it up, add the onion, the meat and the seasoning, toss and brown for 10 minutes. Add the vinegar and the rest of the ingredients, put the lid on and cook on High for 20 minutes. Release the pressure naturally for 10 minutes, divide between plates and serve with a side salad.

Nutrition: calories 200, fat 11, fiber 3, carbs 6, protein 15

Lemon Beef

Preparation time: 10 minutes**Cooking time:** 35 minutes**Servings:** 4

Ingredients:

- 2 pounds beef stew meat, cubed
- Juice of ½ lemon
- Zest of 1 lemon, grated
- 2 tablespoons olive oil
- 1 red onion, chopped
- ½ cup beef stock
- A pinch of salt and black pepper
- 1 tablespoon rosemary, chopped

Directions:

Set your instant pot on Sauté mode, add the oil, heat it up, add the onion, lemon juice, zest and rosemary and cook for 5 minutes. Add the beef and the rest of the ingredients, put the lid on and cook on High for 30 minutes. Release the pressure naturally for 10 minutes, divide everything between plates and serve.

Nutrition: calories 210, fat 5, fiber 3, carbs 8, protein 12

Parsley Pork and Fennel

Preparation time: 10 minutes**Cooking time:** 30 minutes**Servings:** 4

Ingredients:

- 2 pounds pork stew meat, roughly cubed
- 2 tablespoons avocado oil
- 2 scallions, chopped
- ½ teaspoon oregano, dried
- 2 fennel bulbs, sliced
- Juice of 1 lime
- ½ teaspoon cumin, ground
- ½ teaspoon coriander, ground
- 2 teaspoons chili powder
- 1 cup beef stock
- Salt and black pepper to the taste

Directions:

Set the instant pot on Sauté mode, add the oil, heat it up, add the scallions, oregano, chili powder and the meat and brown for 10 minutes. Add the lime juice and the remaining ingredients, toss, put the lid on and cook on High for 20 minutes. Release the pressure naturally for 10 minutes, divide the mix between plates and serve right away.

Nutrition: calories 248, fat 11, fiber 3, carbs 6, protein 15

Pork Chops and Sprouts

Preparation time: 10 minutes**Cooking time:** 30 minutes**Servings:** 4

Ingredients:
- 2 pounds pork chops
- 2 tablespoons olive oil
- 1 cup Brussels sprouts, trimmed and halved
- 1 cup beef stock
- ½ teaspoon chili powder
- 4 teaspoons sweet paprika
- A pinch of salt and black pepper
- 1 tablespoon cilantro, chopped

Directions:
In the instant pot, combine the pork chops with the sprouts and the other ingredients, toss, put the lid on and cook on High for 30 minutes. Release the pressure naturally for 10 minutes, divide everything between plates and serve.

Nutrition: calories 233, fat 9, fiber 3, carbs 7, protein 14

Beef and Avocado Mix

Preparation time: 10 minutes**Cooking time:** 30 minutes**Servings:** 4

Ingredients:
- 2 pounds beef stew meat, roughly cubed
- 2 tablespoons avocado oil
- 1 cup avocado, peeled, pitted and cubed
- ½ cup tomato passata
- 1 tablespoon dill, chopped
- 2 scallions, chopped
- 1 teaspoon chili powder
- A pinch of salt and black pepper

Directions:
Set your instant pot on Sauté mode, add the oil, heat it up, add the scallions, chili powder and the meat and cook for 10 minutes. Add the rest of the ingredients, put the lid on and cook on High for 20 minutes. Release the pressure naturally for 10 minutes, divide the mix between plates and serve.

Nutrition: calories 227, fat 14, fiber 4, carbs 6, protein 16

Lamb and Corn

Preparation time: 10 minutes**Cooking time:** 30 minutes**Servings:** 4

Ingredients:

- 2 pounds lamb chops
- 2 cups corn
- 2 scallions, chopped
- 1 tablespoon lime juice
- 1 tablespoon olive oil
- ½ cup chives, chopped
- 1 cup beef stock
- 1 teaspoon sweet paprika
- 1 tablespoon chives, chopped

Directions:

Set your instant pot on Sauté mode, add the oil, heat it up, add the scallions, paprika and the meat and cook for 10 minutes. Add the corn and the rest of the ingredients, toss, put the lid on and cook on High for 20 minutes. Release the pressure naturally for 10 minutes, divide the mix between plates and serve.

Nutrition: calories 236, fat 12, fiber 2, carbs 7, protein 15

Masala Pork

Preparation time: 10 minutes**Cooking time:** 30 minutes**Servings:** 4

Ingredients:

- 1 pounds pork stew meat, roughly cubed
- 1 teaspoon garam masala
- ½ teaspoon turmeric powder
- 1 cup beef stock
- 2 tablespoons lemon zest, grated
- 2 tablespoons lemon juice
- 2 tablespoons olive oil
- A pinch of salt and black pepper

Directions:

Set the instant pot on Sauté mode, add the oil, heat it up, add the meat and brown for 5 minutes. Add the garam masala and the rest of the ingredients, put the lid on and cook on High for 25 minutes. Release the pressure naturally for 10 minutes, divide the mix between plates and serve.

Nutrition: 273, fat 12, fiber 4, carbs 7, protein 17

Lamb with Peppercorns

Preparation time: 10 minutes**Cooking time:** 40 minutes**Servings:** 4

Ingredients:

- 2 pounds lamb stew meat, roughly cubed
- 2 tablespoons olive oil
- 3 scallions, chopped
- 1 tablespoon peppercorns, crushed
- 1 cup beef stock
- 4 garlic cloves, minced
- A pinch of salt and black pepper
- 1 tablespoon rosemary, chopped

Directions:

Set your instant pot on sauté mode, add the oil, heat it up, add the scallions, peppercorns, garlic and the meat and brown for 10 minutes. Add the rest of the ingredients, put the lid on and cook on High for 30 minutes. Release the pressure naturally for 10 minutes, divide the mix between plates and serve.

Nutrition: calories 244, fat 12, fiber 2, carbs 5, protein 16

Ground Lamb and Veggies

Preparation time: 10 minutes**Cooking time:** 30 minutes**Servings:** 4

Ingredients:

- 2 pounds lamb stew meat, ground
- 1 zucchini, cubed
- 1 cup fresh peas
- 1 red onion, sliced
- 1 eggplant, cubed
- 2 tablespoons olive oil
- 1 carrot, peeled and sliced
- 1 parsnip, peeled and sliced
- 1 and ½ cups beef stock
- 1 tablespoon chives, chopped
- A pinch of salt and black pepper

Directions:

Set the instant pot on Sauté mode, add the oil, heat it up, add the onion and the meat and brown for 10 minutes. Add the peas, onion and the rest of the ingredients, toss, put the lid on and cook on High for 20 minutes. Release the pressure naturally for 10 minutes, divide the mix into bowls and serve.

Nutrition: calories 254, fat 14, fiber 3, carbs 6, protein 17

Lamb and Peppers

Preparation time: 10 minutes**Cooking time:** 30 minutes**Servings:** 4

Ingredients:

- 2 pounds lamb stew meat, cubed
- 1 red bell pepper, cut into strips
- 1 green bell pepper, cut into strips
- 1 yellow onion, chopped
- ½ teaspoon red pepper flakes, crushed
- 2 tablespoons olive oil
- A pinch of salt and black pepper
- 1 tablespoon smoked paprika
- 1 cup beef stock
- 1 tablespoon cilantro, chopped

Directions:

Set your instant pot on Sauté mode, add the oil, heat it up, add the onion, pepper flakes, paprika and the meat and brown for 10 minutes. Add the rest of the ingredients, toss, put the lid on and cook on High for 20 minutes. Release the pressure naturally for 10 minutes, divide the mix between plate sand serve.

Nutrition: calories 263, fat 14, fiber 3, carbs 6, protein 20

Beef, Zucchinis and Corn

Preparation time: 10 minutes**Cooking time:** 30 minutes**Servings:** 4

Ingredients:

- 2 pounds beef stew meat, cubed
- 2 zucchinis, cubed
- 1 cup corn
- 1 red onion, sliced
- 2 tablespoons avocado oil
- ½ cup tomato passata
- A pinch of salt and black pepper
- 1 teaspoon cayenne pepper
- 1 tablespoon cilantro, chopped

Directions:

Set the instant pot on Sauté mode, add the oil, heat it up, add the onion, cayenne and the meat and brown for 10 minutes. Add the rest of the ingredients, toss, put the lid on and cook on High for 20 minutes. Release the pressure naturally for 10 minutes, divide mix between plates and serve.

Nutrition: calories 283, fat 13, fiber 4, carbs 6, protein 16

Cinnamon Pork and Potatoes

Preparation time: 10 minutes**Cooking time:** 30 minutes**Servings:** 4

Ingredients:

- 2 pounds pork stew meat, roughly cubed
- 1 cup sweet potatoes, peeled and cubed
- 1 teaspoon cinnamon powder
- 1 red onion, chopped
- 2 tablespoons avocado oil
- 3 garlic cloves, minced
- 1 tablespoon oregano, chopped
- 1 and ½ cups beef stock
- 1 tablespoon chives, chopped

Directions:

Set your instant pot on Sauté mode, add the oil, heat it up, add the onion, garlic, the meat and cinnamon and brown for 10 minutes. Add the stock and the rest of the ingredients, put the lid on and cook on High for 20 minutes. Release the pressure naturally for 10 minutes, divide the mix between plates and serve.

Nutrition: calories 253, fat 14, fiber 2, carbs 6, protein 18

Lamb and Greens

Preparation time: 10 minutes**Cooking time:** 30 minutes**Servings:** 4

Ingredients:

- 2 pounds lamb shoulder, cubed
- 2 tablespoons garlic, minced
- 1 cup baby spinach
- 1 cup baby kale
- 1 tablespoon olive oil
- 1 yellow onion, chopped
- A pinch of salt and black pepper
- ¼ cup beef stock
- 1 tablespoon chives, chopped

Directions:

Set your instant pot on Sauté mode, add the oil, heat it up, add the onion, garlic and the meat and brown for 10 minutes. Add the spinach and the rest of the ingredients, toss, put the lid on and cook on High for 20 minutes. Release the pressure naturally for 10 minutes, divide everything between plates and serve.

Nutrition: calories 264, fat 14, fiber 3, carbs 6, protein 17

Coriander Beef

Preparation time: 10 minutes**Cooking time:** 30 minutes**Servings:** 4

Ingredients:
- 2 tablespoons avocado oil
- 2 pounds beef stew meat, roughly cubed
- 1 red onion, chopped
- 1 cup tomato passata
- A pinch of salt and black pepper
- ½ teaspoon cumin, ground
- 1 tablespoon coriander, chopped

Directions:
Set your instant pot on Sauté mode, add the oil, heat it up, add the onion, cumin and the meat and brown for 10 minutes. Add the rest of the ingredients, toss, put the lid on and cook on High for 20 minutes. Release the pressure naturally for 10 minutes, divide the mix into bowls and serve.

Nutrition: calories 273, fat 13, fiber 2, carbs 6, protein 15

Orange Beef Mix

Preparation time: 10 minutes**Cooking time:** 30 minutes **Servings:** 4

Ingredients:
- 2 pounds beef stew meat, cubed
- Juice of 2 oranges
- 4 scallions, chopped
- 2 tablespoons olive oil
- ½ cup beef stock
- ½ teaspoon turmeric powder
- A pinch of salt and black pepper
- 1 tablespoon ginger, grated
- 1 tablespoon chives, chopped

Directions:
Set the instant pot on Sauté mode, add the oil, heat it up, add the scallions, ginger and the meat and brown for 10 minutes Add the rest of the ingredients, toss, put the lid on and cook on High for 20 minutes. Release the pressure naturally for 10 minutes, divide the mix between plates and serve.

Nutrition: calories 274, fat 14, fiber 2, carbs 6, protein 16

Curry Pork

Preparation time: 10 minutes**Cooking time:** 35 minutes**Servings:** 4

Ingredients:
- 2 pounds pork shoulder, boneless and cubed
- 2 garlic cloves, minced
- 1 tablespoon green curry paste
- 4 scallions, chopped
- A pinch of salt and black pepper
- 1 cup beef stock
- 1 tablespoon cilantro, chopped

Directions:
In your instant pot, mix the pork shoulder with the curry paste and the other ingredients, toss, put the lid on and cook on High for 35 minutes. Release the pressure naturally for 10 minutes, divide the mix between plates and serve with a side salad.

Nutrition: calories 264, fat 14, fiber 2, carbs 8, protein 12

Hot Lamb

Preparation time: 10 minutes**Cooking time:** 30 minutes**Servings:** 4

Ingredients:
- 2 pounds lamb stew meat, roughly cubed
- 1 red chili pepper, minced
- 1 teaspoon hot paprika
- ½ teaspoon rosemary, dried
- ½ teaspoon turmeric powder
- 4 scallions, chopped
- A pinch of salt and black pepper
- 2 tablespoons hot sauce
- 1 cup beef stock

Directions:
In your instant pot, combine the lamb with the chili pepper, paprika and the other ingredients, toss, put the lid on and cook on High for 30 minutes. Release the pressure naturally for 10 minutes, divide the mix between plates and serve with a side salad.

Nutrition: calories 200, fat 9, fiber 2, carbs 6, protein 12

Lamb Roast

Preparation time: 10 minutes**Cooking time:** 40 minutes**Servings:** 4

Ingredients:
- 2 pounds lamb shoulder, sliced
- 1 tablespoon sweet paprika
- 1 tablespoon capers, drained
- 2 tablespoons olive oil
- A pinch of salt and black pepper
- 2 cups beef stock

Directions:

In your instant pot, combine the lamb shoulder with the oil, paprika and the other ingredients, put the lid on and cook on High for 40 minutes. Release the pressure naturally for 10 minutes, slice the lamb, divide roast between plates and serve with a side salad.

Nutrition: calories 234, fat 11, fiber 3, carbs 7, protein 15

Lamb and Artichokes

Preparation time: 10 minutes**Cooking time:** 30 minutes**Servings:** 4

Ingredients:
- 2 pounds lamb meat, cubed
- 1 cup canned artichoke hearts, drained and quartered
- 1 yellow onion, chopped
- ½ teaspoon turmeric powder
- ½ teaspoon chili powder
- ½ teaspoon coriander, ground
- 1 cup beef stock
- 2 tablespoons olive oil
- 1 tablespoon cilantro, chopped

Directions:

Set the instant pot on Sauté mode, add the oil, heat up, add the onion and the meat and brown for 10 minutes. Add the artichokes, turmeric and the other ingredients, toss, put the lid on and cook on High for 20 minutes. Release the pressure naturally for 10 minutes, divide the mix between plates and serve.

Nutrition: calories 273, fat 14, fiber 2, carbs 6, protein 15

Balsamic Chops and Apples

Preparation time: 10 minutes**Cooking time:** 30 minutes**Servings:** 4

Ingredients:
- 1 pound lamb chops
- 2 apples, cored and cut into wedges
- 1 tablespoon olive oil
- 4 garlic cloves, minced
- 1 tablespoon balsamic vinegar
- 1 cup beef stock
- A pinch of salt and black pepper
- 1 tablespoon chives, chopped

Directions:
In your instant pot, mix the lamb chops with the oil, garlic and the other ingredients, toss, put the lid on and cook on High for 30 minutes. Release the pressure naturally for 10 minutes, divide everything between plates and serve.

Nutrition: calories 292, fat 12, fiber 3, carbs 7, protein 16

Creamy Pork

Preparation time: 10 minutes**Cooking time:** 30 minutes**Servings:** 4

Ingredients:
- 2 pounds pork stew meat, cubed
- 1 cup coconut ream
- 2 tablespoons olive oil
- 3 scallions, chopped
- 1 tablespoon cilantro, chopped
- A pinch of salt and black pepper

Directions:
Set the instant pot on Sauté mode, add the oil, heat it up, add the scallions and the meat and brown for 10 minutes. Add the rest of the ingredients, put the lid on and cook on High for 20 minutes. Release the pressure naturally for 10 minutes, divide everything into bowls and serve.

Nutrition: calories 277, fat 14, fiber 3, carbs 7, protein 17

Walnut Beef Mix

Preparation time: 10 minutes**Cooking time:** 35 minutes**Servings:** 4

Ingredients:
- 2 pounds beef stew meat, cubed
- 2 tablespoons olive oil
- 2 tablespoons walnuts, chopped
- 1 cup beef stock
- ½ teaspoon rosemary, dried
- ½ teaspoon Italian seasoning
- 1 yellow onion, minced
- A pinch of salt and black pepper
- 1 tablespoon parsley, chopped

Directions:

Set the instant pot on Sauté mode, add the oil, heat up, add the onion and the meat and brown for 10 minutes. Add the walnuts and the other ingredients, toss, put the lid on and cook on High for 25 minutes. Release the pressure naturally for 10 minutes, divide everything between plates and serve.

Nutrition: calories 274, fat 12, fiber 4, carbs 7, protein 16

Lamb and Okra

Preparation time: 10 minutes**Cooking time:** 30 minutes**Servings:** 4

Ingredients:
- 2 pounds lamb stew meat, cubed
- 1 cup okra, halved
- 1 tablespoon olive oil
- 2 garlic cloves, minced
- 2 scallions, chopped
- A pinch of salt and black pepper
- 1 cup beef stock
- 1 tablespoon chives, chopped

Directions:

Set the instant pot on Sauté mode, add the oil, heat it up, add the scallions, garlic and the meat and brown for 10 minutes. Add the okra and the rest of the ingredients, put the lid on and cook on High for 20 minutes. Release the pressure naturally for 10 minutes, divide the mix between plates and serve.

Nutrition: calories 269, fat 12, fiber 3, carbs 5, protein 16

Lamb and Beets

Preparation time: 10 minutes**Cooking time:** 30 minutes**Servings:** 4

Ingredients:
- 2 pounds lamb stew meat, cubed
- 2 beets, peeled and cut into wedges
- 1 red onion, chopped
- 1 cup beef stock
- 2 tablespoons olive oil
- 2 garlic cloves, minced
- A pinch of salt and black pepper
- ½ teaspoon rosemary, dried
- ½ teaspoon chili powder
- ½ teaspoon sweet paprika
- 2 tablespoons cilantro, chopped

Directions:

Set the instant pot on Sauté mode, add the oil, heat it up, add the onion, garlic, rosemary, chili powder, paprika and the meat and brown fro 10 minutes. Add the rest of the ingredients, put the lid on and cook on High for 20 minutes. Release the pressure naturally for 10 minutes, divide everything between plates and serve.

Nutrition: calories 293, fat 14, fiber 4, carbs 6, protein 18

Lamb, Cauliflower and Tomatoes

Preparation time: 10 minutes**Cooking time:** 30 minutes**Servings:** 4

Ingredients:
- 1 red onion, chopped
- 2 tablespoons olive oil
- 2 pounds lamb stew meat, cubed
- 1 cup cauliflower florets
- 1 cup cherry tomatoes, halved
- 1 tablespoon chives, chopped
- 1 cup beef stock
- A pinch of salt and black pepper
- 1 cup tomato puree
- 1 tablespoon cilantro, chopped

Directions:

Set the instant pot on Sauté mode, add the oil, heat it up, add the onion and the meat and brown for 10 minutes. Add the cauliflower and the rest of the ingredients, put the lid on and cook on High for 20 minutes. Release the pressure naturally for 10 minutes, divide the mix between plates and serve.

Nutrition: calories 263, fat 12, fiber 3, carbs 6, protein 13

Pork and Radish Mix

Preparation time: 10 minutes**Cooking time:** 30 minutes**Servings:** 4
Ingredients:

- 2 pounds pork shoulder, cubed
- 1 cup radishes, halved
- 2 tablespoons olive oil
- 1 yellow onion, chopped
- ½ teaspoon cumin, ground
- ½ teaspoon rosemary, dried
- ½ cup beef stock
- ½ cup tomato passata
- 2 garlic cloves, minced
- 2 tablespoons parsley, chopped
- Salt and black pepper to the taste

Directions:

Set the instant pot on Sauté mode, add the oil, heat up, add the onion, cumin, rosemary and the meat and brown for 10 minutes. Add the radishes and the other ingredients, toss, put the lid on and cook on High for 20 minutes. Release the pressure naturally for 10 minutes, divide everything between plates and serve.

Nutrition: calories 454, fat 26.5, fiber 0.3, carbs 1.1, protein 35.6

Nutmeg Lamb Mix

Preparation time: 10 minutes**Cooking time:** 40 minutes**Servings:** 6
Ingredients:

- 2 pounds lamb shoulder, cubed
- 1 teaspoon nutmeg, ground
- 1 red onion, sliced
- 1 tablespoon lime juice
- ½ teaspoon chili powder
- 1 tablespoon olive oil
- 1 cup beef stock
- 1 tablespoon rosemary, chopped
- 2 garlic cloves, minced
- A pinch of salt and black pepper
- 1 tablespoon chives, chopped

Directions:

Set the instant pot on Sauté mode, add the oil, heat it up, add the onion, nutmeg, chili powder, garlic and the meat and cook for 10 minutes. Add the lime juice and the remaining ingredients, toss, put the lid on and cook on High for 30 minutes. Release the pressure naturally for 10 minutes, divide the mix between plates and serve.

Nutrition: calories 352, fat 26.5, fiber 0.3, carbs 0.7, protein 26.5

Sage Pork Mix

Preparation time: 10 minutes**Cooking time:** 30 minutes**Servings:** 6

Ingredients:

- 2 pounds pork shoulder, cubed
- 2 tablespoons olive oil
- 1 red onion, sliced
- ½ teaspoon cumin, ground
- 1 teaspoon chili powder
- 2 tablespoons sage, chopped
- 2 garlic cloves, minced
- 1 cup beef stock
- A pinch of salt and black pepper

Directions:

Set your instant pot on Sauté mode, add the oil, heat it up, add the onion, cumin, chili, garlic and the meat and cook for 10 minutes. Add the stock and the rest of the ingredients, put the lid on and cook on High for 20 minutes. Release the pressure naturally for 10 minutes, divide everything between plates and serve right away.

Nutrition: calories 373, fat 25, fiber 1.6, carbs 6.9, protein 28.8

Pork and Cilantro Sauce

Preparation time: 10 minutes**Cooking time:** 30 minutes**Servings:** 4

Ingredients:

- 2 pound pork stew meat, cubed
- 2 tablespoons avocado oil
- 1 tablespoon walnuts, chopped
- 2 tablespoons cilantro, chopped
- 1 cup beef stock
- 1 tablespoon lime juice
- 1 tablespoon lime zest, grated
- 2 garlic cloves, minced
- A pinch of salt and black pepper

Directions:

Set your instant pot on Sauté mode, add half of the oil, heat it up, add the meat and cook for 10 minutes. Meanwhile, in a blender, combine the rest of the oil with the walnuts, cilantro and the other ingredients and pulse well. Add this over the meat, toss, put the lid on and cook on High for 20 minutes. Release the pressure naturally for 10 minutes, divide the mix between plates and serve.

Nutrition: calories 285, fat 14.6, fiber 0.6, carbs 3.1, protein 33.9

Pork with Kale and Chard

Preparation time: 10 minutes**Cooking time:** 30 minutes**Servings:** 4

Ingredients:
- 2 pounds pork stew meat, cubed
- 1 tablespoon olive oil
- 1 cup baby kale
- 1 cup Swiss chard, torn
- 2 scallions, chopped
- ½ teaspoon chili powder
- 2 garlic cloves, minced
- A pinch of salt and black pepper
- 1 cup beef stock
- 1 tablespoon hives, chopped

Directions:

Set your instant pot on Sauté mode, add the oil, heat up, add the scallions, garlic and the meat and brown for 10 minutes. Add the rest of the ingredients, put the lid on and cook on High for 20 minutes. Release the pressure naturally for 10 minutes, divide the mix between plates and serve.

Nutrition: calories 353, fat 17.4, fiber 0.4, carbs 1.2, protein 34.2

Pork with Spinach

Preparation time: 10 minutes**Cooking time:** 30 minutes**Servings:** 4

Ingredients:
- 2 pounds pork shoulder, cubed
- 1 yellow onion, chopped
- ½ pound baby spinach
- 1 cup beef stock
- ½ teaspoon sweet paprika
- ½ teaspoon coriander, ground
- 2 tablespoons olive oil
- A pinch of salt and black pepper
- 1 tablespoon chives, chopped

Directions:

Set your instant pot on Sauté mode, add the oil, heat it up, add the onion, the meat, paprika and coriander, stir and cook for 10 minutes. Add the stock and the rest of the ingredients, put the lid on and cook on High for 20 minutes. Release the pressure naturally for 10 minutes, divide the mix between plates and serve.

Nutrition: calories 384, fat 26.5, fiber 1.8, carbs 5, protein 28.4

Ground Beef with Radishes and Kale

Preparation time: 10 minutes**Cooking time:** 30 minutes**Servings:** 4

Ingredients:

- 2 pounds pork shoulder, ground
- 1 cup radishes, halved
- 1 cup baby kale
- 1 yellow onion, chopped
- 1 tablespoon avocado oil
- A pinch of salt and black pepper
- 1 cup beef stock
- ½ teaspoon smoked paprika
- 2 garlic cloves, minced
- 1 tablespoons chives, chopped

Directions:

Set the instant pot on Sauté mode, add the oil, heat it up, add the onion, garlic, paprika and the meat and cook for 5 minutes. Add the radishes, kale and the rest of the ingredients, put the lid on and cook on High for 25 minutes. Release the pressure naturally for 10 minutes, divide the mix into bowls and serve.

Nutrition: calories 367, fat 24.5, fiber 1.3, carbs 6.8, protein 28.2

Lemon Pork with Green Beans

Preparation time: 10 minutes**Cooking time:** 30 minutes**Servings:** 4

Ingredients:

- 2 tablespoons olive oil
- 2 pounds pork stew meat, cubed
- 1 cup green beans, trimmed and halved
- 1 cup tomato passata
- 2 tablespoons lemon juice
- ½ teaspoon Italian seasoning
- ½ teaspoon oregano, dried
- 2 tablespoons basil, chopped
- A pinch of salt and black pepper

Directions:

Set the instant pot on Sauté mode, add the oil, heat up, add the meat, seasoning and oregano, stir and brown for 5 minutes. Add the green beans, passata and the other ingredients, toss, put the lid on and cook on High for 25 minutes. Release the pressure naturally for 10 minutes, divide the mix between plates and serve.

Nutrition: calories 272, fat 14.5, fiber 0.1, carbs 0.3, protein 33.3

Oregano Pork

Preparation time: 10 minutes**Cooking time:** 30 minutes**Servings:** 4

Ingredients:
- 1 pound pork shoulder, cubed
- 1 red onion, sliced
- 2 tablespoons olive oil
- 1 cup beef stock
- ½ teaspoon chili powder
- ½ teaspoon rosemary, dried
- ½ teaspoon smoked paprika
- 2 tablespoons chives, chopped
- A pinch of salt and black pepper
- 2 tablespoons oregano, chopped

Directions:

Set your instant pot on Sauté mode, add the ghee, heat it up, add the onion, chili powder, rosemary, paprika and the meat and cook for 10 minutes. Add the stock and the rest of the ingredients, put the lid on and cook on High for 20 minutes. Release the pressure naturally for 10 minutes, divide the mix between plates and serve.

Nutrition: calories 393, fat 13, fiber 0.1, carbs 0.2, protein 27.2

Pork and Zucchinis

Preparation time: 10 minutes**Cooking time:** 30 minutes**Servings:** 4

Ingredients:
- 2 pounds pork shoulder, cubed
- 1 tablespoon avocado oil
- 2 zucchinis, cubed
- ½ teaspoon coriander, ground
- A pinch of red pepper flakes, crushed
- 1 yellow onion, chopped
- 1 cup beef stock
- 1 tablespoon cilantro, chopped
- A pinch of salt and black pepper

Directions:

Set your instant pot on Sauté mode, add the oil, heat it up, add the onion, pepper flakes, coriander and the meat and cook for 10 minutes. Add the zucchinis and the rest of the ingredients, put the lid on and cook on High for 20 minutes. Release the pressure naturally for 10 minutes, divide everything between plates and serve.

Nutrition: calories 396, fat 26.4, fiber 2.3, carbs 5.5, protein 28.5

Mediterranean Diet Instant Pot Vegetable Recipes

Spicy Black Beans

Preparation time: 5 minutes**Cooking time:** 20 minutes**Servings:** 4
Ingredients:
- 2 cups canned black beans, drained and rinsed
- 2 tablespoons olive oil
- 1 red onion, sliced
- 1 tablespoon lime juice
- ½ cup veggie stock
- 1 green chili, minced
- ½ teaspoon red pepper flakes, crushed
- A pinch of salt and black pepper

Directions:
Set the instant pot on Sauté mode, add the oil, heat up, add the onion, green chili and pepper flakes and cook for 5 minutes. Add the beans and the other ingredients, toss, put the lid on, and cook on High for 15 minutes. Release the pressure fast for 5 minutes, divide everything between plates and serve.

Nutrition: calories 121, fat 2, fiber 1, carbs 5, protein 6

Italian Beets

Preparation time: 5 minutes**Cooking time:** 25 minutes**Servings:** 4
Ingredients:
- 1 pound beets, peeled and cut into wedges
- 2 scallions, chopped
- 2 garlic cloves, minced
- ½ teaspoon hot paprika
- 2 tablespoons olive oil
- A pinch of salt and black pepper
- ¼ cup veggie stock
- 1 tablespoon chives, chopped
- 1 teaspoon Italian seasoning

Directions:
Set the instant pot on Sauté mode, add the oil, heat up, add the garlic and scallions and cook for 5 minutes. Add the beets, paprika and the other ingredients, toss, put the lid on and cook on High for 20 minutes. Release the pressure fast for 5 minutes, divide the mix between plates and serve.

Nutrition: calories 120, fat 1, fiber 2, carbs 4, protein 2

Dill Fennel
Preparation time: 5 minutes**Cooking time:** 15 minutes**Servings:** 4

Ingredients:
- 2 fennel bulbs, sliced
- 1 tablespoon olive oil
- 2 garlic cloves, minced
- ½ cup veggie stock
- 2 scallions, chopped
- 1 tablespoon dill, chopped
- A pinch of salt and black pepper

Directions:
Set the instant pot on Sauté mode, add the oil, heat up, add the scallions and garlic and cook for 2 minutes. Add the fennel and the other ingredients, toss, put the lid on and cook on High for 13 minutes. Release the pressure fast for 5 minutes, divide the mix between plates and serve.

Nutrition: calories 110, fat 2, fiber 2, carbs 4, protein 3

Creamy Artichokes
Preparation time: 5 minutes**Cooking time:** 15 minutes**Servings:** 4

Ingredients:
- 2 cups canned artichoke hearts, drained and quartered
- 2 tablespoons avocado oil
- ½ teaspoon cumin, ground
- ½ teaspoon garam masala
- 1 teaspoon chili powder
- ½ cup veggie stock
- 1 tablespoon coriander, ground
- 2 garlic cloves, chopped
- A pinch of salt and black pepper

Directions:
Set the instant pot on Sauté mode, add the oil, heat up, add the garlic, cumin, chili and garam masala, stir and cook for 3 minutes. Add the artichoke hearts and the other ingredients, toss, put the lid on and cook on High for 12 minutes. Release the pressure fast for 5 minutes, divide the mix between plates and serve.

Nutrition: calories 140, fat 2, fiber 2, carbs 5, protein 2

Creamy Endives

Preparation time: 5 minutes**Cooking time:** 15 minutes**Servings:** 4

Ingredients:
- 2 endives, shredded
- 1 cup coconut cream
- 1 tablespoon lime juice
- ½ teaspoon turmeric powder
- A pinch of salt and black pepper
- 1 tablespoon chives, chopped

Directions:

In your instant pot, combine the endives with the cream, lime juice and the other ingredients, toss, put the lid on and cook on High for 15 minutes. Release the pressure fast for 5 minutes, divide the mix between plates and serve.

Nutrition: calories 120, fat 2, fiber 3, carbs 5, protein 6

Lime Green Beans

Preparation time: 10 minutes**Cooking time:** 15 minutes**Servings:** 4

Ingredients:
- 1 tablespoon avocado oil
- 2 garlic cloves, minced
- 1 pound green beans, trimmed and halved
- 1 tablespoon lime juice
- ½ cup tomato passata
- 1 tablespoon dill, chopped
- A pinch of salt and black pepper
- A pinch of red pepper flakes, crushed

Directions:

Set the instant pot on Sauté mode, add the oil, heat it up, add the garlic and cook for 3 minutes. Add the green bean and the other ingredients, toss, put the lid on and cook on High for 12 minutes. Release the pressure naturally for 10 minutes, divide the mix between plates and serve.

Nutrition: calories 142, fat 2, fiber 2, carbs 4, protein 3

Chili Beets
Preparation time: 5 minutes**Cooking time:** 25 minutes**Servings:** 4

Ingredients:
- 1 pounds beets, peeled and cut into wedges
- 1 red chili, minced
- ½ teaspoon chili powder
- 2 tablespoons avocado oil
- A pinch of salt and black pepper
- ½ cup veggie stock
- 2 tablespoons cilantro, chopped

Directions:
In your instant pot, combine the beets with the chili, chili powder and the other ingredients, toss, put the lid on and cook on High for 25 minutes. Release the pressure fast for 5 minutes, divide everything between plates and serve.

Nutrition: calories 120, fat 2, fiber 2, carbs 4, protein 2

Creamy Tomato Mix
Preparation time: 5 minutes**Cooking time:** 15 minutes**Servings:** 4

Ingredients:
- 1 pound cherry tomatoes, halved
- 3 scallions, chopped
- ½ teaspoon oregano, dried
- ½ teaspoon basil, dried
- ½ teaspoon Italian seasoning
- A pinch of salt and black pepper
- 1 cup coconut cream
- 1 tablespoon chives, chopped

Directions:
Set the instant pot on Sauté mode, add the oil, heat it up, add the scallions and cook for 3 minutes. Add the tomatoes and the other ingredients, toss, put the lid on and cook on High for 12 minutes. Release the pressure fast for 5 minutes, divide the mix between plates and serve.

Nutrition: calories 134, fat 2, fiber 3, carbs 4, protein 5

Chili Radish Mix

Preparation time: 5 minutes**Cooking time:** 15 minutes**Servings:** 4

Ingredients:
- 2 cups radishes, halved
- 2 tablespoons olive oil
- 2 scallions, chopped
- 1 cup veggie stock
- ½ teaspoon sweet paprika
- 1 teaspoon rosemary, dried
- 1 teaspoon chili powder
- A pinch of salt and black pepper

Directions:
In your instant pot, combine the radishes with the oil, scallions and the other ingredients, toss, put the lid on and cook on High for 15 minutes. Release the pressure fast for 5 minutes, divide the mix between plates and serve.

Nutrition: calories 121, fat 3, fiber 2, carbs 3, protein 3

Chives Radishes

Preparation time: 10 minutes**Cooking time:** 20 minutes**Servings:** 4

Ingredients:
- 2 cups radishes, halved
- 1 tablespoon olive oil
- 3 garlic cloves, minced
- 1 red onion, sliced
- ½ cup veggie stock
- A pinch of salt and black pepper
- 1 tablespoon chives, chopped

Directions:
Set the instant pot on Sauté mode, add the oil, heat it up, add the onion and the garlic and cook for 5 minutes. Add the radishes and the rest of the ingredients, toss, put the lid on and cook on High for 15 minutes. Release the pressure naturally for 10 minutes, divide everything between plates and serve.

Nutrition: calories 162, fat 3, fiber 1, carbs 4, protein 5

Creamy Cabbage

Preparation time: 10 minutes**Cooking time:** 20 minutes**Servings:** 4

Ingredients:

- 1 pound red cabbage, shredded
- 1 red onion, chopped
- 2 tablespoons avocado oil
- 1 cup coconut cream
- ½ teaspoon Italian seasoning
- ½ teaspoon rosemary, dried
- A pinch of salt and black pepper
- 1 tablespoon dill, chopped

Directions:

Set the instant pot on Sauté mode, add the oil, heat it up, add the onion, seasoning and the rosemary and cook for 5 minutes. Add the cabbage and the other ingredients, toss, put the lid on and cook on High for 15 minutes. Release the pressure naturally for 10 minutes, divide the mix between plates and serve.

Nutrition: calories 142, fat 2, fiber 1, carbs 3, protein 4

Coconut Broccoli

Preparation time: 10 minutes**Cooking time:** 20 minutes**Servings:** 4

Ingredients:

- 1 pound broccoli florets
- 3 scallions, chopped
- 1 tablespoon coconut, unsweetened and shredded
- 1 cup coconut cream
- ½ teaspoon cumin, ground
- ½ teaspoon chili powder
- 2 tablespoons olive oil
- 1 teaspoon fennel seeds, crushed
- 1 tablespoon chives, chopped

Directions:

Set the instant pot on Sauté mode, add the oil, heat it up, add the scallions, cumin, chili powder and fennel seeds and cook for 5 minutes. Add the broccoli and the remaining ingredients, toss, put the lid on and cook on High for 15 minutes. Release the pressure naturally for 10 minutes, divide the mix between plates and serve.

Nutrition: calories 152, fat 2, fiber 2, carbs 4, protein 5

Chili Brussels Sprout

Preparation time: 10 minutes**Cooking time:** 15 minutes**Servings:** 4
Ingredients:

- 1 pound Brussels sprouts, trimmed and halved
- 1 red chili pepper, minced
- 2 garlic cloves, minced
- 1 red onion, chopped
- 2 tablespoons avocado oil
- ½ cup veggie stock
- ½ teaspoon rosemary, dried
- A pinch of salt and black pepper
- 1 tablespoon chives, chopped

Directions:

Set the instant pot on Sauté mode, add the oil, heat it up, add the chili pepper, garlic and the onion and cook for 3 minutes. Add the sprouts and the other ingredients, toss, put the lid on and cook on High for 12 minutes. Release the pressure naturally for 10 minutes, divide the mix between plates and serve.

Nutrition: calories 121, fat 2, fiber 2, carbs 4, protein 5

Radish and Spinach

Preparation time: 5 minutes**Cooking time:** 15 minutes**Servings:** 4
Ingredients:

- 2 cups radishes, halved
- 1 cup baby spinach
- 3 scallions, chopped
- 1 tablespoon lime juice
- 2 tablespoons avocado oil
- 3 spring onions, chopped
- 1 tablespoon almonds, chopped
- ½ teaspoon rosemary, dried
- 1 tablespoon chives, hopped
- 1 cup veggie stock

Directions:

In your instant pot, combine the radishes with the scallions, lime juice and the other ingredients, toss, put the lid on and cook on High for 15 minutes. Release the pressure naturally for 10 minutes, divide the mix between plates and serve.

Nutrition: calories 110, fat 2, fiber 2, carbs 4, protein 4

Tomato and Peppers Mix

Preparation time: 5 minutes**Cooking time:** 15 minutes**Servings:** 4

Ingredients:
- 1 pound cherry tomatoes, halved
- 1 cup roasted red peppers, cut into strips
- 1 red onion, chopped
- 2 tablespoons olive oil
- ¼ cup veggie stock
- A pinch of salt and black pepper
- 1 tablespoon lemon juice
- 1 tablespoon chives, chopped

Directions:
In your instant pot, mix the tomatoes with the peppers, onion and the other ingredients, toss, put the lid on and cook on High for 15 minutes. Release the pressure naturally for 5 minutes, divide the mix between plates and serve.

Nutrition: calories 151, fat 2, fiber 3, carbs 5, protein 4

Chili Pearl Onions

Preparation time: 10 minutes**Cooking time:** 15 minutes**Servings:** 4

Ingredients:
- 2 cups pearl onions, peeled
- 1 teaspoon chili powder
- ½ cup veggie stock
- 1 tablespoon olive oil
- Juice of 1 lime
- A pinch of salt and black pepper
- 1 tablespoon parsley, chopped
- 2 tablespoons chives, chopped

Directions:
Set the instant pot on Sauté mode, add the oil, heat up, add the pearl onions and cook for 5 minutes. Add the chili powder and the other ingredients, toss, put the lid on and cook on High for 10 minutes. Release the pressure naturally for 10 minutes, divide the mix between plates and serve.

Nutrition: calories 126, fat 1, fiber 2, carbs 4, protein 4

Cumin Sweet Potatoes

Preparation time: 10 minutes**Cooking time:** 20 minutes**Servings:** 4

Ingredients:
- 4 sweet potatoes, peeled and cut into wedges
- 1 cup veggie stock
- 1 teaspoon cumin, ground
- ½ teaspoon sweet paprika
- 2 scallions, chopped
- A pinch of salt and black pepper
- 1 tablespoon parsley, chopped

Directions:

In your instant pot, mix the sweet potatoes with the stock, cumin and the other ingredients, toss, put the lid on and cook on High for 20 minutes. Release the pressure naturally for 10 minutes, divide the mix between plates and serve.

Nutrition: calories 162, fat 8, fiber 2, carbs 4, protein 7

Greek Beets Mix

Preparation time: 5 minutes**Cooking time:** 20 minutes**Servings:** 4

Ingredients:
- 1 pound beets, peeled and cut into wedges
- 1 tablespoon olive oil
- ½ teaspoon garam masala
- 2 spring onions, chopped
- 1 cup Greek yogurt
- A pinch of salt and black pepper

Directions:

In your instant pot, combine the beets with the garam masala, oil and the other ingredients, toss, put the lid on and cook on High for 20 minutes. Release the pressure fast for 5 minutes, divide the mix between plates and serve.

Nutrition: calories 182, fat 4, fiber 2, carbs 4, protein 5

Smoked Leeks Mix

Preparation time: 10 minutes**Cooking time:** 15 minutes**Servings:** 4

Ingredients:
- 4 leeks, sliced
- 1 tablespoon avocado oil
- ½ cup veggie stock
- ½ teaspoon turmeric powder
- ½ teaspoon oregano, dried
- A pinch of salt and black pepper
- 1 tablespoon smoked paprika
- 1 tablespoon chives, chopped

Directions:

Set your instant pot on Sauté mode, add the oil, heat it up, add the leeks and cook for 5 minutes. Add the stock and the rest of the ingredients, put the lid on and cook on High for 10 minutes more. Release the pressure naturally for 10 minutes, divide the mix between plates and serve.

Nutrition: calories 188, fat 2, fiber 2, carbs 4, protein 5

Zucchini Saute

Preparation time: 10 minutes**Cooking time:** 15 minutes**Servings:** 4

Ingredients:
- 2 tablespoons avocado oil
- 1 pound zucchinis, roughly cubed
- 1 yellow onion, chopped
- ½ teaspoon coriander, ground
- ½ teaspoon rosemary, dried
- 1 teaspoon turmeric powder
- A pinch of salt and black pepper
- 1 cup tomato passata
- 1 tablespoon chives, chopped

Directions:

Set the instant pot on Sauté mode, add the oil, heat up, add the onion, coriander, rosemary and turmeric and cook for 5 minutes. Add the zucchinis and the other ingredients, toss gently, put the lid on and cook on High for 10 minutes. Release the pressure naturally for 10 minutes, divide the mix between plates and serve.

Nutrition: calories 162, fat 2, fiber 2, carbs 5, protein 6

Hot Eggplant Mix

Preparation time: 10 minutes**Cooking time:** 15 minutes**Servings:** 4

Ingredients:

- 2 big eggplants, roughly cubed
- 1 red chili pepper, minced
- ½ teaspoon hot paprika
- 2 garlic cloves, minced
- ¼ cup veggie stock
- A pinch of salt and black pepper
- ½ cup tomato passata
- ½ tablespoon dill, chopped

Directions:

In your instant pot, combine the eggplant cubes with the chili pepper and the other ingredients, toss, put the lid on and cook on High for 15 minutes. Release the pressure naturally for 10 minutes, divide the mix between plates and serve.

Nutrition: calories 162, fat 4, fiber 3, carbs 5, protein 7

Parsley Carrots Mix

Preparation time: 10 minutes**Cooking time:** 20 minutes**Servings:** 4

Ingredients:

- 1 pound baby carrots, peeled
- ½ teaspoon chili powder
- ½ teaspoon rosemary, dried
- 1 tablespoon olive oil
- A pinch of salt and black pepper
- 1 cup veggie stock
- 1 tablespoon parsley, chopped

Directions:

In your instant pot, combine the carrots with the chili powder, rosemary and the other ingredients, toss, put the lid on and cook on High for 20 minutes. Release the pressure naturally for 10 minutes, divide the mix between plates and serve.

Nutrition: calories 121, fat 2, fiber 2, carbs 4, protein 2

Spinach and Kale Mix

Preparation time: 5 minutes**Cooking time:** 12 minutes**Servings:** 4

Ingredients:
- 2 cups baby kale
- 1 cup baby spinach
- 1 red onion, chopped
- 1 tablespoon olive oil
- ½ cup veggie stock
- 1 tablespoon sweet paprika
- A pinch of salt and black pepper
- 1 tablespoon chives, chopped

Directions:
Set the instant pot on Sauté mode, add the oil, heat up, add the onion and the paprika and cook for 2 minutes. Add the kale, spinach and the other ingredients, toss, put the lid on and cook on High for 10 minutes. Release the pressure fast for 5 minutes, divide the mix into bowls and serve.

Nutrition: calories 100, fat 1, fiber 2, carbs 2, protein 1

Coriander Tomato and Okra Mix

Preparation time: 10 minutes**Cooking time:** 14 minutes**Servings:** 4

Ingredients:
- 2 cups okra
- 2 cups cherry tomatoes, halved
- 1 tablespoon coriander, ground
- ½ teaspoon chili powder
- ½ teaspoon basil, dried
- A pinch of salt and black pepper
- 1 cup tomato passata
- 2 tablespoon parsley, chopped

Directions:
In your instant pot, mix the cherry tomatoes with the okra, coriander and the other ingredients, toss, put the lid on and cook on High for 14 minutes. Release the pressure naturally for 10 minutes, divide the mix between plates and serve.

Nutrition: calories 121, fat 2, fiber 2, carbs 4, protein 4

Balsamic Potatoes

Preparation time: 10 minutes**Cooking time:** 20 minutes**Servings:** 4

Ingredients:
- 1 pound sweet potatoes, peeled and cut into wedges
- 1 cup veggie stock
- 2 tablespoons balsamic vinegar
- ½ teaspoon chili powder
- ½ teaspoon coriander, ground
- A pinch of salt and black pepper
- 1 tablespoon dill, chopped

Directions:
In your instant pot, combine the potato wedges with the stock, vinegar and the other ingredients, toss, put the lid on and cook on High for 20 minutes. Release the pressure naturally for 10 minutes, divide mix between plates and serve.

Nutrition: calories 123, fat 1, fiber 2, carbs 3, protein 2

Hot Kale

Preparation time: 10 minutes**Cooking time:** 12 minutes**Servings:** 4

Ingredients:
- 1 pound baby kale
- ½ teaspoon hot paprika
- ½ teaspoon red pepper flakes, crushed
- 1 cup veggie stock
- A pinch of salt and black pepper
- 1 tablespoon dill, chopped

Directions:
In your instant pot, combine the kale with the hot paprika, pepper flakes and the other ingredients, toss, put the lid on and cook on High for 12 minutes. Release the pressure naturally for 10 minutes, divide the mix between plates and serve warm.

Nutrition: calories 122, fat 2, fiber 2, carbs 5, protein 3

Peppers and Sauce

Preparation time: 10 minutes**Cooking time:** 15 minutes**Servings:** 4

Ingredients:
- 1 orange bell pepper, cut into strips
- 1 red bell pepper, cut into strips
- 1 green bell pepper, cut into strips
- ½ cup coconut cream
- 1 teaspoon sweet paprika
- ½ teaspoon turmeric powder
- A pinch of salt and black pepper
- 1 tablespoon cilantro, chopped

Directions:
In your instant pot, mix the peppers with the cream, paprika and the other ingredients, toss, put the lid on and cook on High for 15 minutes. Release the pressure naturally for 10 minutes, divide the mix into bowls and serve.

Nutrition: calories 130, fat 2, fiber 2, carbs 4, protein 6

Spinach and Mango

Preparation time: 5 minutes**Cooking time:** 8 minutes**Servings:** 4

Ingredients:
- 3 scallions, chopped
- 1 pound baby spinach
- 1 cup mango, peeled and cubed
- A pinch of salt and black pepper
- Juice of 1 lime
- 1 tablespoon chives, chopped

Directions:
In your instant pot, combine the spinach with the scallions, mango and the other ingredients, toss, put the lid on and cook on High for 8 minutes. Release the pressure fast for 5 minutes, divide the mix into bowls and serve.

Nutrition: calories 140, fat 2, fiber 2, carbs 5, protein 7

Artichokes and Spinach

Preparation time: 10 minutes**Cooking time:** 12 minutes**Servings:** 4

Ingredients:
- 1 cup canned artichoke hearts, drained and halved
- 1 cup baby spinach
- 2 spring onions, chopped
- A pinch of salt and black pepper
- ½ cup veggie stock
- ½ teaspoon cumin, ground
- 1 tablespoon chives, chopped

Directions:

In your instant pot, combine the artichoke hearts with the spinach and the other ingredients, toss, put the lid on and cook on High for 12 minutes. Release the pressure naturally for 10 minutes, divide the mix between plates and serve.

Nutrition: calories 114, fat 2, fiber 2, carbs 4, protein 4

Cinnamon Yams

Preparation time: 10 minutes**Cooking time:** 20 minutes**Servings:** 4

Ingredients:
- 2 yams, peeled and cut into wedges
- 1 teaspoon cinnamon powder
- 1 tablespoon olive oil
- 1 teaspoon turmeric powder
- A pinch of salt and black pepper
- ½ cup coconut milk

Directions:

In your instant pot, combine the yams with the cinnamon and the other ingredients, toss, put the lid on and cook on High for 20 minutes. Release the pressure naturally for 10 minutes, divide the mix into bowls and serve.

Nutrition: calories 124, fat 2, fiber 1, carbs 3, protein 4

Greek Coriander Sprouts

Preparation time: 10 minutes**Cooking time:** 15 minutes**Servings:** 4

Ingredients:
- 2 cups Brussels sprouts, halved
- 1 tablespoon coriander, chopped
- 1 tablespoon lemon juice
- 1 tablespoon olive oil
- 1 cup Greek yogurt
- A pinch of salt and black pepper
- ½ teaspoon garam masala

Directions:
In your instant pot, mix the sprouts with the coriander, lemon juice and the other ingredients, toss, put the lid on and cook on High for 15 minutes. Release the pressure naturally for 10 minutes, divide the mix between plates and serve.

Nutrition: calories 121, fat 1, fiber 1, carbs 4, protein 5

Creamy Corn

Preparation time: 10 minutes**Cooking time:** 15 minutes**Servings:** 4

Ingredients:
- 2 cups corn
- 2 scallions, chopped
- ½ cup coconut cream
- 1 teaspoon turmeric powder
- A pinch of salt and black pepper
- 1 tablespoon chives, chopped

Directions:
In your instant pot, combine the corn with the scallions, cream and the other ingredients, toss, put the lid on and cook on High for 15 minutes. Release the pressure naturally for 10 minutes, divide the mix into bowls and serve cold.

Nutrition: calories 200, fat 7, fiber 2, carbs 4, protein 6

Carrots Sauté

Preparation time: 5 minutes**Cooking time:** 15 minutes**Servings:** 4

Ingredients:
- 1 pound baby carrots, peeled
- 2 garlic cloves, minced
- A pinch of salt and black pepper
- 1 teaspoon rosemary, dried
- ½ cup veggie stock
- 1 tablespoon balsamic vinegar

Directions:
In your instant pot, mix the carrots with the garlic, rosemary and the other ingredients, toss, put the lid on and cook on High for 15 minutes. Release the pressure fast for 5 minutes, divide the mix between plates and serve.

Nutrition: calories 124, fat 2, fiber 2, carbs 4, protein 5

Olives Sauté

Preparation time: 5 minutes**Cooking time:** 15 minutes**Servings:** 4

Ingredients:
- 1 cup green olives, pitted and halved
- 1 cup black olives, pitted and halved
- 1 cup kalamata olives, pitted and halved
- 4 scallions, chopped
- 1 tablespoon olive oil
- 1 teaspoon turmeric powder
- A pinch of salt and black pepper
- ½ cup veggie stock
- 1 tablespoon rosemary, chopped

Directions:
Set the instant pot on Sauté mode, add the oil, heat it up, add the scallions and turmeric powder and cook for 5 minutes. Add the olives and the rest of the ingredients, put the lid on and cook on High for 10 minutes. Release the pressure fast for 5 minutes, divide the mix into bowls and serve.

Nutrition: calories 135, fat 5, fiber 2, carbs 3, protein 4

Curry Eggplant

Preparation time: 10 minutes**Cooking time:** 14 minutes**Servings:** 4

Ingredients:
- 1 pound eggplant, roughly cubed
- 1 tablespoon yellow curry paste
- 1 tablespoon olive oil
- 2 scallions, chopped
- 1 teaspoon chili powder
- A pinch of salt and black pepper
- ½ cup veggie stock
- 1 tablespoon dill, chopped

Directions:
Set the instant pot on Sauté mode, add the oil, heat up, add the scallions, curry paste and the chili powder and sauté for 4 minutes. Add the eggplants and the other ingredients, toss, put the lid on and cook on High for 10 minutes. Release the pressure naturally for 10 minutes, divide the mix between plates and serve.

Nutrition: calories 128, fat 3, fiber 2, carbs 4, protein 5

Chard Sauté

Preparation time: 10 minutes**Cooking time:** 12 minutes**Servings:** 4

Ingredients:
- 2 cups red chard, torn
- 1 tablespoon lime juice
- A pinch of salt and black pepper
- ½ cup veggie stock
- ½ teaspoon chili powder
- 1 tablespoon sweet paprika
- 1 tablespoon cilantro, chopped

Directions:
In your instant pot, combine the chard with the lime juice, stock and the other ingredients, toss, put the lid on and cook on High for 12 minutes. Release the pressure naturally for 10 minutes, divide the mix into bowls and serve.

Nutrition: calories 146, fat 4, fiber 2, carbs 4, protein 6

Chili Carrots and Spinach

Preparation time: 5 minutes**Cooking time:** 14 minutes**Servings:** 4

Ingredients:

- 2 cups baby spinach
- ½ pound baby carrots, peeled
- ½ teaspoon coriander, ground
- ½ teaspoon turmeric powder
- 1 red chili, minced
- ½ teaspoon chili powder
- 2 garlic cloves, chopped
- ½ cup veggie stock
- 1 tablespoon rosemary, chopped

Directions:

In your instant pot, mix the spinach with the carrots, coriander and the other ingredients, toss, put the lid on and cook on High for 15 minutes. Release the pressure fast for 5 minutes, divide the mix into bowls and serve.

Nutrition: calories 146, fat 4, fiber 2, carbs 4, protein 7

Radish and Mango Mix

Preparation time: 10 minutes**Cooking time:** 20 minutes**Servings:** 4

Ingredients:

- 2 cups radishes, halved
- 1 cup mango, peeled and cubed
- 2 tablespoons olive oil
- 1 red onion, chopped
- ½ teaspoon chili powder
- ½ teaspoon cayenne pepper
- ½ cup veggie stock
- 1 teaspoon hot paprika
- A pinch of salt and black pepper
- ½ tablespoon cilantro, chopped

Directions:

Set your instant pot on Sauté mode, add the oil, heat it up, add the onion, chili powder and cayenne, stir and cook for 5 minutes. Add the radishes, mango and the other ingredients, put the lid on and cook on High for 15 minutes. Release the pressure naturally for 10 minutes, divide the mix into bowls and serve.

Nutrition: calories 134, fat 2, fiber 2, carbs 5, protein 5

Beet and Tomato Mix

Preparation time: 5 minutes**Cooking time:** 20 minutes**Servings:** 4

Ingredients:
- 2 scallions, chopped
- 1 tablespoon olive oil
- 2 beets, peeled and cubed
- ½ pound cherry tomatoes, halved
- 1 teaspoon chili powder
- ½ teaspoon oregano, dried
- ½ teaspoon basil, dried
- 1 tablespoon lime juice
- A pinch of salt and black pepper
- ½ cup veggie stock
- 1 tablespoon chives, chopped

Directions:

Set the instant pot on Sauté mode, add the oil, heat it up, add the scallions, beets, chili powder, oregano and basil, stir and sauté for 5 minutes. Add the tomatoes and the rest of the ingredients, put the lid on and cook on High for 15 minutes. Release the pressure fast for 5 minutes, divide the mix into bowls and serve.

Nutrition: calories 129, fat 4, fiber 2, carbs 3, protein 2

Potato and Radish Bowls

Preparation time: 10 minutes**Cooking time:** 20 minutes**Servings:** 4

Ingredients:
- 1 pound sweet potatoes, peeled and roughly cubed
- 1 tablespoon olive oil
- 1 red onion, sliced
- 1 cup radishes, halved
- 1 cup veggie stock
- ½ cup baby spinach
- 1 tablespoon balsamic vinegar
- A pinch of salt and black pepper
- 1 tablespoon chives, chopped

Directions:

In your instant pot, combine the sweet potatoes with the oil, onion and the other ingredients, toss, put the lid on and cook on High for 20 minutes. Release the pressure naturally for 10 minutes, divide the mix into bowls and serve.

Nutrition: calories 119, fat 2, fiber 2, carbs 4, protein 5

Lemon Asparagus
Preparation time: 5 minutes**Cooking time:** 10 minutes**Servings:** 4

Ingredients:
- 1 pound asparagus, trimmed
- Juice of 1 lime
- ½ teaspoon chili powder
- ½ teaspoon cumin, ground
- 1 tablespoon sweet paprika
- 2 cups chicken stock
- A pinch of salt and black pepper

Directions:
In your instant pot, combine the asparagus with the lime juice, chili powder and the rest of the ingredients, put the lid on and cook on High for 10 minutes. Release the pressure fast for 5 minutes, divide between plates and serve.

Nutrition: calories 56, fat 1.8, fiber 0.4, carbs 0.5, protein 5.6

Basil Asparagus
Preparation time: 5 minutes**Cooking time:** 10 minutes**Servings:** 4

Ingredients:
- 1 pound asparagus, trimmed and halved
- A pinch of salt and black pepper
- ¼ cup lime juice
- 1 teaspoon basil, chopped
- ½ teaspoon coriander, ground
- A pinch of cayenne pepper

Directions:
In your instant pot, combine the asparagus with the lime juice and the other ingredients, toss, put the lid on and cook on High for 10 minutes. Release the pressure fast for 5 minutes, divide the mix between plates and serve.

Nutrition: calories 10, fat 1.1, fiber 0.8, carbs 1.6, protein 0.6

Coconut Cabbage
Preparation time: 5 minutes**Cooking time:** 20 minutes**Servings:** 4

Ingredients:
- 2 cups red cabbage, shredded
- ½ teaspoon chili powder
- ½ teaspoon turmeric powder
- ½ cup coconut cream
- 1 tablespoon dill, chopped
- A pinch of salt and black pepper

Directions:
In your instant pot, combine the cabbage with the turmeric, chili powder and the other ingredients, toss, put the lid on and cook on High for 20 minutes. Release the pressure fast for 5 minutes, divide the mix between plates and serve.

Nutrition: calories 148, fat 7.8, fiber 2.9, carbs 5.4, protein 5.5

Leeks and Capers
Preparation time: 5 minutes**Cooking time:** 15 minutes**Servings:** 4

Ingredients:
- 4 leeks, sliced
- ½ cup veggie stock
- 1 tablespoon capers, drained
- 1 tablespoon sweet paprika
- 2 garlic cloves, chopped
- 1 tablespoon chives, chopped

Directions:
In your instant pot, mix the leeks with the stock, capers and the other ingredients, toss, put the lid on and cook on High for 15 minutes Release the pressure fast for 5 minutes, divide the mix between plates, and serve.

Nutrition: calories 106, fat 1.9, fiber 0.2, carbs 0.5, protein 7.8

Creamy Asparagus

Preparation time: 5 minutes**Cooking time:** 10 minutes**Servings:** 4

Ingredients:
- 1 pound asparagus, trimmed and halved
- ½ cup coconut cream
- A pinch of salt and black pepper
- 1 tablespoon basil, chopped
- 1 teaspoon coriander, ground
- ½ teaspoon garam masala
- 1 tablespoon chives, chopped

Directions:

In your instant pot, mix the asparagus with the cream, basil and the other ingredients, toss, put the lid on and cook on High for 10 minutes. Release the pressure fast for 5 minutes, divide mix between plates and serve.

Nutrition: calories 42, fat 1.2, fiber 0.7, carbs 1, protein 3.5

Asparagus and Avocado Mix

Preparation time: 5 minutes**Cooking time:** 10 minutes**Servings:** 4

Ingredients:
- 1 pound asparagus, trimmed and halved
- 1 cup avocado, peeled, pitted and cubed
- 2 tablespoons olive oil
- A pinch of salt and black pepper
- 1 teaspoon garlic powder
- ½ teaspoon chili powder
- ¼ cup chives, chopped
- ¼ cup lemon juice

Directions:

In your instant pot, mix the asparagus with the avocado, oil and the other ingredients, toss, put the lid on and cook on High for 10 minutes. Release the pressure fast for 5 minutes, divide everything between plates and serve.

Nutrition: calories 102, fat 7.5, fiber 3, carbs 6.1, protein 3.4

Oregano Radish and Zucchini Mix

Preparation time: 5 minutes**Cooking time:** 15 minutes**Servings:** 4

Ingredients:
- 1 cup radishes, halved
- 2 zucchinis, roughly cubed
- 1 teaspoon turmeric powder
- 2 tablespoons oregano, chopped
- ½ cup coconut cream
- A pinch of salt and black pepper
- 1 tablespoon chives, chopped

Directions:

In your instant pot, mix the radishes with the zucchinis, turmeric and the other ingredients, toss, put the lid on and cook on High for 15 minutes. Release the pressure fast for 5 minutes, divide everything between plates and serve.

Nutrition: calories 121, fat 11.5, fiber 1.8, carbs 4.1, protein 1.9

Radishes and Quinoa

Preparation time: 5 minutes**Cooking time:** 20 minutes**Servings:** 4

Ingredients:
- 1 cup quinoa
- 2 cups veggie stock
- ½ teaspoon chili powder
- 1 cup radishes, cubed
- A pinch of salt and black pepper
- ½ teaspoon coriander, ground
- 1 tablespoon chives, chopped

Directions:

In your instant pot, mix the quinoa with the stock, chili powder and the other ingredients, toss, put the lid on and cook on High for 20 minutes. Release the pressure fast for 5 minutes, divide the mix between plates and serve.

Nutrition: calories 45, fat 0.6, fiber 0.1, carbs 0.4, protein 2

Bulgur and Zucchinis

Preparation time: 5 minutes**Cooking time:** 20 minutes**Servings:** 4

Ingredients:
- 2 zucchinis, cubed
- 1 cup bulgur
- 2 cups veggie stock
- 1 tablespoon lemon juice
- 2 teaspoons lemon zest, grated
- 1 teaspoon chili powder
- A pinch of salt and black pepper
- 1 tablespoon basil, chopped

Directions:
In your instant pot, combine the bulgur with the zucchinis, stock and the other ingredients, toss, put the lid on and cook on High for 20 minutes. Release the pressure fast for 5 minutes, divide the mix between plates and serve.

Nutrition: calories 82, fat 2.5, fiber 1.9, carbs 2.1, protein 5.6

Green Beans and Olives

Preparation time: 10 minutes**Cooking time:** 20 minutes**Servings:** 4

Ingredients:
- 1 cup kalamata olives, pitted and halved
- 1 pound green beans, trimmed and halved
- 1 teaspoon sweet paprika
- 1 cup veggie stock
- A pinch of salt and black pepper
- 2 garlic cloves, minced
- 1 tablespoon dill, chopped

Directions:
In your instant pot, mix the green beans with the olives, paprika and the other ingredients, toss, put the lid on and cook on High for 20 minutes. Release the pressure naturally for 10 minutes, divide between plates and serve.

Nutrition: calories 46, fat 1.7, fiber 0.1, carbs 0.6, protein 2.7

Broccoli and Cauliflower Bowls

Preparation time: 5 minutes**Cooking time:** 20 minutes**Servings:** 4

Ingredients:
- 1 cup broccoli florets
- 1 cup cauliflower florets
- 1 tablespoon balsamic vinegar
- 1 cup chicken stock
- 2 garlic cloves, minced
- A pinch of salt and black pepper
- 1 tablespoon dill, chopped

Directions:

In your instant pot, mix the broccoli with the cauliflower and the other ingredients, toss, put the lid on and cook on High for 20 minutes. Release the pressure fast for 5 minutes, divide the mix into bowls and serve.

Nutrition: calories 71, fat 2.1, fiber 1.1, carbs 1.3, protein 4.4

Bell Peppers and Quinoa

Preparation time: 10 minutes**Cooking time:** 20 minutes**Servings:** 4

Ingredients:
- 1 pound red bell peppers, chopped
- 1 tablespoon olive oil
- 1 tablespoon lime juice
- 1 cup veggie stock
- 1 cup quinoa
- 1 tablespoon sweet paprika
- 1 tablespoon chives, chopped

Directions:

In your instant pot, mix the quinoa with the bell peppers and the other ingredients, toss, put the lid on and cook on High for 20 minutes. Release the pressure naturally for 10 minutes, divide the mix between plates and serve.

Nutrition: calories 70, fat 1.8, fiber 1.1, carbs 1.4, protein 0.6

Carrots and Potatoes

Preparation time: 5 minutes**Cooking time:** 20 minutes**Servings:** 4

Ingredients:
- 1 pound baby carrots, peeled
- ½ pound sweet potatoes, peeled and cubed
- ½ cup chicken stock
- ½ teaspoon turmeric powder
- ½ teaspoon chili powder
- A pinch of salt and black pepper
- 1 tablespoon cilantro, chopped

Directions:

In your instant pot, mix the carrots with the sweet potatoes and the other ingredients, toss, put the lid on and cook on High for 20 minutes. Release the pressure fast for 5 minutes, divide the mix between plates and serve.

Nutrition: calories 63, fat 5.7, fiber 0.4, carbs 2.8, protein 0.7

Black Beans and Quinoa

Preparation time: 5 minutes**Cooking time:** 20 minutes**Servings:** 4

Ingredients:
- 1 cup canned black beans, drained and rinsed
- 1 cup quinoa
- 2 cups veggie stock
- 1 teaspoon smoked paprika
- A pinch of salt and black pepper
- 1 tablespoon chives, chopped

Directions:

In your instant pot, combine the beans with the quinoa, stock and the other ingredients, toss, put the lid on and cook on High for 20 minutes. Release the pressure fast for 5 minutes, divide the mix between plates and serve.

Nutrition: calories 68, fat 4.2, fiber 2.3, carbs 3.4, protein 2.4

Mustard Greens Sauté

Preparation time: 5 minutes**Cooking time:** 15 minutes**Servings:** 4

Ingredients:
- 1 pound mustard greens
- 3 scallions, chopped
- 1 tablespoon olive oil
- 1 tablespoon lime juice
- A pinch of salt and black pepper
- ½ cup veggie stock
- 1 teaspoon chili powder
- 1 teaspoon chives, chopped

Directions:
Set the instant pot on Sauté mode, add the oil, heat up, add the scallions and cook for 5 minutes. Add the mustard greens and the other ingredients, toss, put the lid on and cook on High for 10 minutes. Release the pressure fast for 5 minutes, divide the mix between plates and serve.

Nutrition: calories 32, fat 3.4, fiber 2.3, carbs 2.9, protein 2.3

Lime Radish Mix

Preparation time: 10 minutes**Cooking time:** 20 minutes**Servings:** 4

Ingredients:
- 1 pound radishes, halved
- Juice of 1 lime
- 1 teaspoon sweet paprika
- A pinch of salt and black pepper
- ½ cup veggie stock
- 1 teaspoon coriander, ground

Directions:
In your instant pot, combine the radishes with the lime juice, paprika and the other ingredients, toss, put the lid on and cook on High for 20 minutes. Release the pressure naturally for 10 minutes, divide mix between plates and serve.

Nutrition: calories 38, fat 1.5, fiber 0.2, carbs 0.4, protein 2.5

Italian Veggie Mix

Preparation time: 10 minutes**Cooking time:** 20 minutes**Servings:** 4

Ingredients:
- 1 cup cherry tomatoes, halved
- 1 cup black olives, pitted and halved
- 1 tablespoon olive oil
- 1 cup zucchini, cubed
- 1 cup eggplant, cubed
- ½ cup veggie stock
- A pinch of salt and black pepper
- 1 teaspoon chili powder
- 1 tablespoon chives, chopped

Directions:
In your instant pot, mix the tomatoes with the olives, the oil, zucchini and the other ingredients, toss, put the lid on and cook on High for 20 minutes. Release the pressure naturally for 10 minutes, divide the mix between plates and serve.

Nutrition: calories 161, fat 10.1, fiber 3.1, carbs 4.5, protein 9.6

Dill Tomatoes Mix

Preparation time: 10 minutes**Cooking time:** 15 minutes**Servings:** 4

Ingredients:
- 2 cups cherry tomatoes, halved
- 3 garlic cloves, minced
- 1 tablespoon olive oil
- ½ cup veggie stock
- ½ teaspoon smoked paprika
- A pinch of salt and black pepper
- 1 tablespoon dill, chopped

Directions:
In your instant pot, mix the tomatoes with the garlic, oil and the other ingredients, toss, put the lid on and cook on High for 15 minutes. Release the pressure naturally for 10 minutes, divide the mix between plates and serve.

Nutrition: calories 165, fat 14.5, fiber 2.8, carbs 6.4, protein 2.7

Creamy Kale

Preparation time: 10 minutes**Cooking time:** 14 minutes**Servings:** 4

Ingredients:
- 1 pound kale, torn
- 1 tablespoon olive oil
- 4 garlic cloves, minced
- 2 scallions, chopped
- 1 cup coconut cream
- ½ teaspoon garam masala
- ½ teaspoon sweet paprika
- ½ teaspoon coriander, ground
- A pinch of salt and black pepper
- 1 tablespoon cilantro, chopped

Directions:

Set your instant pot on Sauté mode, add the oil, heat it up, add the garlic and the scallions and sauté for 2 minutes. Add the kale, cream and the rest of the ingredients, put the lid on and cook on High for 12 minutes more. Release the pressure naturally for 10 minutes, divide the mix into bowls and serve.

Nutrition: calories 95, fat 3.7, fiber 1.9, carbs 2.4, protein 3.8

Eggplant and Tomato Quinoa

Preparation time: 10 minutes**Cooking time:** 20 minutes**Servings:** 4

Ingredients:
- 1 cup quinoa
- 2 cups veggie stock
- 1 cup cherry tomatoes, halved
- 2 eggplants, cubed
- A pinch of salt and black pepper
- 1 yellow onion, chopped
- 1 tablespoon olive oil
- 1 teaspoon turmeric powder
- 1 tablespoon chives, chopped

Directions:

Set the instant pot on Sauté mode, add the oil, heat up, add the onion and turmeric and cook for 4 minutes. Add quinoa, eggplant and the other ingredients, toss, put the lid on and cook on High for 16 minutes. Release the pressure naturally for 10 minutes, divide the mix between plates and serve.

Nutrition: calories 181, fat 11.8, fiber 4.2, carbs 5.9, protein 3.6

Mediterranean Diet Instant Pot Dessert Recipes

Dates Cream Pudding
Preparation time: 10 minutes**Cooking time:** 30 minutes**Servings:** 4

Ingredients:
- 3 cups dates, chopped
- 2 tablespoons brown sugar
- 1 teaspoon almond extract
- 1 cup coconut cream
- 2 eggs, whisked
- Cooking spray
- 1 cup water

Directions:
In a blender, combine the dates with the sugar and the other ingredients except the cooking spray and the water, and pulse well. Grease 4 ramekins with the cooking spray and divide the dates cream in each. Add the water to the instant pot, add the steamer basket, put the ramekins inside, put the lid on and cook on High for 30 minutes. Release the pressure naturally for 10 minutes, cool the cream down and serve.

Nutrition: calories 152, fat 5, fiber 2, carb 6, protein 3

Walnuts and Mango Bowls
Preparation time: 10 minutes**Cooking time:** 10 minutes**Servings:** 4

Ingredients:
- 1 cup walnuts, chopped
- 1 cup mango, peeled and roughly cubed
- 1 cup coconut cream
- 1 teaspoon almond extract
- 1 tablespoon brown sugar

Directions:
In your instant pot, combine the mango with the walnuts and the other ingredients, toss, put the lid on and cook on High for 10 minutes. Release the pressure naturally for 10 minutes, divide the mix into bowls and serve.

Nutrition: calories 220, fat 4, fiber 2, carbs 4, protein 6

Berries and Avocado Salad

Preparation time: 10 minutes**Cooking time:** 15 minutes**Servings:** 4

Ingredients:
- 2 tablespoons brown sugar
- 1 tablespoon lime juice
- 1 cup blackberries
- 1 cup strawberries
- 1 avocado, peeled, pitted and cubed
- ¼ cup coconut cream

Directions:

In your instant pot, combine the berries with the avocado and the other ingredients, toss, put the lid on and cook on High for 15 minutes. Release the pressure naturally for 10 minutes, divide the mix into bowls and serve.

Nutrition: calories 262, fat 7, fiber 2, carbs 5, protein 8

Coconut Apples

Preparation time: 10 minutes**Cooking time:** 20 minutes**Servings:** 4

Ingredients:
- 2 teaspoons almond extract
- 1 tablespoon walnuts, chopped
- 4 apples, cored and halved
- 1 tablespoon brown sugar
- ½ cup coconut cream

Directions:

In your instant pot, mix the apples with the walnuts, almond extract and the other ingredients, toss, put the lid on and cook on High for 20 minutes. Release the pressure naturally for 10 minutes, divide the mix into bowls and serve.

Nutrition: calories 120, fat 2, fiber 2, carbs 4, protein 3

Plums Bowls

Preparation time: 10 minutes**Cooking time:** 15 minutes**Servings:** 4

Ingredients:
- 2 cups plums, pitted and halved
- 1 cup coconut cream
- ½ teaspoon vanilla extract
- ½ cup coconut sugar
- 1 teaspoon almond extract

Directions:
In your instant pot, combine the plums with the cream, vanilla and the other ingredients, toss, put the lid on and cook on High for 15 minutes. Release the pressure naturally for 10 minutes, divide the mix into bowls and serve.

Nutrition: calories 162, fat 2, fiber 2, carbs 4, protein 5

Almond Pudding

Preparation time: 5 minutes**Cooking time:** 15 minutes**Servings:** 4

Ingredients:
- 1 cup coconut cream
- 2 eggs, whisked
- ½ teaspoon baking soda
- 1 cup Greek yogurt
- 1 cup almonds, chopped
- 1 teaspoon coconut sugar
- ½ teaspoon cinnamon powder

Directions:
In your instant pot, combine the cream with the yogurt and the other ingredients, whisk, put the lid on and cook on High for 15 minutes. Release the pressure fast for 5 minutes, divide the pudding into bowls and serve.

Nutrition: calories 172, fat 2, fiber 3, carbs 4, protein 5

Strawberries Cream

Preparation time: 10 minutes**Cooking time:** 20 minutes**Servings:** 4

Ingredients:
- 1 cup strawberries, chopped
- 1 cup Greek yogurt
- 2 tablespoons brown sugar
- ½ teaspoon vanilla extract
- 1 cup water

Directions:
In a blender, combine the berries with the yogurt and the other ingredients except the water, pulse well and divide into 4 ramekins. Add the water to your instant pot, add the steamer basket, add the ramekins inside, put the lid on and cook on High for 20 minutes. Release the pressure naturally for 10 minutes, and serve cold.

Nutrition: calories 200, fat 5, fiber 3, carbs 4, protein 5

Cinnamon Apple Cream

Preparation time: 10 minutes**Cooking time:** 25 minutes**Serving:** 4

Ingredients:
- 2 apples, peeled, cored and chopped
- 2 eggs, whisked
- 1 cups water
- 1 cup Greek yogurt
- 2 tablespoons brown sugar
- 1 teaspoon cinnamon powder

Directions:
In a blender, combine the apples with the eggs and the other ingredients except the water, pulse well and divide into 4 ramekins. Add the water to the instant pot, add the steamer basket, put the ramekins inside, put the lid on and cook on High for 25 minutes. Release the pressure naturally for 10 minutes, cool the cream down and serve.

Nutrition: calories 200, fat 5, fiber 2, carbs 5, protein 6

Dates and Quinoa Pudding

Preparation time: 10 minutes**Cooking time:** 20 minutes**Servings:** 4

Ingredients:
- 1 cup quinoa
- 2 cups coconut milk
- ½ cup dates, chopped
- 2 tablespoons honey
- 1 teaspoon cinnamon powder

Directions:

In your instant pot, mix the quinoa with the milk and the other ingredients, whisk, put the lid on and cook on High for 20 minutes. Release the pressure naturally for 10 minutes, divide the pudding into bowls and serve.

Nutrition: calories 172, fat 4, fiber 2, carbs 4, protein 5

Avocado Pudding

Preparation time: 10 minutes**Cooking time:** 10 minutes**Servings:** 4

Ingredients:
- 1 cup avocado, peeled, pitted and roughly cubed
- 2 eggs, whisked
- 1 cup coconut milk
- 2 tablespoons honey
- 1 teaspoon vanilla extract
- 1 cup water

Directions:

In a blender, mix the avocado with the eggs and the other ingredients except the water, pulse well and divide into 4 ramekins. Put the water in the instant pot, add the steamer basket, put the ramekins in the pot, put the lid on and cook on Low for 10 minutes. Release the pressure naturally for 10 minutes and serve.

Nutrition: calories 172, fat 2, fiber 2, carbs 4, protein 6

Raisins and Avocado Bowls

Preparation time: 5 minutes**Cooking time:** 10 minutes**Servings:** 4

Ingredients:
- 2 cups raisins
- 1 cup avocado, peeled, pitted and cubed
- 1 cup Greek yogurt
- 1 tablespoon cinnamon powder
- 2 tablespoons honey
- ½ teaspoon vanilla extract

Directions:

In your instant pot, combine the raisins with the avocado and the other ingredients, toss, put the lid on and cook on Low for 10 minutes. Release the pressure fast for 5 minutes, divide into bowls and serve.

Nutrition: calories 172, fat 3, fiber 2, carbs 6, protein 6

Lemon Rice Pudding

Preparation time: 10 minutes**Cooking time:** 20 minutes**Servings:** 4

Ingredients:
- 1 cup white rice
- 2 cups almond milk
- Juice of ½ lemon
- Zest of ½ lemon, grated
- 1 teaspoon vanilla extract
- 2 tablespoons honey

Directions:

In your instant pot, combine the rice with the almond milk and the other ingredients, whisk, put the lid on and cook on High for 20 minutes. Release the pressure naturally for 10 minutes, divide the pudding into bowls and serve right away.

Nutrition: calories 162, fat 2, fiber 2, carbs 4, protein 6

Carrot and Rice Pudding

Preparation time: 10 minutes**Cooking time:** 20 minutes**Servings:** 4

Ingredients:
- 1 cup white rice
- 2 cups almond milk
- 1 cup carrots, peeled and grated
- 2 tablespoons honey
- ½ teaspoon almond extract

Directions:

In your instant pot, combine the rice with the milk and the other ingredients, whisk, put the lid on and cook on High for 20 minutes. Release the pressure naturally for 10 minutes, and serve the pudding cold.

Nutrition: calories 200, fat 4, fiber 2, carbs 5, protein 4

Avocado and Orange Bowls

Preparation time: 5 minutes**Cooking time:** 6 minutes**Servings:** 4

Ingredients:
- 4 oranges, peeled and cut into segments
- 2 avocados, peeled, pitted and cubed
- 1 cup Greek yogurt
- 1 teaspoon vanilla extract
- 1 tablespoon nutmeg, ground

Directions:

In your instant pot, mix the avocados with the oranges and the other ingredients, toss gently, put the lid on and cook on High for 6 minutes. Release the pressure fast for 5 minutes, divide the mix into bowls and serve.

Nutrition: calories 182, fat 4, fiber 2, carbs 4, protein 6

Rhubarb Cream

Preparation time: 10 minutes**Cooking time:** 14 minutes**Servings:** 4

Ingredients:
- 2 cups rhubarb, chopped
- 1 cup Greek yogurt
- 1 tablespoon honey
- 1 tablespoon lime juice
- ½ teaspoon vanilla extract
- 1 cup water

Directions:

In a blender, combine the rhubarb with the yogurt and the other ingredients except the water, pulse well and divide into 4 ramekins. Put the water in the instant pot, add the trivet inside, put the ramekins into the pot, put the lid on and cook on High for 14 minutes. Release the pressure naturally for 10 minutes, and serve the cream cold.

Nutrition: calories 162, fat 2, fiber 2, carbs 4, protein 6

Rice and Blackberries

Preparation time: 10 minutes**Cooking time:** 20 minutes**Servings:** 4

Ingredients:
- 1 cup white rice
- 1 cup blackberries
- 2 cups coconut milk
- 2 tablespoons honey
- 1 teaspoon lime zest, grated
- ½ teaspoon almond extract
- 1 teaspoon vanilla extract

Directions:

In your instant pot, mix the rice with the milk, berries and the other ingredients, whisk, put the lid on and cook on High for 20 minutes. Release the pressure naturally for 10 minutes, divide the mix into bowls and serve.

Nutrition: calories 172, fat 2, fiber 3, carbs 6, protein 6

Lemon Berries Mix
Preparation time: 10 minutes**Cooking time:** 10 minutes**Servings:** 4

Ingredients:
- 1 cup blueberries
- 1 cup blackberries
- 1 cup strawberries, halved
- 1 tablespoon lemon zest, grated
- 1 tablespoon lemon juice
- 1 tablespoon honey
- 1 cup almond milk

Directions:
In your instant pot, mix the berries with the lemon juice and the other ingredients, whisk, put the lid on and cook on High for 10 minutes. Release the pressure naturally for 10 minutes, divide the mix into bowls and serve.

Nutrition: calories 200, fat 5, fiber 2, carbs 4, protein 6

Pumpkin Cream
Preparation time: 10 minutes**Cooking time:** 20 minutes**Servings:** 4

Ingredients:
- 1 cup pumpkin puree
- 2 eggs, whisked
- 1 teaspoon baking powder
- 1 cup coconut cream
- 1 teaspoon ginger, ground
- ½ teaspoon cinnamon powder
- 1 teaspoon vanilla extract

Directions:
In the instant pot, combine the pumpkin puree with the eggs and the other ingredients, whisk well, put the lid on and cook on High for 20 minutes. Release the pressure naturally for 10 minutes, divide the mix into bowls and serve cold.

Nutrition: calories 162, fat 3, fiber 2, carbs 4, protein 3

Nutmeg Pears Mix

Preparation time: 10 minutes**Cooking time:** 20 minutes**Servings:** 4
Ingredients:

- 4 pears, cored and halved
- 1 tablespoon lemon juice
- 1 teaspoon nutmeg, ground
- 1 teaspoon almond extract
- 1 cup water
- 2 tablespoons honey

Directions:

In your instant pot, combine the pears with the lemon juice and the other ingredients, toss, put the lid on and cook on High for 20 minutes. Release the pressure naturally for 10 minutes, divide the mix into bowls and serve.

Nutrition: calories 162, fat 2, fiber 2, carbs 4, protein 4

Orange Jam

Preparation time: 10 minutes**Cooking time:** 30 minutes**Servings:** 6
Ingredients:

- Juice of 1 lime
- 3 tablespoons honey
- 1 pound oranges, peeled and cut into segments
- 3 cups water

Directions:

In your instant pot, combine the oranges with the water and the other ingredients, stir, put the lid on and cook on Low for 30 minutes. Release the pressure naturally for 10 minutes, blend the mix using an immersion blender, divide into jars and serve.

Nutrition: calories 162, fat 1, fiber 2, carbs 3, protein 6

LemonGrapes Stew

Preparation time: 10 minutes**Cooking time:** 20 minutes**Servings:** 4
Ingredients:

- 1 pound grapes, halved
- Juice of 1 lemon
- 2 cups water
- 2 tablespoons honey
- 1 teaspoon vanilla extract

Directions:

In your instant pot, combine the grapes with the lemon juice and the other ingredients, toss,, put the lid on and cook on High for 20 minutes. Release the pressure naturally for 10 minutes, divide the mix into bowls and serve.

Nutrition: calories 100, fat 1, fiber 2, carbs 4, protein 3

Apple and Couscous Mix

Preparation time: 10 minutes**Cooking time:** 20 minutes**Servings:** 4

Ingredients:

- 1 cup couscous
- 2 cups almond milk
- 1 apple, cored and grated
- 2 tablespoons honey
- 1 teaspoon cinnamon powder

Directions:

In your instant pot, combine the couscous with the apple and the other ingredients, toss, put the lid on and cook on High for 20 minutes. Release the pressure naturally for 10 minutes, divide into bowls and serve.

Nutrition: calories 124, fat 2, fiber 2, carbs 4, protein 5

Apples Stew

Preparation time: 10 minutes**Cooking time:** 15 minutes**Servings:** 4

Ingredients:

- 4 apples, cored and roughly cubed
- 1 cup apple juice
- 2 tablespoons honey
- 1 teaspoon almond extract

Directions:

In your instant pot, mix the apples with the apple juice, honey and almond extract, toss, put the lid on and cook on High for 15 minutes. Release the pressure naturally for 10 minutes, divide the stew into bowls and serve.

Nutrition: calories 129, fat 2, fiber 2, carbs 4, protein 7

Simple Quinoa Pudding

Preparation time: 10 minutes**Cooking time:** 20 minutes**Servings:** 4

Ingredients:

- 2 tablespoons honey
- 1 cup quinoa
- 2 cups almond milk
- 1 tablespoon almonds, chopped
- 1 teaspoon vanilla extract

Directions:

In your instant pot, combine the quinoa with the milk and the other ingredients, toss, put the lid on and cook on High for 20 minutes. Release the pressure naturally for 10 minutes, and serve the pudding cold.

Nutrition: calories 120, fat 1, fiber 1, carbs 4, protein 6

Strawberry and Apples Bowls

Preparation time: 10 minutes**Cooking time:** 15 minutes**Servings:** 4
Ingredients:

- 2 cup strawberries, halved
- 1 cup apples, cored and roughly cubed
- 2 tablespoons lime juice
- 2 tablespoons honey
- 1 and ½ cups apple juice

Directions:

In your instant pot, mix the strawberries with the apples, lime juice and the other ingredients, toss, put the lid on and cook on High for 15 minutes. Release the pressure naturally for 10 minutes, divide the mix into bowls and serve cold.

Nutrition: calories 110, fat 2, fiber 2, carbs 4, protein 5

Grape and Berries Compote

Preparation time: 10 minutes**Cooking time:** 15 minutes**Servings:** 4
Ingredients:

- 1 cup grapes
- 1 cup blackberries
- 1 tablespoon lemon zest, grated
- 1 cup water
- 2 tablespoons honey

Directions:

In your instant pot, combine the berries with the grapes and the other ingredients, toss, put the lid on and cook on High for 15 minutes. Release the pressure naturally for 10 minutes, divide the compote into bowls and serve cold.

Nutrition: calories 152, fat 1, fiber 2, carbs 4, protein 5

Rhubarb Compote

Preparation time: 10 minutes**Cooking time:** 15 minutes**Servings:** 4
Ingredients:

- 2 cups rhubarb, sliced
- 1 cup water
- 1 teaspoon almond extract
- 3 tablespoons honey

Directions:

In your instant pot, mix the rhubarb with the water and the other ingredients, toss, put the lid on and cook on High for 15 minutes. Release the pressure naturally for 10 minutes, divide the mix into bowls and serve cold.

Nutrition: calories 110, fat 2, fiber 2, carbs 5, protein 5

Peach Pudding
Preparation time: 10 minutes**Cooking time:** 20 minutes**Servings:** 4

Ingredients:
- 1 cup peaches, cubed
- 1 cup quinoa
- 2 cups almond milk
- 2 tablespoon honey
- 2 tablespoons ghee, melted
- 1 teaspoon vanilla extract

Directions:
In your instant pot, mix the quinoa with the almond milk and the other ingredients, toss, put the lid on and cook on High for 20 minutes. Release the pressure naturally for 10 minutes, divide everything into bowls and serve.

Nutrition: calories 158, fat 4, fiber 1, carbs 5, protein 2

Almond Lime Cream
Preparation time: 10 minutes**Cooking time:** 15 minutes**Servings:** 4

Ingredients:
- 1 cup almonds, chopped
- 1 tablespoon lime juice
- 1 cup heavy cream
- 1 teaspoon nutmeg, ground
- 2 tablespoons honey
- 1 teaspoon vanilla extract

Directions:
In your instant pot, combine the cream with the almonds and the other ingredients, whisk, put the lid on and cook on High for 15 minutes. Release the pressure naturally for 10 minutes, divide the cream into bowls and serve cold.

Nutrition: calories 152, fat 2, fiber 2, carbs 4, protein 4

Apricot Salad

Preparation time: 10 minutes**Cooking time:** 15 minutes**Servings:** 4

Ingredients:
- 2 cups apricots, halved
- 1 cup blackberries
- 1 cup coconut water
- 2 tablespoons honey
- 1 teaspoon cinnamon powder
- 1 teaspoon vanilla extract

Directions:
In your instant pot, combine the apricots with the berries and the other ingredients, toss, put the lid on and cook on High for 15 minutes. Release the pressure naturally for 10 minutes, divide the mix into bowls and serve.

Nutrition: calories 110, fat 1, fiber 2, carbs 4, protein 6

Lime Yogurt Cream

Preparation time: 10 minutes**Cooking time:** 10 minutes**Servings:** 4

Ingredients:
- ½ teaspoon vanilla extract
- 2 eggs, whisked
- 2 cups Greek yogurt
- 2 tablespoons yogurt
- 1 tablespoon lime juice

Directions:
In your instant pot, combine the yogurt with the eggs and the other ingredients, whisk, put the lid on and cook on High for 10 minutes. Release the pressure naturally for 10 minutes, divide the cream into bowls and serve.

Nutrition: calories 200, fat 6, fiber 2, carbs 5, protein 6

Zucchini Pudding

Preparation time: 10 minutes**Cooking time:** 20 minutes**Servings:** 4

Ingredients:
- 2 cups coconut milk
- 1 cup quinoa
- 2 zucchinis, grated
- 2 eggs, whisked
- 1 tablespoon lime juice
- ½ teaspoon vanilla extract

Directions:
In your instant pot, combine the coconut milk with the zucchini and the other ingredients, whisk, put the lid on and cook on High for 20 minutes. Release the pressure naturally for 10 minutes, divide the pudding into bowls and serve.

Nutrition: calories 200, fat 5, fiber 2, carbs 5, protein 6

Yogurt and Cream Cheese Mix

Preparation time: 10 minutes**Cooking time:** 20 minutes**Servings:** 4

Ingredients:
- 1 cup Greek yogurt
- 1 cup cream cheese, soft
- 2 tablespoons honey
- 2 eggs, whisked
- ½ teaspoon vanilla extract
- ½ teaspoon nutmeg, ground

Directions:
In your instant pot, combine the yogurt with the cream cheese and the other ingredients, whisk, put the lid on and cook on High for 20 minutes. Release the pressure naturally for 10 minutes, divide the mix into bowls and serve.

Nutrition: calories 200, fat 4, fiber 2, carbs 6, protein 6

Mango Pudding

Preparation time: 10 minutes**Cooking time:** 20 minutes**Servings:** 4

Ingredients:
- 1 cup mango, peeled and chopped
- 2 cups coconut cream
- 2 eggs, whisked
- 2 tablespoons honey
- ½ teaspoon vanilla extract

Directions:

In your instant pot, combine the cream with the mango and the other ingredients, whisk, put the lid on and cook on High for 20 minutes. Release the pressure naturally for 10 minutes, divide the pudding into bowls and serve.

Nutrition: calories 162, fat 3, fiber 2, carbs 5, protein 6

Pineapple Salad

Preparation time: 10 minutes**Cooking time:** 15 minutes**Servings:** 4

Ingredients:
- 1 cup pineapple, peeled and cubed
- 1 cup strawberries, halved
- 2 tablespoons honey
- 2 mangoes, peeled and cubed
- ½ cup coconut cream

Directions:

In your instant pot, mix the pineapple with the berries and the other ingredients, toss, put the lid on and cook on High for 15 minutes. Release the pressure naturally for 10 minutes, divide the salad into bowls and serve.

Nutrition: calories 128, fat 5, fiber 1, carbs 2, protein 6

Peaches and Pineapple Mix

Preparation time: 10 minutes**Cooking time:** 20 minutes**Servings:** 4

Ingredients:
- 1 cup pineapple, peeled and cubed
- 1 cup peaches, cubed
- 2 cups coconut cream
- 2 tablespoons honey
- 2 teaspoons vanilla extract

Directions:

In your instant pot, combine the pineapple with the peaches and the other ingredients, toss, put the lid on and cook on High for 20 minutes. Release the pressure naturally for 10 minutes, cool the mix down and serve.

Nutrition: calories 187, fat 4, fiber 2, carbs 4, protein 6

Cinnamon Quinoa

Preparation time: 10 minutes**Cooking time:** 20 minutes**Servings:** 4

Ingredients:

- 2 cups coconut milk
- 1 cup quinoa
- 3 tablespoons honey
- 1 tablespoon cinnamon powder
- ½ teaspoon vanilla extract

Directions:

In your instant pot, mix the quinoa with the milk and the other ingredients, toss, put the lid on and cook on High for 20 minutes. Release the pressure naturally for 10 minutes, divide the pudding into bowls and serve.

Nutrition: calories 200, fat 7, fiber 2, carbs 4, protein 6

Pineapple Stew

Preparation time: 10 minutes**Cooking time:** 15 minutes**Servings:** 4

Ingredients:

- 2 cups water
- 1 cup pineapple, peeled and cubed
- 3 tablespoon honey
- 1 tablespoon lemon juice

Directions:

In your instant pot, combine the pineapple with the water, honey and lemon juice, toss, put the lid on and cook on High for 15 minutes. Release the pressure naturally for 10 minutes, divide the mix into bowls and serve cold.

Nutrition: calories 142, fat 2, fiber 2, carbs 4, protein 6

Plums Cake

Preparation time: 10 minutes**Cooking time:** 40 minutes**Servings:** 4

Ingredients:

- 1 cup plums, pitted and chopped
- 1 cup Greek yogurt
- 1 cup coconut flour
- 2 tablespoons avocado oil
- 1 and ½ cups coconut sugar
- ½ teaspoon baking soda
- 4 eggs, whisked
- 1 cup water

Directions:

In a bowl, mix the plums with the yogurt and the other ingredients except the water, and whisk well. Line a cake pan with parchment paper and pour the cake mix in it. Add the water to the instant pot, add the steamer basket, put the cake pan inside, put the lid on and cook on High for 40 minutes. Release the pressure naturally for 10 minutes, cool the cake down, slice and serve.

Nutrition: calories 182, fat 4, fiber 2, carbs 7, protein 5

Creamy Grapes and Mango Bowls

Preparation time: 10 minutes**Cooking time:** 12 minutes**Servings:** 4

Ingredients:

- 1 cup mango, peeled, and cubed
- 1 cup grapes, halved
- ½ teaspoon ginger, ground
- 2 tablespoons honey
- 1 cup heavy cream

Directions:

In your instant pot, combine the mango with the grapes, ginger and the other ingredients, toss, put the lid on and cook on High for 12 minutes. Release the pressure naturally for 10 minutes, cool the mix, divide into bowls and serve.

Nutrition: calories 200, fat 7, fiber 3, carbs 6, protein 7

Millet and Berries Pudding

Preparation time: 10 minutes**Cooking time:** 20 minutes**Servings:** 4

Ingredients:

- 1 cup millet
- 2 cups almond milk
- ¼ cup blackberries
- 1 tablespoon vanilla extract
- 2 tablespoon honey

Directions:

In your instant pot, combine the millet with the berries and the other ingredients, toss, put the lid on and cook on High for 20 minutes. Release the pressure naturally for 10 minutes and serve the pudding cold.

Nutrition: calories 176, fat 5.5, fiber 3.4, carbs 4.6, protein 7.8

Walnuts Bread

Preparation time: 5 minutes**Cooking time:** 40 minutes**Servings:** 8

Ingredients:

- ¾ cup stevia
- 1/3 cup avocado oil
- 1 cup walnuts, chopped
- 1 teaspoon almond extract
- 3 eggs, whisked
- 1 teaspoon baking powder
- 2 cups almond milk
- 1/3 cup almond flour
- 1 cup water

Directions:

In a bowl, combine the walnuts with the stevia, oil and the other ingredients except the water, whisk well and pour into a loaf pan. Add the water to your instant pot, add the steamer basket, add the loaf pan inside, put the lid on and cook on High for 40 minutes. Release the pressure fast for 5 minutes, cool the bread down, slice and serve.

Nutrition: calories 361, fat 18.2, fiber 3.4, carbs 5.9, protein 5.9

Peach Cake

Preparation time: 10 minutes**Cooking time:** 40 minutes**Servings:** 4

Ingredients:
- 3 eggs, whisked
- ½ cup stevia
- 1 cup peaches, chopped
- 2 tablespoons avocado oil
- 1 cup almond milk
- ¼ cup coconut flour
- ½ teaspoon baking soda
- 1 cup water

Directions:

In a bowl, combine the eggs with the peaches and the other ingredients except the water, whisk well and pour into a loaf pan. Add the water to the pot, add steamer basket, add the cake pan inside, put the lid on and cook on High for 40 minutes. Release the pressure naturally for 10 minutes, cool the cake, slice and serve.

Nutrition: calories 242, fat 23.2, fiber 2.4, carbs 6.8, protein 5.4

Apple Bulgur Mix

Preparation time: 10 minutes**Cooking time:** 20 minutes**Servings:** 4

Ingredients:
- ½ teaspoon vanilla extract
- 2 apples, cored and cubed
- 1 cup bulgur
- 2 cups almond milk
- 1 tablespoon honey

Directions:

In your instant pot, combine the bulgur with the almond milk and the other ingredients, whisk, put the lid on and cook on High for 20 minutes. Release the pressure naturally for 10 minutes, divide the mix into bowls and serve.

Nutrition: calories 70, fat 1, fiber 0.4, carbs 0.9, protein 1.6

Coconut Plums and Avocado

Preparation time: 10 minutes**Cooking time:** 20 minutes**Servings:** 4

Ingredients:
- 1 cup plums, pitted and halved
- 1 cup coconut water
- 1 cup avocado, peeled, pitted and cubed
- 2 tablespoons honey
- 1 teaspoon vanilla extract

Directions:

In your instant pot, combine the plums with the coconut water, avocado and the other ingredients, toss, put the lid on and cook on High for 20 minutes. Release the pressure naturally for 10 minutes, divide the mix into bowls and serve cold.

Nutrition: calories 50, fat 1.2, fiber 0.1, carbs 0.6, protein 0.8

Greek Cocoa Cream

Preparation time: 5 minutes**Cooking time:** 12 minutes**Servings:** 4

Ingredients:
- 2 cups Greek yogurt
- 1 tablespoon cocoa powder
- ½ teaspoon ginger, ground
- 1 tablespoon honey
- ½ teaspoon vanilla extract
- 1 cup water

Directions:

In a bowl, combine the yogurt with the cocoa, ginger and the other ingredients except the water, whisk well and divide into ramekins. Put the water in your instant pot, add the steamer basket, add the ramekins inside, put the lid on and cook on High for 12 minutes. Release the pressure fast for 5 minutes, and serve the cream cold.

Nutrition: calories 360, fat 17.2, fiber 2.9, carbs 6.4, protein 3.9

Pecans and Quinoa

Preparation time: 10 minutes**Cooking time:** 20 minutes**Servings:** 4

Ingredients:

- 1 cup coconut cream
- 2 tablespoons honey
- 1 teaspoon vanilla extract
- 2 tablespoons pecans, chopped
- 1 cup coconut milk
- ½ cup quinoa

Directions:

In your instant pot, combine the cream with the quinoa and the other ingredients, toss, put the lid on and cook on High for 20 minutes. Release the pressure naturally for 10 minutes, divide the mix into bowls and serve cold.

Nutrition: calories 129, fat 11.8, fiber 2.3, carbs 5.1, protein 1.6

Chocolate Cream

Preparation time: 10 minutes**Cooking time:** 15 minutes**Serving:** 4

Ingredients:

- 3 ounces chocolate, unsweetened and melted
- 4 eggs, whisked
- 1 cup almond milk
- 2 tablespoons honey
- ½ teaspoon ginger, grated
- ½ teaspoon nutmeg, ground

Directions:

In your instant pot, combine the melted chocolate with the almond milk and the other ingredients, whisk, put the lid on and cook on High for 15 minutes. Release the pressure naturally for 10 minutes, divide the mix into bowls and serve.

Nutrition: calories 300, fat 15.8, fiber 2.6, carbs 5.8, protein 6.2

Lime Watermelon Bowls

Preparation time: 5 minutes**Cooking time:** 5 minutes**Servings:** 4

Ingredients:

- 1 cup watermelon, peeled and cubed
- 1 cup coconut cream
- 1 teaspoon vanilla extract
- 1 tablespoon honey
- 1 tablespoon lime juice

Directions:

In your instant pot, combine the watermelon and the other ingredients, toss, put the lid on and cook on High for 5 minutes. Release the pressure fast for 5 minutes, divide the mix into bowls and serve.

Nutrition: calories 184, fat 15.6, fiber 2.1, carbs 7.5, protein 3.4

Raspberry and Cantaloupe Bowls

Preparation time: 5 minutes**Cooking time:** 5 minutes**Servings:** 4

Ingredients:
- 1 cup cantaloupe, peeled and cubed
- 1 cup raspberries
- 1 cup coconut milk
- 2 tablespoons stevia
- 1 teaspoon vanilla extract

Directions:
In your instant pot, mix the cantaloupe with the raspberries and the other ingredients, toss, put the lid on and cook on Low for 5 minutes. Release the pressure fast for 5 minutes, divide the mix into bowls and serve.

Nutrition: calories 259, fat 22.3, fiber 3.5, carbs 6.8, protein 5.3

Cantaloupe and Avocado Cream

Preparation time: 10 minutes**Cooking time:** 10 minutes**Servings:** 4

Ingredients:
- 2 cups cantaloupe, peeled and chopped
- 1 avocado, peeled, pitted and cubed
- 1 cup heavy cream
- 1 tablespoon vanilla extract
- 2 tablespoons honey
- 1 cup water

Directions:
In a blender, combine the cantaloupe with the avocado and the other ingredients except the water, pulse and divide into 4 ramekins. Add the water to the instant pot, add the steamer basket, put the ramekins inside, put the lid on and cook on High for 10 minutes. Release the pressure naturally for 10 minutes and serve the mix cold.

Nutrition: calories 136, fat 11.2, fiber 0.2, carbs 7, protein 1.1

Lemon Stew

Preparation time: 10 minutes**Cooking time:** 10 minutes**Servings:** 4
Ingredients:

- 1 cup avocado, peeled, pitted and cubed
- 1 tablespoon lemon zest, grated
- 1 tablespoon lemon juice
- 2 tablespoons honey
- 1 teaspoon vanilla extract
- 1 cup apple juice

Directions:

In your instant pot, combine the avocado with the lemon juice, zest and the other ingredients, toss, put the lid on and cook on High for 10 minutes. Release the pressure naturally for 10 minutes, divide the mix into bowls and serve.

Nutrition: calories 82, fat 1.4, fiber 0.5, carbs 1, protein 0.8

Cantaloupe and Mango Pudding

Preparation time: 10 minutes**Cooking time:** 20 minutes**Servings:** 4
Ingredients:

- 1 cup white rice
- 2 cups almond milk
- 1 cup cantaloupe, peeled and cubed
- 1 mango, peeled and cubed
- ½ teaspoon vanilla extract
- 2 tablespoons honey

Directions:

In your instant pot, combine the rice with the milk and the other ingredients, whisk, put the lid on and cook on High for 20 minutes. Release the pressure naturally for 10 minutes, and serve the pudding cold.
Nutrition: calories 283, fat 11.8, fiber 0.3, carbs 4.7, protein 7.1

Coconut Cocoa Mix

Preparation time: 10 minutes**Cooking time:** 15 minutes**Servings:** 4
Ingredients:

- 2 cups coconut cream
- ½ tablespoon ginger, grated
- 1 teaspoon vanilla extract
- 1 tablespoon cocoa powder
- 2 tablespoons honey

Directions:

In your instant pot, mix the coconut cream with the ginger and the other ingredients, whisk, put the lid on and cook on High for 15 minutes. Release the pressure naturally for 10 minutes, divide the mix into bowls and serve.
Nutrition: calories 72, fat 1.8, fiber 0.2, carbs 0.7, protein 1.6

Ginger Cherry and Avocado Bowls
Preparation time: 5 minutes**Cooking time:** 10 minutes**Servings:** 4

Ingredients:
- 1 cup cherries, pitted
- 1 tablespoon ginger, grated
- 1 cup avocado, peeled, pitted and cubed
- 1 cup coconut water
- ½ teaspoon vanilla extract

Directions:
In your instant pot, mix the cherries with the ginger, avocado and the other ingredients, toss, put the lid on and cook on High for 10 minutes. Release the pressure fast for 5 minutes, divide the mix into bowls and serve cold.

Nutrition: calories 72, fat 3.4, fiber 1, carbs 1.5, protein 0.5

Cherry Pudding
Preparation time: 10 minutes**Cooking time:** 20 minutes**Servings:** 4

Ingredients:
- 1 cup white rice
- 2 cups almond milk
- 1 cup cherries, pitted
- 2 tablespoons swerve
- 1 teaspoon vanilla extract

Directions:
In your instant pot, combine the rice with the milk, cherries and the other ingredients, toss, put the lid on and cook on High for 20 minutes. Release the pressure naturally for 10 minutes, divide the pudding into bowls and serve.

Nutrition: calories 122, fat 12.3, fiber 3.1, carbs 4.6, protein 4.5

Cream Cheese Avocado Ramekins

Preparation time: 5 minutes**Cooking time:** 10 minutes**Servings:** 4

Ingredients:
- 2 cups cream cheese, soft
- 1 cup coconut cream
- 1 cup avocado, peeled, pitted and mashed
- 3 tablespoons honey
- ½ teaspoon ginger, ground
- 1 cup water

Directions:
In a bowl, combine the cream cheese with the avocado and the other ingredients except the water, whisk really well and divide into 4 ramekins. Put the water in your instant pot, add the steamer basket, put the ramekins inside, put the lid on and cook on High for 10 minutes. Release the pressure fast for 5 minutes and serve.

Nutrition: calories 306, fat 13.4, fiber 0, carbs 2.4, protein 5

Nuts Cream Pudding

Preparation time: 10 minutes**Cooking time:** 20 minutes**Servings:** 4

Ingredients:
- 2 eggs, whisked
- 1 teaspoon baking soda
- 2 cups almond milk
- 1 cup walnuts, chopped
- 1 tablespoon macadamia nuts, chopped
- 1 tablespoon pecans, chopped
- 3 tablespoons honey
- 1 cup coconut cream

Directions:
In your instant pot, combine the almond milk with the nuts and the other ingredients, whisk well, put the lid on and cook on High for 20 minutes. Release the pressure naturally for 10 minutes and serve.

Nutrition: calories 342, fat 14.8, fiber 3.4, carbs 6.4, protein 6.2

Lime Jam

Preparation time: 10 minutes**Cooking time:** 20 minutes**Servings:** 4
Ingredients:

- Juice of 1 lime
- 1 orange, peeled and cut into segments
- 2 teaspoon vanilla extract
- 1 cup water
- 2 tablespoons lime zest, grated
- 2 tablespoons honey

Directions:

In your instant pot, combine the water with the lime juice and the other ingredients, whisk, put the lid on and cook on High for 20 minutes. Release the pressure naturally for 10 minutes, divide into jars and serve.

Nutrition: calories 342, fat 22.7, fiber 2.7, carbs 7.4, protein 8.3

Avocado Stew

Preparation time: 5 minutes**Cooking time:** 5 minutes**Servings:** 4
Ingredients:

- 1 cup avocado, peeled, pitted and roughly cubed
- 1 tablespoon lemon zest, grated
- 1 cup stevia
- 1 cup water

Directions:

In your instant pot, combine the avocado with the stevia and the other ingredients, toss, put the lid on and cook on Low for 5 minutes. Release the pressure fast for 5 minutes, divide into bowls and serve.

Nutrition: calories 42, fat 1.7, fiber 0.2, carbs 0.3, protein 0.4

Raspberries Stew

Preparation time: 10 minutes**Cooking time:** 12 minutes**Servings:** 4
Ingredients:

- 2 cups raspberries
- 2 tablespoons honey
- 1 tablespoon lime juice
- 1 teaspoon vanilla extract
- 1 cup water

Directions:

In your instant pot, combine the raspberries with the water and the other ingredients, toss, put the lid on and cook on High for 12 minutes. Release the pressure naturally for 10 minutes and serve the sweet pudding cold.

Nutrition: calories 346, fat 15.8, fiber 2.7, carbs 6.5, protein 3.8

Strawberry Salad

Preparation time: 5 minutes**Cooking time:** 5 minutes**Servings:** 4

Ingredients:

- 2 cups strawberries, halved
- 2 tablespoons lime juice
- 1 teaspoon lime zest, grated
- 2 tablespoons honey
- 1 mango, peeled and cubed
- 1 avocado, peeled, pitted and cubed
- 1 tablespoon cinnamon powder
- ½ cup coconut water

Directions:

In your instant pot, combine the strawberries with the lime juice, zest and the other ingredients, toss, put the lid on and cook on High for 5 minutes. Release the pressure fast for 5 minutes, divide the salad into bowls and serve.

Nutrition: calories 374, fat 22.1, fiber 3.2, carbs 5.9, protein 8.8

Watermelon Salad

Preparation time: 5 minutes**Cooking time:** 5 minutes**Servings:** 4

Ingredients:

- 2 cups watermelon, peeled and cubed
- ½ cup mango, peeled, pitted and cubed
- 1 cup pineapple, peeled and cubed
- 1 cup water
- 2 tablespoons honey
- 1 teaspoon vanilla extract

Directions:

In your instant pot, combine the watermelon with the mango, pineapple and the other ingredients, toss, put the lid on and cook on High for 5 minutes. Release the pressure fast for 5 minutes, divide the mix into bowls and serve.

Nutrition: calories 41, fat 1.7, fiber 0.7, carbs 1, protein 0.8

Ginger Cream

Preparation time: 10 minutes**Cooking time:** 15 minutes**Servings:** 4

Ingredients:
- 2 tablespoons stevia
- 1 tablespoon ginger, grated
- 2 cups coconut cream
- 1 teaspoon almond extract
- 1 cup water

Directions:
In a bowl, mix the cream with the stevia and the rest of the ingredients except the water, whisk and divide into 4 ramekins. Put the water in the instant pot, add the steamer basket, put the ramekins inside, put the lid on and cook on High for 15 minutes. Release the pressure naturally for 10 minutes, and serve the cream cold.

Nutrition: calories 235, fat 14.1, fiber 3.8, carbs 4.1, protein 5

Sweet Pear Cream

Preparation time: 5 minutes**Cooking time:** 20 minutes**Servings:** 4

Ingredients:
- 1 cup pear, peeled, chopped
- 2 tablespoons lime juice
- 2 tablespoons honey
- 2 cups coconut cream
- 1 teaspoon vanilla extract

Directions:
In your instant pot, combine the pear with the cream and the other ingredients, whisk, put the lid on and cook on High for 20 minutes. Release the pressure fast for 5 minutes, divide the cream into bowls and serve.

Nutrition: calories 78, fat 2, fiber 1.2, carbs 1.5, protein 1.4

Cantaloupe Compote

Preparation time: 10 minutes**Cooking time:** 10 minutes**Servings:** 4

Ingredients:

- 2 cups cantaloupe, peeled and cubed
- 2 tablespoons lemon juice
- 2 cups water
- 2 tablespoons honey
- 1 teaspoon vanilla extract

Directions:

In your instant pot, mix the cantaloupe with the lemon juice and the other ingredients, toss, put the lid on and cook on High for 10 minutes. Release the pressure naturally for 10 minutes, divide the compote into bowls and serve.

Nutrition: calories 43, fat 1.2, fiber 0.1, carbs 1, protein 0.5

Orange Compote

Preparation time: 5 minutes**Cooking time:** 10 minutes**Servings:** 4

Ingredients:

- 2 cups oranges, peeled and cut into segments
- 2 cups water
- 3 tablespoons stevia
- ½ teaspoon almond extract

Directions:

In your instant pot, mix the oranges with the water and the other ingredients, toss, put the lid on and cook on High for 10 minutes. Release the pressure fast for 5 minutes, divide the mix into bowls and serve.

Nutrition: calories 40, fat 1, fiber 0.1, carbs 0.2, protein 0.6

Vanilla Cream

Preparation time: 5 minutes**Cooking time:** 15 minutes**Servings:** 4

Ingredients:

- 2 cups coconut cream
- 2 tablespoons honey
- 1 teaspoon vanilla extract

Directions:

In your instant pot, combine the cream with the honey and the other ingredients, whisk, put the lid on and cook on High for 8 minutes. Release the pressure fast for 5 minutes, divide the cream into bowls and serve cold.

Nutrition: calories 195, fat 17.9, fiber 4, carbs 7.5, protein 1.4

Pineapple Cream

Preparation time: 10 minutes**Cooking time:** 15 minutes**Servings:** 4

Ingredients:
- 2 cups pineapple, peeled and chopped
- 1 cup coconut cream
- 4 tablespoons stevia
- 1 teaspoon vanilla extract
- 1 cup water

Directions:

In a blender, combine the pineapple with the cream and the other ingredients, pulse well, and divide into 4 ramekins. Put the water in the instant pot, add the steamer basket inside, add the ramekins, put the lid on and cook on High for 15 minutes. Release the pressure naturally for 10 minutes and serve cold.

Nutrition: calories 176, fat 17.6, fiber 2.2, carbs 5, protein 1.7

Cocoa Bread

Preparation time: 10 minutes**Cooking time:** 30 minutes**Servings:** 4

Ingredients:
- 1 cup almond milk
- 3 eggs, whisked
- 3 tablespoons honey
- 2 cups coconut flour
- 2 tablespoons avocado oil
- 2 tablespoons cocoa powder
- ½ teaspoon almond extract
- ¼ teaspoon baking powder
- 2 cups water
- Cooking spray

Directions:

In a bowl, mix the eggs with the milk, honey and the other ingredients except the cooking spray and the water and whisk well. Grease a loaf pan with the cooking spray and pour the sweet bread mix inside. Add the water to the instant pot, add the trivet inside, put the loaf pan inside, put the lid on and cook on High for 30 minutes. Release the pressure naturally for 10 minutes, cool the bread, slice and serve.

Nutrition: calories 253, fat 19.7, fiber 1.8, carbs 6.8, protein 5.2

Conclusion

Following a Mediterranean diet can be so easy and so much fun. This is much more than a simple weight loss program. This amazing diet is a healthy lifestyle that you should embrace in order to look and feel great.

The Mediterranean diet is not a restrictive and complex one as you can see for yourself. There are so many delicious, flavored and rich Mediterranean dishes you can prepare. We gathered in this great cooking journal the best ones you can make in the comfort of your own home.
The best thing about this collection is that it contains some wonderful Mediterranean diet meals you can prepare using the ultimate cooking tool: the instant pot.
This way, you get your Mediterranean meals done a lot faster and in a healthier way.

So, what are you still waiting for? Get the Mediterranean diet instant pot collection today and start a new and healthy life right away.

Made in the USA
Monee, IL
31 January 2020